Mentoring and Tutoring by Students

Mentoring and Tutoring by Students

EDITED BY

Sinclair Goodlad

published in association with BP

London • Stirling

First published in 1998

Kogan Page Limited
120 Pentonville Road
London N1 9JN
and
22883 Quicksilver Drive
Stirling, VA 20166, USA

British Library Cataloguing in Publication Data

A CIP record for this book is available from the British Library.

ISBN 0 7494 2559 8

Typeset by Kogan Page Ltd
Printed and bound in Great Britain by Clays Ltd, St Ives plc

CONTENTS

PART C: EMBEDDING TUTORING IN THE SYSTEM: ACCREDITATION AND QUALITY ASSURANCE

PART D: HELP FOR TRANSITIONAL STUDENTS

PART E: MEETING NATIONAL NEEDS

PREFACE AND ACKNOWLEDGEMENTS

Like its companion volume, *Students as Tutors and Mentors* (Goodlad, 1995a) this is not a book of conference proceedings. It was, however, stimulated by a conference planned by John C Hughes and Julie Nicholls of British Petroleum. Without their good work and without the financial support of BP, the conference would not have happened and the book would not have been written. They were assisted in the task of planning the conference by a team consisting of Roger Banfield (England), Amos Carmeli (Israel), Russell Elsegood (Australia), Nigel Giles (England), Sinclair Goodlad (England), Joe Hogan (Scotland), Tonya Hunter (USA), Danny Saunders (Wales), Elaine Slater-Simons (England), Jo-Anne Vorster (South Africa), and Jerry Wilbur (USA). They were assisted in the refereeing of papers for the conference and for this book by Toni Beardon, Fritz Becker, Marc Freedman, Barbara Fresko, Meenal Gupta, Jane Hofmeister, Joan Leach, Glen Odenbrett, and Keith Topping.

We are grateful to Kluwer publishers for permission to reproduce a paper by Keith Topping (Chapter 4 of this book) that first appeared in their journal *Higher Education*.

Caroline Gatenby, Charles Lewis and Trijntje Ytsma helped greatly with typing and the reproduction of tables. Pat Lomax of Kogan Page was the commissioning editor and Claire Cohen the desk editor. To all, I, as editor, am very grateful; I gladly take responsibility for any infelicities of style that remain.

Sinclair Goodlad
Imperial College
London, July 1997

FOREWORD

Following our second BP International Conference – Students as Tutors and Mentors, early in 1997 it is a pleasure for me to provide the Foreword to this book.

As a managing director of a major international company that believes that sharing best practice across the globe is a way to grow and learn, I am pleased to see evidence of experience from so many countries in this book – the conference itself had delegates from over 30 countries. This rich cultural diversity encouraged learning and this book now helps to extend those lessons learnt to you.

BP's community affairs programmes are one of the most visible demonstrations of our wish to be a source of positive influence wherever we operate. BP believes that it is the company's duty to be a good neighbour and to earn the trust of the community by being a responsible corporate citizen. We therefore aim to work in partnership with the communities around our business sites. In so doing we aim to maintain and enhance our valued good reputation and thus our ability to perform.

With continuous change and uncertainty about the future nature of work, the need for an educated society and business to work closely together is greater now than at any time. BP contributes to these partnerships in a variety of ways including this project on mentoring and tutoring.

University students who act as tutors and mentors are provided with the opportunity to develop their transferable skills, which helps them find rewarding and challenging careers. School pupils who have student tutors/mentors are provided with positive role models to raise their aspirations to continue with their education and training and also get added assistance with their learning.

This is the seventh year of our partnership with Imperial College, University of London, on the International Mentoring and Tutoring Project. In that time we have run two international conferences, many country seminars and published a range of resources to help with the establishment of new programmes. It is inspiring to be involved with a project that has put into practice the true spirit of tutoring and mentoring. We have been able to use our international presence to help educational practitioners to think globally while acting locally to help more than 500,000 young people in over 30 countries.

Dr Chris Gibson-Smith
Managing Director
The British Petroleum Company plc

For more information on the range of educational and related resources published by BP please contact:

BP Educational Service
PO Box 934
Poole
BH17 7BR
United Kingdom

Tel +44 (0) 1202 669940
Fax +44 (0) 1202 661999
e-mail: bpes@bp.com
http://www.bp.com

CONTRIBUTORS

L A (Toni) Beardon lectures in the University of Cambridge School of Education, and is Director of the Cambridge STIMULUS peer education project and the National Royal Institution Cambridge University Mathematics Enrichment Online Maths Project (NRICH Maths http://www.nrich.maths.org.uk). She is an OFSTED school inspector with 15 years' school teaching experience and 20 years in universities teaching mathematics, training teachers, running a peer tutoring scheme and publishing research on the pedagogical issues surrounding peer education, software for teaching mathematics and statistics, and papers and articles on mathematics teaching and student profiling. Toni is active in popularizing and promoting the public understanding of mathematics.

Fritz Becker, who is Professor of Geography and Head of the Department of Geography and Environmental Studies, University of Namibia (UNAM), took his higher doctoral degree at the Ruhr University, Bochum, FRG. He worked for UNESCO in Asia, taught at the Ruhr University, the National Institute of Public Administration in Sana'a, Yemen and the Asian Institute of Technology in Bangkok, Thailand. He has conducted research in Asia and Africa since 1974. His engagement at UNAM, where he served the Faculty of Humanities and Social Sciences as Dean (1992–1994) introduced him to the challenges of student tutoring and mentoring in higher education.

Linda Brennan is currently a lecturer in marketing management at Monash University, Clayton campus, and is coordinator of advanced marketing for Honours students. Linda has a Bachelor of Business (Marketing) (Hons), a Diploma of Marketing Research and is currently completing a PhD in the marketing of institutional services. Linda also operates as an independent marketing consultant to privately owned and non-profit organizations, including facilitation in the development of strategic and marketing plans. In the 15 years prior to joining Monash, Linda held various marketing positions within industry. She is a full member of the Marketing Research

Society of Australia and an Executive Committee Member of the Monash Marketing Alumni Association.

Val Clulow is a Senior Lecturer in the Department of Marketing, Faculty of Business and Economics at Monash University, where she is Course Director for retail studies at both undergraduate and postgraduate level. She has a Diploma of Teaching, Bachelor of Arts degree and a Master of Education degree. She has extensive experience in the Australian retail industry. She is currently undertaking her PhD at the University of Melbourne, in the Faculty of Education. She has written a number of unique retail subjects for delivery by distance education. Her teaching specializations include retail management, retail consumer behaviour, and retail technology. She has research interests and publications in the fields of mentoring, peer tutoring, experiential learning and retail case studies. She is co-leader of Monash University's Marketing International Study Program. She consults to businesses and is a Chartered Member of the Australian Human Resources Institute.

Moira de Groot holds the position of Senior Tutor in the Department of Psychology at the University of the Witwatersrand, Johannesburg. She holds postgraduate degrees in the fields of both education and psychology. Her primary interest and publications lie in academic development work, focusing on the needs of students who are 'underprepared' for university-level study due to disadvantage in educational background. One of her research interests with respect to tutoring and mentoring is in the role of ethnically-similar advanced peer tutors in academic development.

Russell Elsegood, Public Relations Manager at Murdoch University in Perth, Western Australia, is also Director of the BP Australia-sponsored Science/Technology Awareness Raising (STAR) Peer Tutoring Programme. The STAR Programme, launched in 1994 as a pilot programme with six peer tutors in three schools, now has 60 peer tutors working regularly in 19 high schools and two primary schools, and it is the model for similar programmes in universities throughout Australia. The STAR Programme evolved from the success of using university students as peer tutors in the WA Science Summer School – a one-week, fully-residential programme – of which Russell is also Director. STAR was awarded two $100,000AUD National Priority grants by the Australian government to develop the scheme as an Australian model, and this year STAR was cited in Western Australia's Science and Technology Policy and granted $50,000AUD to launch peer tutoring via the Internet to high schools throughout this vast state.

Joan Freeman is the author of 11 books, many of which have been translated into other languages, as well as hundreds of scientific and popular publications on the development of exceptionally high-level abilities. She has given invited presentations on the subject in most parts of the world to universities, schools and conferences based on considerable research in this area over more than 25 years: most notably her national 14-year comparison study of gifted and non-gifted children across Britain. She received her doctorate in Child Psychology from the University of Manchester and is now Visiting Professor at Middlesex University, London. She is an elected Fellow of the British Psychological Society. She was the Founding President of the European Council for High Ability (ECHA), an association that promotes the development of talent during the life-span, and is now Editor in Chief of the academic journal *High Ability Studies*.

Barbara Fresko is head of the Research and Evaluation Unit at Beit Berl College in Israel where she also teaches statistics and research methodology to prospective teachers and school counsellors. She has been affiliated with the PERACH Project at the Weizmann Institute of Science since 1978 and has published numerous articles and research reports about tutoring/mentoring in PERACH.

Peter Fridjhon is a senior lecturer in the Department of Statistics and Actuarial Sciences at the University of the Witwatersrand, Johannesburg, and obtained his undergraduate degree in science. He holds a Masters degree in Education from the University of Lancaster, and lectures in the Department of Psychology in the fields of statistics and research methodology. He has published widely, both in the prediction of academic performance, as well as in teaching and learning at tertiary level.

Sinclair Goodlad is Director of the Humanities Programme at the Imperial College of Science, Technology and Medicine, University of London. He has taught in India and at MIT and has been visiting associate at the University of California, Berkeley. He has written and edited a number of books about tutoring, including the companion volume to this book, *Students as Tutors and Mentors* (Kogan Page, 1995). One of his recent books, *The Quest for Quality: Sixteen forms of heresy in higher education,* (SRHE and Open University Press, 1995) locates tutoring in the wider context of a systematic philosophy of higher education. With Stephanie McIvor, he has recently completed a study extending the 'tutoring' idea to museum interpretation – *Museum Volunteers* (Routledge, forthcoming).

Ian Gregory is a production technologist working for Shell International Exploration and Production in the Netherlands. He studied a Master's degree in Mechanical Engineering at Imperial College, London, for which he was awarded the New Graduate Engineering prize from the Royal

Academy of Engineering. While in London he was involved with the Pimlico Connection Student Tutoring Project, both as a tutor and chairperson of the student committee. In 1996 he undertook six months' voluntary educational development work in South Africa, based at Rhodes University, Grahamstown, together with Line Sorensen. Current interests include educational partnerships between industry and schools, particularly raising awareness of environmental issues.

Ruth Hickey lectures in Science Education at Murdoch University School of Education, and coordinates a unit in Peer Tutoring and Mentoring in Science. She has been a teacher and primary school principal and has worked extensively in curriculum design for primary and secondary students in science and social studies. Her interests include the effect of science knowledge on teaching, and on the development of the school practice component in teaching qualifications.

Jane Hofmeister has been, since 1986, a university professor at the University of Amsterdam in the Faculty of Pedagogical and Educational Sciences for the In-service Teacher Training Department and since 1991 also in the Central Bureau of the University for the Expertise Centre of Academic Affairs as a general manager (coordinator) of the Alignment Pre University – University scheme.

Bruce Jeffreys has been the co-ordinator of the STAR Programme since 1995 and, most recently, has been instrumental in developing the procedures for using the Internet and e-mail to launch peer tutoring for science students in Australia's far-flung regional schools.

Ray Kingdon is Special Projects Manager within the Educational Development Unit at the University of Glamorgan. His main interests are in the recording of student achievement, and he is module leader for the student tutoring scheme that accredits students for their work within local schools. His background is in information systems and the training of staff within higher education who have an interest in educational technology applications.

Ronen Kowalsky received a Masters degree with high honours from Tel Aviv University in clinical child psychology and has begun doctoral studies in political psychology. For the past three years he has been involved with evaluation of the PERACH Project.

Claudia Landsman obtained an Honours degree in Psychology from the University of the Witwatersrand, Johannesburg and is currently completing her Masters degree in Psychology by coursework and research report. She is currently employed as a full-time tutor in the department. Her research interests include issues in educational psychology such as peer-tutoring, tutoring, teaching and learning, as well as social cognition and child sexual abuse.

Judith MacCallum is a Lecturer in Educational Psychology in the School of Education, Murdoch University and has been involved in teaching in secondary and tertiary institutions since 1974. Originally a science teacher, her main teaching and research interests are student motivation and using social interaction and collaboration for learning. Judith runs workshops on collaborative learning for teacher groups and facilitates the use of peer tutoring and collaborative groups for learning in tertiary courses.

Mmanosi Daisy Matlou is a student counsellor at the University of the Witwatersrand offering to students within the College of Science an academic development programme designed to increase access of educationally disadvantaged students. She has a BA honours degree in Sociology, and is currently doing a Masters degree in Psychology.

Barnabas Otaala is Professor of Educational Psychology and Dean of the Faculty of Education, University of Namibia. He has previously worked at Makarere University, Kampala, Uganda; Kenyatta University, Nairobi, Kenya; the University of Botswana, Gaborone, Botswana; and the National Teacher Training College, Maseru, Lesotho. He is one of the International Advisers for the Child-to-Child Trust at the Institute of Education, University of London, with which he has been associated since 1979.

Joseph T Pascarelli has designed, developed, installed and evaluated youth mentoring programmes and systems in New York, Oregon, the US Virgin Islands, and other states and school districts. He has been actively engaged in research and development in educational reform, including effective teaching and learning programmes, instructional design, and professional development in the United States and the US Trust Territories. He is an action researcher in systems change and is presently on the faculty of the University of Portland, School of Education in Portland, Oregon.

Ceasar Pirs obtained his first degree in 1996 at the University of the Witwatersrand, Johannesburg, majoring in psychology. He has been involved as a part-time tutor in the department in 1996 and 1997, and is currently completing his Honours degree in physical education at the University. His interests lie in human movement studies and sports psychology, as well as in teaching and learning, with particular emphasis on peer tutoring.

Michael Pitman obtained his BA with distinction from the University of the Witwatersrand, Johannesburg in 1994. He then continued his studies at Wits, obtaining a first class Honours in Applied Psychology in 1995, and a first class Honours in Philosophy in 1996. Michael worked part-time as a tutor in the Department of Psychology in 1994 and 1995, and as a tutorial supervisor in 1996. He was then appointed to a full-time position as a tutor in the department in 1997, where he coordinates and supervises the tutorial programme for the undergraduate research design and analysis courses.

Charles Potter is an educational psychologist by training, and holds a number of degrees, including a Masters degree in Educational Psychology (*cum laude*) from the University of South Africa, and a PhD in curriculum development from the University of the Witwatersrand, Johannesburg. He is a senior lecturer in the Department of Psychology at Wits, where he lectures in research methodology and in programme evaluation. The majority of his publications are in the field of evaluation, with particular emphasis on the evaluation of innovatory projects and programmes. He has also published in the areas of student development and peer tutoring. He is the editor of both the *Journal of Educational Evaluation* and the *Bulletin of Assessment and Evaluation.*

Meira Puterman received her Honours in Applied Psychology in 1996 and graduated top of her class. She has been involved in tutoring in the department for one and a half years. She is currently undergoing a psychometric internship at the Johannesburg General Hospital, and continues to assist in the development of tutorial programmes in the department.

Margaret Rutherford was born and educated in the UK, taking her first degree in aeronautical engineering at Imperial College, London. Her research interests moved to physics and then to physics education (for her PhD studies). She is currently Director of the College of Science, University of the Witwatersrand, Johannesburg, and involved in programmes for increasing access with success for educationally disadvantaged students. Her major research activities are in language and communication in science for second-language students and in relevant explanations in science.

Danny Saunders is head of the Educational Development Unit at the University of Glamorgan, Wales. He has a strong interest in experiential learning and is the series editor of the *Simulation and Gaming Yearbook* (Kogan Page) as well as the *Complete Student Handbook* (Blackwell). His background is in social psychology and the analysis of communication within society, and he is dedicated to the pursuit of strategic innovation and change within higher education.

Line Sørensen is a facilities engineer with Shell International Exploration and Production, although currently working with the development of global human resourcing systems, based in the corporate centre, The Hague, Netherlands. She studied a Master's degree in mechanical engineering at the Norwegian Institute of Technology in Trondheim, Norway and at Aachen University of Technology, Germany, where she was involved with small group tutoring of engineering students. In 1996 she undertook six months' voluntary educational development work in South Africa, based at Rhodes University, Grahamstown, together with Ian Gregory.

Carol Taylor, who took her BA in Toronto and her BEd in Nottingham, is a senior tutor in the Department of Social Anthropology at the University of the Witwatersrand, Johannesburg. She has been a member of the department since 1991, with special responsibility for academic development. Her area of special interest is multicultural education.

Keith Topping is Director of the Centre for Paired Learning in the Department of Psychology at the University of Dundee. He develops and researches the effectiveness of methods for non-professionals (such as parents or peers) to tutor others in fundamental skills (eg, reading, spelling, writing) and higher order learning (science, maths, etc), for use across a wide age range and in many different contexts. He is also Director of postgraduate professional training in educational psychology and the Scottish Office project on Promoting Social Competence in Schools, and has interests in electronic literacy and computer-aided assessment. He is responsible for ten books and 140 other publications including multimedia in-service training and distance learning packs, and presents, trains, consults and engages in collaborative action and research around the world.

Megan Virtue is a qualified nurse and subsequently obtained her Honours degree in Applied Psychology from the University of the Witwatersrand, Johannesburg with distinction. She is currently registered for her Masters degree in Applied Psychology, while doing her internship as a clinical psychologist at Tara Hospital and at the Transvaal Memorial Institute. She has been involved in tutoring in the Department of Psychology at Wits since 1993, both as a part-time tutor for two years and as a tutorial supervisor.

Jim Wood took a BSc in Mathematics at Manchester University in 1976 and a PGCE Secondary at Newcastle Polytechnic in 1977. He was appointed to the newly created position of manager for the Tyneside Students into Schools Project in 1993 after 16 years teaching mathematics in comprehensive schools in Newcastle. In 1996, the project was submitted by Newcastle and Northumbria Universities as their joint entry for the Queen's Anniversary Awards for Further and Higher Education.

PART A: INTRODUCTION

Chapter 1

STUDENTS AS TUTORS AND MENTORS

Sinclair Goodlad

Schemes involving students as tutors and mentors are now in place in many countries, with numerous students, schoolchildren and teachers benefiting from the activity. The key task now is to build student tutoring and mentoring into the basic structures of academic institutions so that systems acquire a greater degree of stability. After a brief section of revision of matters addressed in the companion volume to this one, Students as Tutors and Mentors *(Goodlad, 1995a), attention is given to ways in which the training that all student tutors and mentors require can become the focus of much fruitful academic work.*

Preamble

The aim of this book is to stimulate and encourage the use of an educational technique through which teachers in tertiary and secondary education can massively amplify and extend their influence – namely the deployment of students as tutors and mentors. To this end, the book offers:

- reviews of relevant research;
- case studies of mature projects;
- ideas for new uses of student tutoring and mentoring;
- practical suggestions of ways of implementing tutoring and mentoring.

A key emerging issue is that of embedding in institutions' regular arrangements, procedures that are often seen as useful additions to teaching but not a fundamental part of it. For this reason, several chapters of this book (including this introduction) focus on ways in which tutoring and mentoring can become part of the assessed/accredited activity of students in higher education.

Peer teaching has been going on in various forms of education for hundreds, indeed thousands, of years (see Wagner, 1990). Having been neglected as an educational technique since the mid-nineteenth century, following the development of teaching as an organized profession, it was rediscovered in the 1960s as a way of meeting situations of acute need (see Goodlad, 1979; Goodlad and Hirst, 1989; Topping, 1988). It is now recognized as a way of enriching education, and achieving goals that cannot be achieved by other means. (See, for example, Cohen *et al.*, 1982; Devin-Sheehan *et al.*, 1976; Feldman *et al.*, 1976; Wilkes, 1975.) The field is vast and steadily growing.

Psychologists have become increasingly interested in the possibilities of children helping children (see Allen, 1976; Foot *et al.*, 1990) and in the wider field of group and interactive learning (see Foot, Howe *et al.*, 1994). Peer tutoring techniques have been used to help the learning disabled (see review by Byrd, 1990) and as a way of assisting students who are seen as not socially accepted (see Garcia-Vazquez and Ehly, 1992).

Within higher education itself, experiments are proliferating (see Goodlad, 1997b, 1997c). There is even, now, a staff development pack available (Topping, 1997) and a do-it-yourself manual for staff and students (Donaldson and Topping, 1997). Reciprocal peer tutoring has been shown to improve examination scores, reduce stress, and offer student satisfaction (Fantuzzo *et al.*, 1989) and, provided there is mutual exchange in a structured manner, other academic benefits (Riggio *et al.*, 1991).

Moore-West *et al.* (1990) found that 75 per cent of US medical schools responding to a questionnaire had student-based peer advising or peer tutoring in place. Some medical schools have been doing this for over 25 years – for example Case Western Reserve University School of Medicine (Schaffer *et al.*, 1990). In the UK, Carroll (1996) found that a scheme could be successful if the commitment of student tutors was limited and there were tightly-defined goals.

As an adjunct to problem-based learning, peer tutoring has been shown to stimulate students' interest in learning law (Moust *et al.*, 1989; Moust and Schmidt, 1994b), although, in medicine, staff were marginally more effective than students with higher-level work that drew on breadth of knowledge and experience (Schmidt *et al.*, 1995).

However, the thrust of this book, and the IC/BP International Mentoring and Tutoring Project that stimulated it, has been primarily on college-level students helping younger students (usually schoolchildren). This type of tutoring is operating on a massive scale, particularly in the USA (see Cahalan and Farris, 1990; Reisner *et al.*, 1990), in Israel through the much-evaluated PERACH scheme (see Eisenberg *et al.*, 1980a, 1980b, 1981, 1982, 1983a, 1983b; Fresko, 1988; Fresko and Carmeli, 1990; Fresko and Chen, 1989; Fresko and Eisenberg, 1985; PERACH, 1984), and in Australasia (see Jones, 1989, 1990, 1993a, 1993b). At the most recent count there were over 180 schemes in the United Kingdom, (CSV, 1996), and at the IC/BP conference presentations were made about schemes in many other countries including China, The Czech Republic, India, Lithuania, Namibia, The Netherlands, Norway, Russia, South Africa, Thailand, and The Ukraine. For those who have not read the companion volume to this book (*Students as Tutors and Mentors*, Goodlad, 1995a), I will set the scene by recapping some key points; those who have read the first book are asked to see what follows as revision! Although there is now a growing literature in peer tutoring, peer assisted learning, and other activities in which learners help each other, the definitions offered below deliberately limit the field of discourse to activities involving *students* as tutors and mentors. For those who wish to start this type of scheme, there is a splendid resource pack produced by BP (Hughes, 1991).

Definitions of Student Tutoring and Mentoring

Student tutoring and mentoring involve:

- students from colleges and universities
- helping pupils in local schools
- on a sustained and systematic basis
- under the direction and supervision of teachers.

The key differences are as follows:

	Tutoring	**Mentoring**
Focus	Academic learning	Life skills
Location	Usually in classroom	Often outside classroom
Mode	1 to several	1 to 1
Duration	A few weeks	Several months/years

The basic ideas are very old and very fruitful. The word 'mentor' derives from the name of the teacher of Telemakhos in Homer's *Odyssey*, Book 3: 'Mentor, how can I do it?'

One of the pioneers was Andrew Bell, a minister of religion in Madras, India, and superintendent of the Military Male Asylum (a charity school for the orphaned boys of soldiers) at Egmore. Having observed children drawing in the sand on the beach at Madras, Bell became enthused with the idea of using trays of sand as a cheap writing material with which to teach children the alphabet. Having failed to convince his colleagues of the economic virtues of trays of sand, he started, in 1791 and 1792, to use monitors to teach with these materials. He soon realized that the use of children to teach children was an educational discovery far more important than that of trays of sand!

Before he left Madras, Andrew Bell presented to the directors of the asylum an account of his work there. This was published in October 1797 as *Experiment in Education* which commends tutoring in observations such as these:

> 'The tutors enable their pupils to keep pace with their classes.'
>
> Andrew Bell *Experiment in Education*, 1797

> '(It) establishes such habits of industry, morality and religion, as have a tendency to form good scholars, good men, good subjects, and good Christians.'
>
> Andrew Bell *Experiment in Education*, 1797

Another pioneer was the more flamboyant Joseph Lancaster (born 25 November 1778) who opened his first school on New Year's Day 1798 to provide education to poor children. In June 1801, he moved into a room to accommodate 350 boys in Belvedere Place, Borough Road, London (near the location of the present University of the South Bank). Finding 350 boys somewhat difficult to teach single-handed, he adopted ideas from Andrew Bell (whom he met in 1804 when Bell was back in England as Rector of Swanage), and developed the monitorial system of instruction for which he claimed many benefits, eg:

> 'Lively, active-tempered boys are the most frequent transgressors of good order, and the most difficult to reduce to reason; the best way to form them is by making monitors of them.'
>
> Joseph Lancaster *Improvements in Education*, 1805

I quote these worthies so that we may remind ourselves that we have not invented something new: we stand on the shoulders of giants! (Extracts from the works of Bell and Lancaster are reproduced in Salmon, 1932.)

The Known Benefits of Student Tutoring

My own first foray into student tutoring was through a scheme in 1975 involving 12 engineering students from Imperial College visiting a local comprehensive school weekly for two terms to assist with the teaching of science, mathematics and design technology. Their purpose was to try to make these subjects more interesting to the pupils, many of whom gave them up at the earliest opportunity. The school was The Pimlico School, hence the name of our scheme 'The Pimlico Connection' – the name being a deliberate invocation of two famous film titles, *Passport to Pimlico* and *The French Connection* that made people think that they must have heard of the scheme before!

The first experiments, funded by a grant from the Leverhulme Trust, were within the framework of socio-technical group projects in which the students not only did the tutoring but also carried out a detailed evaluation. In every subsequent year, the scheme has been evaluated, with strikingly similar patterns of results, which suggest that the effects derive from the *system* rather than from the personalities or capabilities of individuals. The evaluation was:

- originally by psychometric tests
- then by depth interviews, plus
- open-ended questionnaires
- ultimately by a combination of specific questions and open-ended replies.

The principal findings (replicated frequently in other schemes stimulated by BP and by CSV since then) were as follows:

Pupils:

- lessons more interesting
- lessons easier to follow
- lessons more enjoyable
- seemed to learn more.

Students:

- practice in communication skills
- feeling of doing something useful with what already learned
- getting to know about people from different social backgrounds
- gaining insight into how other people saw subjects
- increased self-confidence

- reinforcing knowledge of subject
- no great interference with college studies.

Teachers:

- lessons were easier to handle
- teaching was more enjoyable
- pupils seemed to learn more.

Numerical values on these items are recorded in, for example, Goodlad, 1985 and Chapter 5 of Goodlad and Hirst (1989). Strikingly similar effects have been found in other schemes elsewhere in the UK (eg, Beardon, 1990; CSV, 1995a, 1995b; Green and Hughes, 1992; Hector Taylor, 1992; Potter, 1994, 1995). Two papers by Keith Topping and Shirley Hill (Hill and Topping, 1995; Topping and Hill, 1995) offer a comprehensive summary of the outcomes for the various types of participants in schemes.

Student Tutoring and Mentoring as Study Service

In the companion volume, I urged that student tutoring and mentoring should always be seen as *solutions to problems*, not activities undertaken just for the sake of it (or as educational experiments). Study service is the wider field of activity into which tutoring and mentoring fall. Study service is activity in which students do work of direct, practical social value as part of their curriculum (see Goodlad, 1982, 1995b; Whitley, 1980, 1982).

A common phenomenon in higher education, particularly perhaps that of scientists and engineers, is for the main ingredients of professional formation to exist as separate spheres of activity (see Figure 1.1). My intention for over 30 years at Imperial College has been to bring about a fruitful merging of these concerns, as shown in Figure 1.2. Each sphere is crucial: the problem is how best to achieve the benefits from each sphere without doing damage to the others. The issues are discussed below.

Main academic work

The key values of traditional academic work consist of the:

- focusing power of disciplines
- systematic limiting of the field of discourse in the interests of precision and economy
- acceleration of learning.

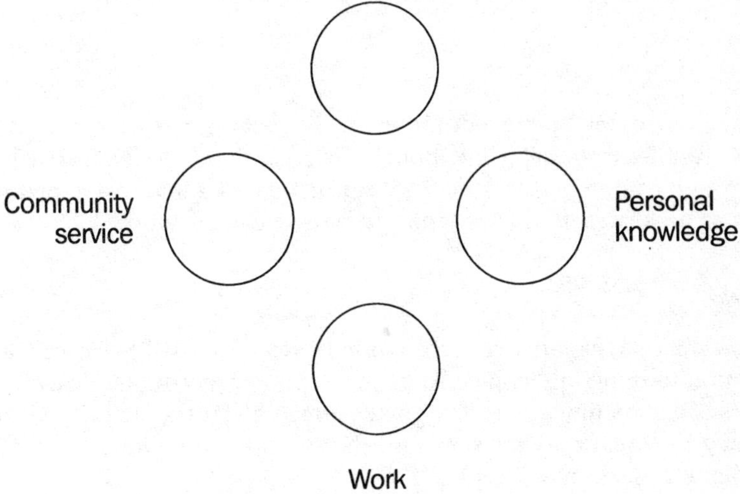

Figure 1.1 The separation of the elements of professional formation

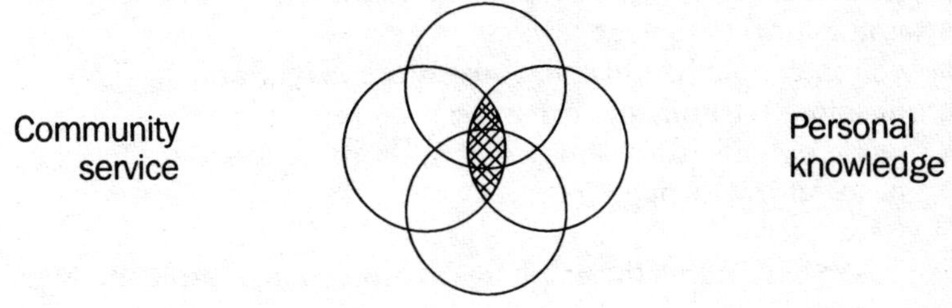

Figure 1.2 The merging of the elements of professional formation

They need to be complemented by opportunities for reflection and social action.

Personal knowledge

Some courses in higher education deliberately and systematically offer opportunities for reflection. Often, however, this is by 'lateral enrichment' – through commentating or 'liberal studies' courses that can sometimes be seen as peripheral to the students' primary academic work.

Work

In like manner, experience of the world of work is usually secured through vacation training/internships/co-op and similar procedures. However, students are sometimes only marginally involved in the main work of the agency to which they are sent, and there is often little interweaving with academic reflection.

Student community action

Student community action is one way in which students engage with social problems in the localities in which they live and work. Usually such action is outside the curriculum, with:

- the elderly (cleaning, decorating, shopping)
- the homeless (soup runs)
- the educationally handicapped (groupwork)
- immigrants (language tuition)
- young people (youth clubs, adventure playgrounds)
- hospitals (visiting, performances)
- welfare rights (stalls and neighbourhood centres)
- fund-raising through 'rags'.

The problem of bringing these spheres of professional formation together is but one example of the wider problem in all forms of higher education of retaining a balance between theory and practice, and the individual and society. (See Goodlad, 1995b for more on this idea.)

Many forms of project work or problem-based learning in higher education try to effect a balance between domains. In addition, they can stimulate in students:

- commitment
- initiative
- cooperation
- communication skills
- knowledge of the organization of knowledge
- a sense of responsibility.

The missing ingredients in college-based projects and problem-based learning are sometimes responsibility to a definable client and direct contact with an ultimate beneficiary. Study service seeks to make good these deficiencies by holding onto one key idea: *to concentrate on work that could not otherwise be done.*

Good practice in any form of study service involves fidelity to two major principles:

- reciprocity – to avoid exploitation of students
- competence – to avoid exploitation of clients.

To qualify as study service, activities that integrate the claims of theory and practice, society and the individual, need to meet the following criteria:

- students (not staff alone) involved
- an integral part of the curriculum – and preferably assessed
- direct contact between students and intended beneficiaries
- effect detectable at individual or small-group level.

From these it will be seen that student tutoring and mentoring are ideal as a form of study service.

Although the idea of tutoring and mentoring is simple, the process of managing schemes is complex. indeed, as a scheme grows in either conceptual or administrative complexity, so the need emerges for a paid coordinator – which may be the most difficult part of a scheme to sustain!

Chapter 16 of this book offers practical suggestions, based on large-scale research, for making mentoring work; Chapter 17 identifies some key factors in making a student tutoring scheme work. Appendix A serves as a sort of checklist for those about to start schemes.

The Fertility of Student Tutoring and Mentoring Encounters as a Focus for Academic Study

Many of us have come to believe that student tutoring and mentoring will only attain stability if they are seen to be *central to the objects of the institutions from which the students come* – further and higher education establishments. And it is the primary obligation of these institutions to educate their students. I therefore turn now to the question of the learning opportunities for students from tutoring and mentoring.

Whatever additional instruction tutors and mentors receive, they must be given certain *basic training* in such matters as the following:

- how to start a tutoring or mentoring session by establishing a friendly atmosphere
- familiarity with the content of the tutees' syllabus
- what to do when the tutee gives a correct answer
- what to do when the answer is wrong
- what to do if a session goes badly
- how to vary the content of tutoring or mentoring sessions
- how to end a tutoring or mentoring session
- record keeping.

But students' education can, and should, go way beyond the inculcation of personal and professional skills. To illustrate the fertility of placements in service learning for generating theoretical questions, let us revert once more to peer tutoring. Some, but not all, of the students who take part in the 'Pimlico Connection' attend a course on the 'Communication of Scientific Ideas' offered by the Humanities Programme at Imperial College. In place of one of the coursework essays, the students can write an analytical report on some aspect of their tutoring. We do *not* at present assess the tutoring itself because the students' tutoring assignments differ widely – from working with cheerful and eager primary school children to coping with sullen and/or disruptive secondary school pupils.

When I have been teaching the Communication of Scientific Ideas course, frequently, in tutorials and seminars, students ask: 'Well, I can report what I did; but what analytic ideas should I pursue?' One technique is to use what I call the 'Gestalt Fix': asking them to think about the tutoring they have done and then to say the first words or phrases that come into their heads. The notion here is that the figure/ground perception that the question elicits will indicate the current configuration in which the students' ideas are located. This will give a frame of reference into and onto which other ideas can be woven. Typically the words the students utter are: 'noise'; 'enthusiasm'; 'chaos'; 'satisfaction'; 'bad discipline'; 'friendly'; 'mixed ability'; 'teachers under siege'; 'frustration'; and so on. My response to such suggestions is: 'Fine, you have the beginnings of an essay!'

As I have indicated, the key task of academic disciplines is to bring order into the chaos of individual perceptions. By identifying through the 'Gestalt Fix' their principal concerns students are offered the opportunity for academic engagement.

Take a typical tutoring scene from the 'Pimlico Connection': eager student (motivated, enthusiastic with a high level of success in the education system) trying to interest wriggling pupil (inner-city child who does not see the relevance of education and whose family has no history of post-16 involvement) in some aspect of science. The situation bristles with potent questions. The basic question – of why science does not seem to appeal to large numbers of pupils in inner-city schools – offers points of purchase for many disciplines. I will not attempt a complete cut and shuffle of disciplines, but rather highlight a few of the questions that might arise for the students and to which the disciplines (in brackets) offer fruitful approaches.

Selection: What aspect of science is being studied? Facts? Principles? Processes? From all the infinite variety of observations made by scientists, and all the procedures for making them, and theories to account for them, why have these particular ones been chosen for special attention by pupils on this day, in this school, in this place? How do these questions of science relate either to the fundamental structures of the discipline (that scientists might wish to pass on to others) or to the world picture that students and pupils use in practice to make sense of things? (*Science, Philosophy, Sociology*)

Relevance: Do these studies, and should they, relate in any way to the chosen careers either of tutors or tutees? (*Economics, Sociology*)

Demography: Why is it that the children of professional workers are so much more successful in the British educational system than those of other social classes? Why, for example, is not the typical scheme that of black tutor and a white child? (*History, Sociology, Psychology, Social Psychology*)

Culture: Where have these people come from? What are the differential life chances of people from different backgrounds? Should education be adapted specifically for the interests and needs of recent arrivals, who may speak languages other than English? Should there be a uniformity of cultural approach or some form of multicultural approach? (*History, Anthropology, Sociology, Literature, Economics*)

Ambience: What other influences are at work on the pupils? Granted, as research shows, schoolchildren spend some 26 hours a week watching television compared to some 24 hours a week actually in study at school, what is the impact on their thinking of the world shown by television? If, as is often the case, they seem to have greater interest in the content of television than in the content of their studies, could/should the content of television programmes be brought into the teaching as subject material? If not, how can teachers compete with the glamour and glitter of the rival media? Who, in any case, should determine what is studied? (*Political Science, Sociology, Psychology, Social Psychology, Economics*)

Curriculum: Where has the curriculum come from? Who controls what is done in schools and why, and with what authority? Who pays for what is done? Who determines how long pupils should stay in school? What areas of public life should be left to the market and what areas should be the subject of detailed state or local political intervention? What place should the National Curriculum have in our society? (*Political Science, Anthropology, History, Sociology, Economics*)

Measurement: If pupils seem to perform differently in their scientific studies (as they manifestly do) why is this? Are there differences in intelligence that can be separated out from differences in application, dedication and experience? How do educational measurements differ from measurements in other spheres? (*Science, Political Science, Anthropology, History, Philosophy, Psychology, Social Psychology, Sociology*)

Locating the experience of student tutors and mentors within academic frameworks

The questions above pertaining to a single situation in tutoring offer fuel for a number of academic disciplines. The value of student peer tutoring as an element in teacher training is self-evident. Intending teachers need to think about such matters in depth *before* entering their professional careers. (Tutoring is, incidentally valuable for those thinking of the *possibility* of going into teaching – as a way of helping them to make up their minds. Research on the 'Pimlico Connection' indicates that this is a motivating factor for many tutors.) However, many of the issues raised by the tutoring encounter penetrate to the heart of academic disciplines, such as history, sociology, social geography, anthropology, psychology, economics, political science, etc, and, indeed, science itself (and its numerous sub-disciplines).

At first sight, tutoring and mentoring may seem attractive only in the area of professional development; for instance in promoting the core personal and professional skills. But the professional skills encapsulate many questions that are fundamental not only to professional education but also to other types of education.

The original, and continuing, object of the 'Pimlico Connection' was to provide an opportunity for students of science and engineering to get realistic and demanding practice in the communication of technical information. Skill in communication is not just a frill; it is at the very core of professional practice. Whatever else professionals do, a key part of their work is that of making clear to people less well-informed than the professionals the areas of their choice in technical matters. For example, doctors explain to patients that this or that mode of treatment (or none at all) is possible; the patients then have to choose what they wish to do – with or without the help and intervention of the doctor. Again, lawyers explain to their clients the ways in which the law affects the client's situation; but the client ultimately gives instructions to the lawyer. Likewise, architects ascertain their clients' general wishes and explain the technical options (usually with drawings and/or models); the client then decides what is to be done. The fact that professionals usually go on to execute the wishes of their clients should not obscure the fact that the primary task of professionals is that of indicating to clients the grounds of the choices available to them (see Chapter 1 of Goodlad, 1984).

In all professions, it is necessary for the professional to communicate ideas and information simply and effectively to others. In some professional schools (in engineering, for example), specific instruction in communication skills is included, through report-writing exercises and so on. Such reports are often tedious for the students and boring for the faculty. Communication, strictly defined, means 'sharing'. One cannot communicate unless one has something one wishes to share. Most students know how dispiriting it can be to write reports for their professors when they know that the professor knows everything that they, the students, could possibly write. Communication exercises are, however, transformed when they are done for real. That is why experiential learning in general, (ie, learning from experiences outside the classroom) and study service learning in particular, are so attractive to students who may work with actual clients and have the interest and responsibility of writing reports/making statements that someone positively wants to read or listen to. Similarly, intending professionals can get tremendous stimulus from trying to explain technical ideas to other people in peer tutoring schemes. Many of the Imperial College students who have taken part in the 'Pimlico Connection' have had no intention of becoming teachers; nevertheless they have greatly valued and enjoyed the experience of explaining things to other people.

At the basic level of developing communication skills, the experience of communicating relatively low-level technical knowledge can be more challenging than explaining complex information to people who already have a highly-developed framework of ideas in which to 'locate' it. To explain ideas to non-specialists requires the communicator to:

- build a framework of ideas into which new material can be placed
- respond to the needs of a specific audience
- decide the specific purpose of communication
- organize ideas in some sort of structure
- choose the order of presentation
- make precise use of simple words, etc.

All these communication skills can readily be practised in tutoring and mentoring.

What is often overlooked is that with minimal prompting, students can be invited to think about the framework of ideas itself – in short, to confront the theoretical foundations of their academic disciplines by testing, through their essay writing, the capacity of the disciplines to illuminate the situations that the students have met. Indeed, some have argued that the type of active, deep, thoughtful learning identified by Marton and Saljo in the 1970s (Marton and Saljo, 1976a, 1976b) is to be found in the process of tutoring (see Benware and Deci, 1984). It is important to note in passing that the benefits to student tutors seem to result from actually *doing* the tutoring, rather than just preparing to do it (see Annis, 1983).

The teaching methods required in study service (of which student tutoring and mentoring are leading examples) are basically ones that work upwards and outwards from specific problems to the coordinating concepts of disciplines, rather than setting out the concepts and then allowing students to find examples. An analogy is that of teaching map reading. One fruitful approach is to drop students in the countryside and let them figure out where they are, and thereby determine how useful or otherwise the map is. A contrasting approach is to have a lecture course on maps (the history of map-making, the design and printing of maps, theory and practice of notation, etc) and then, when the students have passed some examinations in cartography, to let them loose. The art of curriculum planning in study service (service learning) is to know how much of which technique to use when. To drop students into (possibly hostile) unfamiliar terrain with no map at all is simply irresponsible: to talk them through every detail of the map before they can have a look round is likely to bore them and to miss opportunities for learning. Some interweaving of thought and action is called for.

Although tutoring and mentoring, like all study service, must treat the needs of clients as primary, my judgement is that the academic orientation of Study Service activities for facilitators and students must be from detail towards the coordinating ideas of academic disciplines.

Ten years ago, in *Educating the Reflective Practitioner*, Donald Schön (1987:3) identified a crisis of confidence in professional knowledge:

> 'In the varied topography of professional practice, there is a high, hard ground overlooking a swamp. On the high ground, manageable problems lend themselves to solution through the application of research-based theory and technique. In the swampy lowland, messy, confusing problems defy technical solution. The irony of this situation is that the problems of the high ground tend to be relatively unimportant to individuals or society at large, however great their technical interest may be, while in the swamp lie the problems of greatest human concern. The practitioner must choose. Shall he remain on the high ground where he can solve relatively unimportant problems according to prevailing standards of rigor, or shall he descend to the swamp of important problems and non-rigorous inquiry?'

In much higher education, abstraction is equated with virtue; the high, hard ground of theory is seen as the proper concern of universities. 'Swamp' problems are shunned. The reasons are well-known: 'international visibility' is difficult to achieve from the swamp. For better or worse, most academics are rewarded for the outward and visible signs of their activity, not for the inward and spiritual qualities that give rise to them. The principal tangible currency is publication, and the safest form of currency-minting is that done within very strict confines where principles of exclusion and concentration lead to clarity of vision, and where the process of assay (peer review) can work effectively.

There is nothing intrinsically wrong with this process. It leads to great competitiveness in universities and, at best, the emphasis on refinement of concept leads to very fruitful intellectual insights, and many practical benefits from even the most seemingly esoteric pursuits (for example, solid state physics). The institutional pressure on academics to publish is not, however, very conducive to involvement with study service.

The implications are these: new teaching and learning methods which, like study service, seek to unite thought and action, must, if they are to survive, *recognize institutional realities*. That is to say, unless we are to abandon the idea of universities as specialized institutions making their own uniquely important contribution to society, new teaching and learning methods must emphasize theory – presenting occasions for students to reflect upon their social action with a view to discerning underlying themes, regularities, patterns, concepts, and organizing principles. Service learning facilitators, including organizers of tutoring projects, need to help students to discern in the bewildering details of their placements *the connectedness of things*. Faculty and students need to develop skill in demonstrating to colleagues how study of even the grittiest administrative detail can lead to some perception by the students of intellectual order.

Recommended Action: Build the Preparation of the Tutors and Mentors into their Formal Education

By concentrating on the need to create academic contexts in which students can reflect about their tutoring and mentoring, I do not wish to diminish the importance of other matters. For example, tutoring and mentoring schemes may not get off the ground at all unless and until senior administrators in further and higher education institutions and in the government ministries that pay for them can be shown solid evaluation reports of schemes that have already been in operation.

I have stressed previously how important it was for us in the 'Pimlico Connection' to have produced reports each year from its inception. Having had a warm response to circulating copies of the students' group project reports, we have in every year since 1975 produced an annual report. These reports (the production of which is one of the main costs of the tutoring) have been useful in many ways, including:

- helped give local visibility to the scheme
- used for informing teachers and tutors new to the idea
- valuable for fund-raising
- a tangible reward to students for their efforts.

It was not until the 'Pimlico Connection' had been running for six years and evaluation had revealed similar patterns of response each year, that administrators began to take notice – helped perhaps by the fact that the title of one annual report, *The Wednesday Thousand*, highlighted the fact that then, as now, over 1000 people (tutors, teachers and school pupils) are involved with the activity every Wednesday afternoon.

An image

Let me end with an image of how we might usefully see student tutoring and mentoring. In Dinorwig in North Wales there is a special type of power station used to meet demand for electricity at peak periods. During periods of low demand, electricity is used to pump water from a lower reservoir to a higher one. When the electricity supply system is exposed to (usually predictable) surges in demand, water from the upper reservoir is released through generating turbines back into the lower reservoir, providing a boost in the supply of electricity to the grid.

Perhaps too often our tutoring schemes are like cascades (I use the word advisedly) in a remote and beautiful spot that visitors may come to see. We need to translate these cascades into highly-directed torrents that can be released in a concentrated and directed manner to meet situations of great need. But herein lies the moral of my tale: as King Lear said to his daughter Cordelia, 'Nothing comes of nothing'. Filling the reservoir is, to coin a phrase, an uphill struggle. If student tutors and mentors are to have their time and talents properly directed, organizers of schemes must put a great deal of work into preparing them. This costs money. The money can best be justified if the work is seen as part of the education of the tutors and mentors – and if that form of education is seen as part of the institutional mission of our further and higher education institutions. So: turn your cascade into a power station!

Address for correspondence: Professor Sinclair Goodlad, Humanities Programme, Room 440 MED, Imperial College of Science, Technology and Medicine, Exhibition Road, London SW7 2BX. Tel. +44 (0) 171 594 8752. Fax +44 (0) 171 594 8759. e-mail s.goodlad@ic.ac.uk

PART B: THE BENEFITS OF TUTORING: WHAT THE RESEARCH SHOWS

Chapter 2

STUDY AND STARS: THE ROLE OF RELATIONSHIP CONSTELLATIONS

Val Clulow and Linda Brennan

This chapter builds on the study by Clulow (1993) which showed that students interact with different people in their network, including peers, who provide a mentoring function to varying degrees. The extent to which these different relationships can contribute to career, study and personal matters was explored in this study.

Introduction

The nature of the mentoring relationship can be determined in a wide range of personal interactions. Kram (1986: 171) describes this as follows:

> 'The relationship constellation is the range of relationships with superiors, peers, subordinates, and (outside work) family and friends that support an individual's development at any particular time.... It reflects the fact that mentoring functions frequently are embodied in several relationships rather than just one.'

Clulow's (1993) findings, that a group of adult distance education students were gaining different mentoring functions from a range of individuals, was a useful extension of Kram's work. It has been used at Monash University in a number of ways to develop greater awareness among students about the personal, career and study benefits of linking into one's relationship constellation. The 'Student Briefing' publication now includes a section on mentoring and networking effectively. In addition an orientation booklet distributed to distance education students now includes the diagram of the relationship constellation found to be 'typical' in the study, and describes the idea that students isolated geographically can be proactive in incorporating others into their study processes.

The issue of 'transition' from school to university is receiving considerable attention in Australia, and especially in the state of Victoria. Two key factors are behind this interest. First, a major curriculum and assessment approach introduced into schools in recent years, for the final two years of schooling prior to university entry, has focused attention on the subsequent impact on 'transition' to university. Second, a tightening of funding and resources mechanisms for universities, which rewards student retention, has placed an emphasis on retention practices.

Tinto (1975) has proposed a model in which retention or attrition are viewed as outcomes of commitment to, and integration with, the educational process and the particular institution. This model has been validated in a number of studies (Pascarella and Terenzini, 1977; Terenzini and Wright, 1987).

Support provided by relationships involving psychosocial development affects the person's relationship with particular people, and most importantly self-image (Kram, 1986). In regard to learning, psychosocial development increases awareness of one's competencies, identity and effectiveness (Kram, 1986). The benefits of either of these types of developmental relationships can be seen to enhance awareness of learning opportunities and commitment to that process, at any age. There are fine shades of difference in the nature of such interactions that are characteristic of all relationships.

Kram and Isabella (1985), suggest that peers may be able to function well as mentors. In an earlier study of mentoring relationships (Kram, 1980), many of the individuals involved referred to the importance of relationships with peers when a mentoring relationship was changing or ending. Peer relationships appear to have the potential to provide strong interactive communication in relation to some of the mentoring functions (Clulow, 1993). There is no evidence to suggest that this concept is irrelevant to any age group.

Mentoring relationships are generally formed between people with both a considerable age difference and a difference in status in terms of the situational setting. Either of these attributes could be the same in the peer dyad.

This study indicates that peer relationships are able to fulfil a number of functions similar to those provided by a mentor. The benefits of developing a peer relationship as a student support system should be encouraged due to accessibility to other students as opposed to faculty or staff. In addition, as a peer relationship involves greater reciprocity and mutuality than a mentor relationship, for students, gains in relation to progress with study are mutual (Clulow, 1993).

McKavanagh *et al.* (1996) indicate that students as mentors are more successful because students at risk may not seek help from university administration and support services but from their fellow students and people outside the university system.

The concept of the 'relationship constellation' was introduced by Kram (1986) to account for the phenomenon whereby a network of others may contribute to one's development. It takes into account that there is a range of relationships between people both within an organizational environment and outside the workplace that can support an individual's development during their lifetime. Figure 2.1 illustrates this concept and reflects the idea that students gain different mentoring functions from several relationships. The relationship constellation of individuals varies and changes as needs and circumstances change and offers support for different aspects of an individual's development.

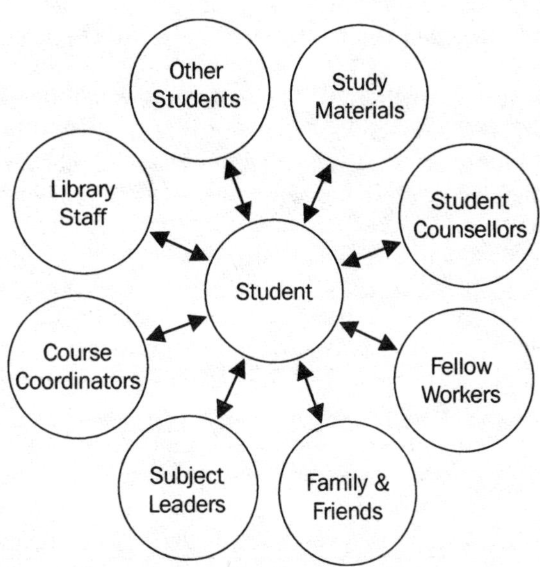

Figure 2.1 Student relationship constellation (Source: Clulow, 1993)

Methodology

In order to examine student relationship constellations, the following hypotheses were tested using a combination of qualitative and quantitative research techniques.

Hypothesis 1: Relationship constellations exist for each of the three areas of individual development; *careers, study and personal support*.
Hypothesis 2: There is a positive relationship between personal support and persistence with study.
Hypothesis 3: Students will differ in the types of relationship constellations according to their age group.

Sample frame

With more than 38,500 students on six campuses – Berwick, Caulfield, Clayton, Gippsland, Parkville and Peninsula – Monash University offers a breadth and depth of courses and programmes unique in Australia. The University has nine faculties – Arts, Business and Economics, Computing and Information Technology, Education, Engineering, Law, Medicine, Pharmacy and Science. The Faculty of Business and Economics comprises the departments of Accounting and Finance, Econometrics and Business Statistics, Economics, Management, Marketing, and Taxation and Business Regulation.

The sample frame consisted of 335 students enrolled in business degrees and business-related subjects at Monash University including open learning and distance education (see Table 2.1). Ages of students varied from 17 to 74, with the majority of students being in the 18–25-year-old groups.

Table 2.1 Sample frame

Mode of study	*Number of students*	*Response rate (%)*	*Mode*
Distance education	122/280	43.6	mail
Open learning	96/800	8.3	mail
On campus	117/800	14.6	lecture

Collection of data

First, three focus group interviews were conducted among university students enrolled in the Faculty of Business and Economics at Monash University. These were conducted to establish the terminology, definitions and possible relationship constellations of university students. These interviews helped to refine the questionnaire.

Secondly, in each of the identified categories, (on campus, distance education and open learning), eight students were interviewed – a total of 24 people in addition to the focus groups. These interviews established the relationships considered to be most important and also the activities undertaken by university students.

Thirdly, the questionnaire was pre-tested before being distributed to 1080 distance education and open learning students by mail. In the case of on-campus students, 800 questionnaires were distributed in lectures. The on-campus groups were selected to match the demographic and study profiles of the external students, so they contained both part-time and full-time students of various ages. Three hundred and thirty-five questionnaires were returned and analysed.

Instruments

A questionnaire contained a series of questions relating to student study practices, prior experience with university study and the people with whom the students were in contact throughout their study. These questions were designed to determine the level of contact in three key areas – careers, study, and personal support. Another series of questions related to personal support provided by the university.

Data analysis

SPSS/PC+ was used to analyse the data, calculate frequencies, and to perform bivariate correlations for the significant variables. Microsoft Excel was used to calculate relative rankings of the identified sets.

Results

Frequency results

The five-point rating scale below was collapsed to a 'talked to' or 'not talked to' scale to increase the numbers in each cell (Malhotra, 1993).

'Which of the following people do you refer to for information or advice regarding **career, study,** or **personal support** issues?'

1 = I **never** talk to ____________ about this issue
2 = I talk to ________________ about this issue **occasionally** (less than once per month)
3 = I talk to ________________ about this issue **often** (at least weekly)
4 = I talk to ________________ about this issue **frequently** (once or twice per week)
5 = I talk to ________________ about this issue on a **daily** basis.

Table 2.2 is the short list of the members of the relationship constellations ranked overall. This indicates the level of contact with various members of the relationship constellations in a general sense. These were ranked using Microsoft Excel.

Table 2.2 First 15 relationship constellation combined ranking

Person	*Careers*	*Study*	*Personal support*
Spouse or partner	68.3	70.8	72.2
Parents	73.8	73.8	67.9
Brothers and/or sisters	58.9	60.9	56.6
Social friends not related to study activities	66.2	64.4	56.0
Friends my own age at work who I see outside of working hours at work-related functions	63.8	65.3	53.4
Other family members	56.9	58.3	51.6
Friends I met at school before coming to university	49.9	48.4	44.9
Friends I met at university	45.8	50.4	38.5
My boss	52.2	46.1	29.7
Older people at work who are not necessarily my 'friend' and who are my equals	45.5	43.1	29.2
Work associates who are my own age and who I would not seek out at social activities	47.2	50.4	28.3

Older people at work who are not necessarily my 'friend' and who are my superiors	49.9	40.5	23.6
Fellow students that I share 'informal' study sessions with	28.9	35.0	22.2
Younger people at work who I see outside of working hours at work-related functions	31.5	33.2	20.7
Business acquaintances	48.7	42.6	19.0

Correlation test

The next phase of analysis undertaken was testing of the identified associations for the strength and direction of the association. To conduct this analysis, bivariate correlations were performed on the constellation members demonstrating significance at the .05 level. Table 2.3 depicts the outcomes of the correlation analysis and the level of significance of the relationships. Those factors that demonstrated an association significant at the .05 level are indicated by an asterisk. A double asterisk marks those where marginal significances were found, ie significances at the .10 level.

Table 2.3 Correlation tests of significance

Person	*Careers*	*Study*	*Personal support*
Friends my own age at work who I see outside of working hours at work-related functions			0.002*
Work associates who are my own age and who I would not seek out at social activities			0.089**
Human resources personnel at work			0.037*
Business acquaintances	0.458		0.002*
Friends I met at school before coming to university		0.001*	0.011*
People I attend classes with who are not 'friends' and whom I do not see outside of class	0.397		

People I attend classes with and some university-related functions	0.316		
Students I share formal study groups with	0.171	0.056**	0.628
Fellow students that I share 'informal' study sessions with	0.130	0.080**	0.201

It can be seen from Table 2.3 that there are a number of significant associations relating to the likelihood of a student's withdrawal from a subject and the people whom they contact about specific issues. Notably they are in the study and personal support area. All of the above associations were *positive* demonstrating a linear relationship between 'never talked to' and persistence with study. For example, in the first cell, 'Friends my own age at work who I see outside of working hours at work-related functions', the relationship between contact and withdrawal is a positive one, hence if a student *never* talks to this person they are *more* likely to withdraw from a subject.

Grouped data analysis and F test by age group

The results were then grouped according to the age of the student into 'over 21 years old' and 'under 21 years old'. Conducting the F tests demonstrated that the relationship constellations are significantly different for the two age groups. The top ten members of the relationship constellations are illustrated in Figures 2.2 and 2.3. Students in the older age category were more likely to withdraw from a subject than to fail a subject; the younger students were more likely to fail than withdraw. There were no significant differences between age groups in the combined failure and withdrawal question. Students in both age groups failed and/or withdrew from subjects at approximately the same rate. The highlighted cells represent the relationship constellation members that were affirmed as being associated with withdrawal or failure.

Discussion

Relationship constellations

In this study students were asked to indicate the extent of their contact with a listing of 24 categories of people, in relation to seeking information or advice on matters concerning careers, study and personal support.

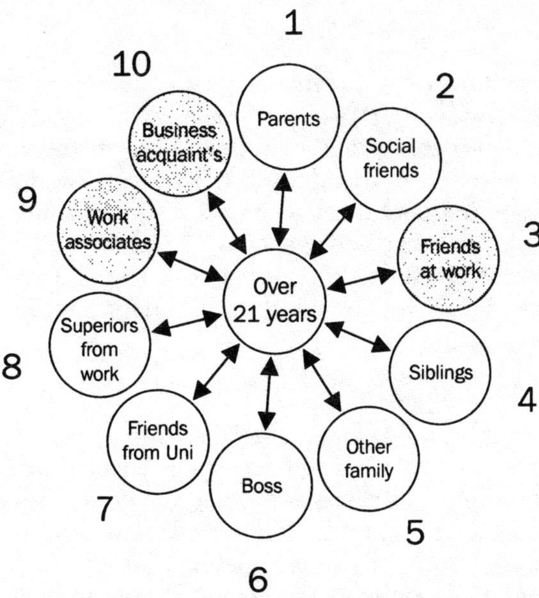

Figure 2.2 Relationship constellation of students over 21 years old

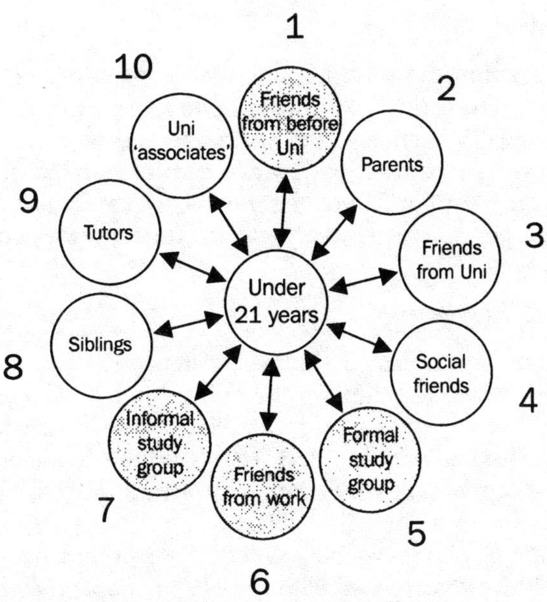

Figure 2.3 Relationship constellation of students under 21 years old

Career

The people listed most by students as their contact person on matters of career were (in ranked order) parents, spouse or partner, social friends, work friends of the same age, siblings and other family members. Although the age range of the sample in this study was between 17 and 74, 73.8 per cent of respondents listed parents as a contact person for matters relating to careers. Perhaps not surprisingly, spouse or partner was the second most listed category. Interestingly 30.3 per cent of respondents listed human resources personnel at work as a contact person for career advice.

Study

The people listed most by students as their contact person on matters of study were (in ranked order) parents, spouse or partner, work friends of the same age, social friends, siblings and other family members. Remarkably, the categories lecturer and tutor were ranked tenth and eleventh respectively as contact persons for matters relating to study. Siblings were listed by 60.9 per cent of respondents as a contact person in matters concerning study. Once again, spouse or partner was the second most listed category.

Personal support

The people listed most by students as their contact person on matters of personal support were (in ranked order) spouse or partner, parents, siblings, social friends, work friends of the same age and other family members. Spouse or partner was listed by 72.2 per cent of respondents as a contact point for personal support. The categories lecturer and tutor were indicated by 10.5 and 9.9 per cent respectively as contact people for personal support.

Persistence with study

The analysis of data collected about persistence with study supports the hypothesis that there is a significant relationship between making contact with people in the personal support relationship constellation and the decision to persist and pass a subject. That is, if they do not talk to people in their personal support network when they face a study crisis point, they are more likely to withdraw or fail a subject.

Results from respondents about whether or not they had withdrawn or failed a subject were correlated with the lists of people they had or had not spoken to. There was a significant relationship between contact made with people from the categories friends my own age at work, human resource personnel, business acquaintances and friends I met at university and whether or not students had withdrawn or failed a subject. That is, there was a positive correlation significant at .05 between those responses indicating that students never spoke to people in these categories and failure or withdrawal from a subject.

At the 0.10 level of significance, the groups, students with whom I share a formal study group, fellow students with whom I share informal study sessions, and work associates of my age were positively correlated with failed or withdrew from a subject. This result is interesting when compared with the respondents' top seven rankings of the most contacted people in the personal support category.

These two student relationship constellations showing the top seven contacts for each are provided as Figures 2.4 and 2.5.

Contrasting these figures with Figures 2.2 and 2.3, it can be seen that older students have three members of the positively correlated group in their relationship constellation: friends my own age at work, work associates and business acquaintances. On the other hand, the younger students had four members of the positively correlated group: friends from before I went to university, informal study group members, and formal study group members and friends at work.

The younger age group might be more at risk of failure than withdrawal than the older group for a number of reasons. First, their relationship constellation has fewer people from outside their university life, which would indicate a lack of breadth in their associations. Second, students who do not have these contacts 'ready made' when entering university may find it difficult to establish the required level of contact for effective crisis-point management. Third, with reference to Tinto (1975), younger students may not at this point be as 'committed to and integrated with' the educational process and the particular institution as their older colleagues. A recognition by the student of the possibility of failure, leading to withdrawal, possibly indicates a greater maturity.

The findings of this study support McKavanagh *et al.*'s (1996) findings which indicated that students do not seek support from formal support structures but more from fellow students. Acceptance of this fact and recognition that at-risk students may remain unobserved by faculty and staff provide further incentive for peer mentoring programmes as proposed by a number of universities and colleges in Australia and the USA. Facilitation of mentoring relationships, such as those described above, becomes a priority as diversity in higher education increases and current systems bear little relationship to the real needs of students.

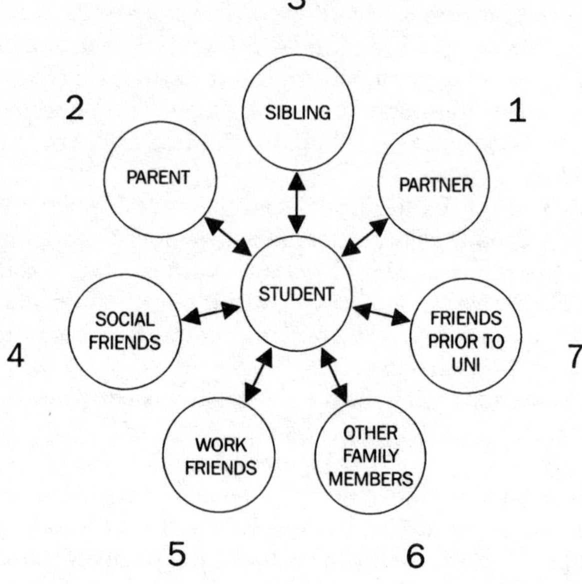

Figure 2.4 Seven most contacted for personal support

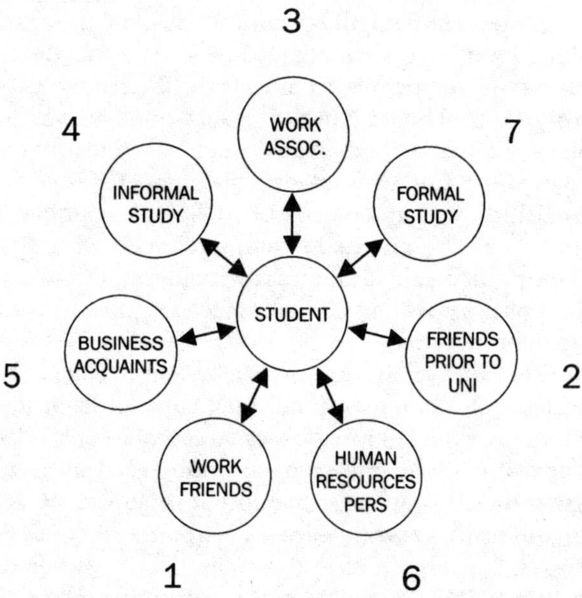

Figure 2.5 Seven contacts for personal support positively correlated with persistence

Implications for Future Research and Conclusion

This study has confirmed that student relationship constellations exist for purposes of career, study and personal support; there may be other categories for which students have relationship constellations. Further investigation of these categories would provide a more comprehensive understanding of the interaction networks of students, which may impact on study and learning outcomes. For example: how relevant and well used are the student support agencies such as counselling, health and study skills, offered on campus?

The study has also shown that there is a positive relationship between personal support and persistence with study and that there is a significant correlation between a group of people never spoken to and likelihood of withdrawal or failure of a subject. This finding has the potential for further investigation as several questions arise: if students had more contact with the seven people shown in Figure 2.5, would they be less likely to withdraw or fail? Examination of this phenomenon would require an experimental research design. The limitations of experimental research in the higher education context (who do you choose to allow to participate and what do you do if they fail?) is a potential barrier to further exploration of this topic as is the proscribing of students' relationships.

Furthermore, what is the *nature* of the contact of students with people in their networks? For example: in relation to matters to do with study, what sort of conversations/assistance/feedback/support do students seek and/or obtain from those in their relationship constellation? What strategies do students living away from home employ? Why do students tend not to contact formal support services and is there anything to be done about this phenomenon? Should universities be concerned at all about students' lives outside university?

A closer study of the value equation of the type and strength of 'support' gained from different members of one's relationship constellations could help to illuminate the concept. The value of the concept of relationship constellations in settings other than higher education are also yet to be explored, for example in the learning of trades, crafts or other non-academic fields.

The results from this essentially exploratory study suggest that universities should not ignore the personal support aspects of student life in relation to study success. Student mentoring is a successful strategy in improving student performance (Hanley, 1996), not least because it facilitates personal support network development for students who might otherwise be at risk if these networks were not in place.

Address for correspondence: V Clulow, Monash University, Department of Marketing, PO Box 197, Caulfield Campus, Victoria, Australia 3145

Chapter 3

HELPING HIGH SCHOOL PUPILS IN THE PERACH PROJECT: A COMPARISON OF MENTORING AND TUTORING APPROACHES

Barbara Fresko and Ronen Kowalsky

Two approaches for helping older pupils are compared as to activities, satisfaction, impact, and difficulties. In the first, university students employed a mentoring approach in which they acted as 'big brothers/sisters' to children while focusing on enrichment and interpersonal relations. In the second, students served as tutors or 'private teachers', working with pupils on homework and test preparation. Results showed that participants in both groups were highly satisfied. Despite the differences in approach, all students reported having contributed greatly to the child's desire to learn, and children in both groups felt that working with a university student had helped them most with their studies. Students who focused on academic work tended to encounter fewer difficulties during the year. There were indications from the data that the academic tutoring approach was more suitable for boys while mentoring which emphasizes enrichment was more appropriate for girls.

Introduction

Mentoring and peer tutoring schemes have become a familiar part of the educational scene around the world. When using either of these terms, individuals are referring to a broad spectrum of activities in which non-professionals assist other individuals through teaching or guiding. Specific programmes tend to differ with respect to a variety of parameters including duration, focus, structure, training and supervision, and participant traits. Goodlad (Chapter 1, this volume) has attempted to distinguish between mentoring and tutoring by defining the characteristics of each along several of these dimensions. For example, mentoring focuses on life skills, often takes place outside the classroom, involves a one-to-one relationship and lasts for a period of several months or even years. In contrast, tutoring concentrates on academic learning, is usually conducted in a classroom setting, involves a one-to-group relationship and takes place over a short period of a few weeks.

Research has shown programme effectiveness to be enhanced by training for mentors or tutors (Cohen *et al.*, 1982; Davis *et al.*, 1984; Niedermeyer, 1970), structuring (Gerber and Kauffman, 1981; Goodlad, 1979), frequency of sessions (Cloward, 1967); and ethnic, gender or age similarity between partners (Cloward, 1967; Cohen *et al.*, 1982; Fresko, 1993, 1996; Fresko and Chen, 1989). Few studies have examined the content of tutoring or mentoring and its effect on participants. At best comparisons have been made concerning the effect of providing academic assistance in different school subjects with the conclusion being that achievement gains for both helpers and those being helped are more readily attained in mathematics than in the area of reading comprehension (Cohen *et al.*, 1982; Fresko and Eisenberg, 1985).

In this chapter we will compare two helping orientations tried out within the context of the PERACH project in Israel. In the first case, assistance to pupils took on strictly academic overtones, while in the second case, it emphasized the provision of enrichment and the development of social skills.

The PERACH Project

PERACH is a nation-wide programme in which Israeli university and college students work with needy schoolchildren. Although termed in the past a tutoring scheme, its core operation actually fits Goodlad's description of mentoring, and therefore will be referred to here as a mentoring programme. Most mentoring in PERACH is individual, though in recent years some group work has been done centring around enrichment programmes in the areas of health, sports, science, nature, and the arts. For the most part, students meet the children twice weekly for two-hour sessions over the course of a school year, and in return they are awarded a partial tuition rebate. Meetings take place outside of school, often in the child's home. In 1996–7 more than 19,000 students were deployed around the country to work with approximately 45,000 schoolchildren. Officially participation is open to virtually any college student; however some screening is done at the start of the school year to weed out unsuitable types.

Unlike many projects that aim at providing remedial help in specific school subjects, PERACH's goals have never been specific nor exclusively academic. Mentors are not expected to deal exclusively with school-related learning. Instead they are to provide enrichment for the children, stimulate in them a desire to learn, reinforce their self-confidence, and serve as a role model. The main scheme is based on one-to-one relationships that take into account the particular needs of each child. Decisions regarding the employment of mentoring time are left to the student–child pair. It is expected that a close bond will develop between mentor and child and that this relationship will serve as the main vehicle by which educational aims are achieved (Attar, 1976).

Traditionally, activity in PERACH has focused on children in the elementary and junior high schools. Children are recommended as candidates for the programme by either their teachers or school counsellors. Over the years there has been a consistent drop in the average age of participants: in 1978 95 per cent of the children in the project were in Grades 5–9 (Eisenberg *et al.*, 1980a and b), whereas in 1994 the majority were attending Grades 3–6 (Fresko and Kowalsky, 1995).

In contrast to this trend the research on PERACH tends to indicate that working with older children may actually be more fruitful, though more difficult. For example, several studies found that older children who were mentored (Grades 5–7) made greater progress in school than others (Grades 3–4) (Fresko and Eisenberg, 1985; Fresko and Kowalsky, 1996). At the same time, mentors who worked with older children encountered greater difficulty setting up work sessions and establishing good interpersonal relationships (Eisenberg *et al.*, 1983a and b).

In 1994 a survey was carried out that included 1864 PERACH mentors (Fresko and Kowalsky, 1995). One variable examined was the mentored child's age. It was discovered that all mentors regardless of the age of their child were very satisfied with participation in the project and reported significant changes in the child as a result of mentoring. It was found, however, that students who worked with junior and senior high school pupils were more likely to stress school-related learning activities. Likewise, these mentors made less use of PERACH libraries, game rooms, and written materials made available to them. The conclusion was that PERACH materials were geared mainly for the younger child rather than for children in the upper grades. This was apparently a result of less attention being given to the mentoring needs of students working with older children.

In an attempt to find a scheme which better suited older children, an arrangement was tried out during 1995–6 in which students worked with children in Grades 11–12 adopting a more academic focus. They were instructed to devote their assistance to school-related learning activities, such as homework or test preparation. The assumption was that older children might find it easier to enter into a task-oriented situation, rather than one in which goals were only loosely defined. Moreover, being in the final stages of secondary schooling it was assumed they would be more motivated to accept assistance which could help them improve their grades as well as their chances of success on national matriculation examinations. In essence the mentoring approach which is traditional to PERACH was replaced by a scheme with a tutoring orientation.

The purpose of the present study is to investigate the success of this experiment. Comparisons are made between the 'experimental' tutoring approach and the 'traditional' mentoring approach in an attempt to answer the following questions:

1. Did students in the tutoring approach only deal with school-related activities or did they also include more 'traditional' PERACH activities of enrichment and personal talks?
2. To what extent were students and pupils satisfied with the academic tutoring arrangement?
3. To what extent and in which areas did tutoring and mentoring help the pupils?
4. What were the difficulties encountered during the tutoring/mentoring period?

The reactions of both students and pupils to the different approaches are examined separately. In addition, gender is also taken into account in data analyses as a variable which may be relevant when determining the merits and failings of each approach.

Data Collection

Sample

The academic tutoring approach was employed by 52 students with children in Grades 11–12. A total of 47 students (90 per cent) and 22 pupils (42 per cent) completed the research questionnaires which were administered on an individual basis by PERACH project coordinators. Insofar as PERACH does not ordinarily work with children at these grade levels, a comparison group that used an enrichment-mentoring approach came from Grades 9–10. In general, few children in these grades can be found in the project; however two groups were located which included 78 pairs, from which 53 students (68 per cent) and 51 children (65 per cent) completed questionnaires. In all 100 students and 73 pupils were studied. Since questionnaires were anonymous, matching between student and pupil responses was not done; rather comparisons were made between groups.

In the experimental group pupils were distributed among five high schools in the area of Haifa; whereas pupils in the comparison group were attending two high schools in the Beer-Sheva region. All pairs were same-gender, and 43 per cent of the students and 34 per cent of the pupils were male. Mentors and tutors were university or college students, 45 per cent of whom had served in PERACH in the past.

Research instruments

Questionnaires were administered to students and pupils towards the end of the 1995–6 school year after eight months of activity. The student questionnaire included items which dealt with project activities, evaluation of their impact on the pupils, reports of difficulties encountered during the year, and satisfaction from the relationship and from project participation. Questionnaires given to pupils contained many similar items as well as several additional ones. Pupils were asked to relate to actual and preferred activities, project effects, difficulty scheduling sessions, and satisfaction from the relationship with the student and from the project. On both questionnaires items tended to be closed-ended and responses were given on a 5-point Likert-type scale. As a result it was possible to calculate group means for most items and comparisons could be made using analysis of variance. English translations of both questionnaires are appended at the end of this chapter.

Results

Areas of activity

As noted above each model had different declared goals: in the academic tutoring model the focus of activity was to be school-related learning, whereas in the traditional PERACH model of mentoring, activity was to include general enrichment, non-formal learning and social activity, along with a 'big brother/sister' relationship. In order to investigate whether activity was actually different in the two groups, both students and pupils were asked to report the extent to which they engaged in different kinds of activities. Responses regarding each area of activity were given on a scale from 1 ('never') to 5 ('to a very great extent'). Average responses are presented in Table 3.1 by group for both students and pupils.

Table 3.1 Average degree of emphasis on different areas of activity, by group and sample (scale 1–5)

	Students		*Children*	
Activity area	*Tutoring group (n=47)*	*Mentoring group (n=52)*	*Tutored group (n=22)*	*Mentored group (n=51)*
School-related	4.64	3.81*	4.32	3.76*
Personal talks	3.17	3.94*	2.52	3.45*
Enrichment	2.06	3.48*	2.38	3.92*

* Significant difference between groups on ANOVA, $p<.05$

The data in Table 3.1 confirm that activity differed between the two groups. Those assigned to the tutoring approach did indeed concentrate on school-related learning while those in the mentoring group tended to divide their time among enrichment, academic studies, and personal talks. It should be noted that the first group did not exclusively engage in academic activities: on occasion interaction became less task-oriented, and student and child carried out discussions of a personal nature or engaged in some enrichment activity.

In order to determine whether pupils were satisfied with the content of the help provided to them, they were requested to indicate to what extent they would like to engage in the different project activities. Results are given in Table 3.2 by group and gender.

It appears from the data that, in general, pupils tended to prefer those activities which characterized their actual experience: pupils who engaged in formal academic activities with their students wanted school-related activities, whereas those who had received mainly enrichment and social activities showed a preference for them. Differences between groups were statistically significant in the latter two areas.

Table 3.2 Children's preferred areas of activity, by group and gender (scale 1–5)

Activity area	*Gender*	*Tutored group*	*Mentored group*
School-related*	male	4.50	3.90
	female	4.38	3.95
Personal talks	male	2.92	2.82
	female	2.88	3.95
Enrichment**	male	3.00	4.18
	female	3.13	4.23

* Significant difference between tutored and mentored groups, between gender groups, and for interaction on ANOVA, $p<.05$

** Significant difference between tutored and mentored groups on ANOVA, $p<.05$

An interaction effect was found in the area of academic activity. Boys in the tutoring model tended to select this area more than girls as the preferred area of concentration, whereas the reverse was the case concerning boys and girls in the mentoring model.

Satisfaction

On both student and pupil questionnaires satisfaction was measured using two items. On the first, respondents were requested to indicate to what extent they were satisfied with the student–child relationship and on the second they were asked whether they would recommend participation in the PERACH project to their friends. In Table 3.3 results are presented by group, sample and gender concerning satisfaction from the relationship.

Generally speaking, satisfaction was high: average scores ranged from 4.14 to 4.41 on a 5-point scale. More specifically, however, the pupils in both groups tended to be more satisfied than the students. Moreover, the pupils most satisfied were the girls in the 'traditional' mentoring group and the boys in the 'experimental' tutoring group.

Comparisons were made between approaches as to the percentage of students and children who would recommend participation to their friends (see Table 3.4). A willingness to recommend was interpreted as an indication of general satisfaction with the project. Overall satisfaction was high and differences between groups were not significant.

Table 3.3 Satisfaction from relationships: means by group, sample and gender (scale 1–5)

	Students		*Children*	
Gender	*Tutoring group*	*Mentoring group*	*Tutored group*	*Mentored group*
Male	4.09	3.81	4.50	3.82*
Female	4.30	4.29	4.00	4.58
All	4.20	4.14	4.32	4.41

* Significant interaction between gender and group for the children on ANOVA, p<.05

Table 3.4 Percentage of students and children recommending participation in PERACH to their friends, by group

	Students		*Children*	
	Tutoring group (n=43)	*Mentoring group (n=49)*	*Tutored group (n=22)*	*Mentored group (n=51)*
Would recommend	91%	96%	86%	90%
Would *not* recommend	9%	4%	14%	10%

Reported effects on the pupils

One would expect a relationship to exist between the area of activity and the area in which mentoring or tutoring has an impact on the pupils. In order to test this assertion, students were asked to evaluate to what extent the project had helped the children in different areas. Evaluations were given on a 5-point scale ranging from 1 ('no impact') to 5 ('great impact'). Results are shown in Table 3.5.

Table 3.5 Student assessments of degree of impact on children in different areas, by group (scale 1–5)

Activity area	*Tutoring group (n=47)*	*Mentoring group (n=50)*
School achievement*	4.11	3.70
Motivation to study	3.83	3.90
Self-confidence	3.74	4.02
Social adjustment*	2.40	3.33
General enrichment*	3.41	3.94

* Significant difference between tutoring and mentoring groups on ANOVA, $p<.05$

As expected, student tutors who engaged in academic learning reported greatest effects in school achievement. In their estimation pupils also received a considerable contribution regarding motivation to study and self-confidence. Unsurprisingly, least affected was social adjustment.

In the mentoring group, students reported greatest impact in the area of self-confidence. In addition contributions were considered great concerning enrichment of general knowledge and motivation to study. Differences between the two groups of students were significant in three areas. Contribution was considered greater in school achievement and lower in social adjustment and general knowledge enrichment for the tutoring group as compared to the mentoring group. It should be noted that, despite the differences in approach, students in both groups felt that they had contributed considerably to the pupils' motivation to learn.

Investigation of the contribution of the PERACH project as seen by the pupils was done indirectly. Pupils were asked to indicate to what extent different activities had helped them. Examination of their responses in Table 3.6 reveals an interesting phenomenon. In both groups, activities related to school-related learning were rated highest, although each group reported dealing with this area to differing degrees (as seen in Table 3.1). Since the tutored group did little other than homework and preparing for examinations, it is not surprising that these pupils rated this activity as most helpful. However, the mentored group engaged in a variety of activities which emphasized enrichment more than formal learning. Although the contribution of enrichment and personal talks was indeed rated higher among them than in the experimental tutored group, school-related activities received the highest contribution rating in this group as well.

Table 3.6 Children's assessments of help received from different activities, by group (scale 1–5)

Activity area	*Tutored group (n=22)*	*Mentored group (n=51)*
School-related	4.27	4.02
Personal talks*	1.95	3.51
Enrichment*	2.52	3.67

* Significant differences between tutored and mentored groups on ANOVA, $p<0.05$

Difficulties

Students were asked to indicate to what extent they encountered difficulties in different areas of their work. They were asked to respond on a scale from 1 ('not at all a problem') to 5 ('a serious problem') for each area. Thus a higher score indicated an area that was more problematic. Results are presented in Table 3.7.

Table 3.7 Students' assessments of difficulties encountered, by group (scale 1–5)

Difficulty	*Tutoring group (n=47)*	*Mentoring group (n=49)*
Scheduling sessions	2.55	2.61
Planning activities*	1.66	2.42
Dealing with emotional problems of child	1.74	2.04
Dealing with requests from child's family	1.62	1.86
Receiving suitable guidance	1.57	1.79

* Significant difference between tutoring and mentoring groups on ANOVA, $p<0.05$

The data in Table 3.7 reveal that mentors encountered more difficulties than tutors. Although only one difference between groups was statistically significant, in all five areas mentors complained of more problems. Differences were particularly great concerning difficulty planning activities and dealing with the emotional problems of the pupil.

Correlations were calculated between satisfaction (recommending participation to a friend) and each of these difficulties. Only one correlation coefficient was statistically significant. Students were less likely to recommend participation to their friends when they encountered difficulty finding suitable guidance (r=.35).

It seems that the most common difficulty encountered by tutors and mentors alike was in scheduling sessions. This problem is not new (see Eisenberg *et al.*, 1983a and b) and is one of the main reasons that PERACH management has been reluctant to increase activity with older children.

Pupils were presented with only one question concerning difficulties: they were asked whether there had been problems setting up work sessions. In the past this was found to be the most common problem when working with older children. Results are shown in Table 3.8 by group and gender; the comparable results for students are also presented. It seems that the pupils regarded arranging meetings as less problematic than the students. Moreover, the boys in the tutoring model and the girls in the mentoring model rated this area as less problematic than the other two groups. It should be recalled that they were also more satisfied with the student–child relationship and more interested in engaging in academic study.

Table 3.8 Degree of difficulty scheduling sessions by sample, group and gender (scale 1–5)

	Students		*Children*	
Gender	*Tutoring group*	*Mentoring group*	*Tutored group*	*Mentored group*
Male	2.71	2.56	1.64	2.64*
Female	2.39	2.64	2.50	1.90
All	2.55	2.61	1.95	2.06

* Significant interaction between gender and group for the children on ANOVA, $p<0.05$

Summary and Conclusions

PERACH activities with older children have always met with certain difficulties, mainly related to setting up work sessions and developing good relationships. In order to find a better approach to assisting older children an experiment was conducted in 1995–6. One group of students worked with high school pupils not in the traditional 'big brother/sister' manner characteristic of mentoring, but rather as tutors whose job was to help with school work. In this study we have examined the reactions of students and high school pupils to this tutoring arrangement and comparisons have been made to their counterparts in the traditional PERACH scheme of mentoring which emphasizes general enrichment and the nurturance of social skills.

It was found that students in the 'experimental' tutoring group dealt with academic studies as planned. Some of them also devoted time to personal talks with the children and other activities, although less frequently than regular PERACH mentors. Apparently, even when helping is highly task-oriented, regular one-to-one interaction between young people relatively close in age encourages the development of some degree of intimacy.

Students thought that the children were helped most in the areas on which they concentrated. In other words, if their emphasis was academic, then they reported that the children benefited most in school achievement, and if they stressed other activities, then they reported greater gains in self-confidence and general knowledge. Both groups of students indicated significant improvement for the children in motivation to study. It appears that both orientations aim at this target, approaching it in different ways.

The children themselves had different perceptions of the effects of mentoring and tutoring. In both groups they reported receiving the greatest benefits in the area of school-related studies. The reason for this might be that it is easier for them to acknowledge getting help in school than it is for them to admit to receiving support in more personal matters.

It appears that students who worked as tutors encountered fewer difficulties in carrying out their responsibilities. Perhaps focusing upon studies gave them a feeling that things were going smoothly. For them, as opposed to the traditional PERACH mentor, the content of activity was concrete, well-defined and concentrated on familiar areas, ie school subjects. Moreover, by definition, emotional problems or special requests from the pupil's family were not supposed to be of any principal concern to them, and were not included in their role specification. It is likely also that their task being clear-cut meant they had relatively less need for guidance. It should be mentioned that the greatest difficulty encountered by both groups of students was setting up regular and convenient sessions. This problem, however, was less troublesome to the children, probably because they saw this as the student's responsibility.

An interesting phenomenon was discovered when the child's gender was taken into account. It seems that boys in the experimental tutoring group and girls in the traditional mentoring group were more satisfied with the student–child relationship, reported fewer problems setting up meetings, and more often wanted project activity to emphasize academic assistance. These findings must be interpreted cautiously. It is indeed possible that the tutoring approach with its focus on school and academic studies suits boys more and that the mentoring approach, which is more social in orientation, is more appropriate for girls. However, since the two samples here were not equivalent with respect to age, clear-cut conclusions cannot yet be drawn. A repetition of this study in more controlled conditions would help ascertain the advantages and disadvantages of the two approaches.

Appendices

A. Student Questionnaire

Dear Student,

Each year PERACH tries to further improve its operation. Therefore your opinion is important to us. We would be grateful if you would spare a few minutes to complete this questionnaire. Your responses will remain anonymous.

1. Out of which PERACH office do you work? ____________________
2. How many years have you been working in PERACH? ________
3. Gender: a. male b. female _____________
4. Mentee's/tutee's school ___________________
5. Grade level of mentee/tutee __________
6. Gender of mentee/tutee: a. male b. female __________
7. To what extent have you engaged in the following activities with your mentee/tutee?

	not at all				to a great extent
Studies and homework	1	2	3	4	5
Personal talks	1	2	3	4	5
Enrichment activities	1	2	3	4	5

8. To what extent has mentoring/tutoring helped the mentee/tutee in each of the following areas?

	not at all				to a great extent
School achievement	1	2	3	4	5
Motivation to study	1	2	3	4	5
Self-confidence	1	2	3	4	5
Social adjustment	1	2	3	4	5
General enrichment	1	2	3	4	5

9. To what extent are you satisfied with the relationship which has developed between you and the mentee/tutee?

not at all				to a great extent
1	2	3	4	5

10. To what extent did you encounter any of the following difficulties in your work as a mentor/tutor?

	not at all				to a great extent
Scheduling sessions	1	2	3	4	5
Planning activities	1	2	3	4	5
Dealing with emotional problems of the child	1	2	3	4	5
Dealing with requests from child's family	1	2	3	4	5
Receiving suitable guidance	1	2	3	4	5

11. Would you recommend to your friends to join PERACH?

    a. yes b. no ________

Additional comments, complaints, suggestions which could help PERACH improve? Write freely. ____

____

____

B. Pupil Questionnaire

Dear Pupil,

Each year PERACH tries to further improve its operation. Therefore your opinion is important to us. We would be grateful if you would spare a few minutes to complete this questionnaire. Your responses will remain anonymous.

Helping high school pupils in the PERACH project

1. Grade ____
2. School __________
3. Gender: a. male b. female _______
4. Student's gender: a. male b. female ______
5. To what extent are you satisfied with the relationship which has developed between you and your student mentor/tutor?

not at all				to a great extent
1	2	3	4	5

6. To what extent did you have trouble setting up convenient meetings with your student?

not at all				to a great extent
1	2	3	4	5

7. To what extent do you and your student engage in the following activities?

	not at all				to a great extent
Studies and homework	1	2	3	4	5
Personal talk	1	2	3	4	5
Enrichment activities	1	2	3	4	5

8. To what extent did each of these activities help you?

	not at all				to a great extent
Studies and homework	1	2	3	4	5
Personal talk	1	2	3	4	5
Enrichment activities	1	2	3	4	5

9. To what extent would you have liked to engage in the following activities with your student?

	not at all				to a great extent
Studies and homework	1	2	3	4	5
Personal talk	1	2	3	4	5
Enrichment activities	1	2	3	4	5

10. What other activities would you like to do with your student?

    ____

11. Would you recommend to your friends to be in PERACH?

    a. yes b. no ________

Additional comments about mentoring/tutoring. Write freely. ____________
____
____

Address for correspondence: Dr Barbara Fresko, Beit Berl College, Doar Beit Berl 44905, Israel

Chapter 4

THE EFFECTIVENESS OF PEER TUTORING IN FURTHER AND HIGHER EDUCATION: A TYPOLOGY AND REVIEW OF THE LITERATURE

Keith J Topping

Quality, outcomes and cost-effectiveness of methods of teaching and learning in colleges and universities are being scrutinized more closely. The increasing use of peer tutoring in this context necessitates a clear definition and typology, which are outlined. The theoretical advantages of peer tutoring are discussed and the research on peer tutoring in schools briefly considered. The substantial existing research on the effectiveness of the many different types and formats of peer tutoring within colleges and universities is then reviewed. Much is already known about the effectiveness of some types of peer tutoring and this merits wider dissemination to practitioners. Directions for future research are indicated.

Research on teaching and learning in further and higher education is much less voluminous than that on teaching and learning in schools. While there have been a number of books on the topic of adult learning (eg, Brookfield, 1983; Entwistle and Ramsden, 1983; Gibbs, 1981; Laurillard, 1993; Lovell, 1980; Marton *et al.*, 1984; Merriam and Caffarella, 1991; Ramsden, 1986; Richardson *et al.*, 1987; Rogers, 1977; Sutherland, 1997; Tight, 1983), both the quantity and quality of research in this area is surprisingly limited, considering the vast resources expended on the tertiary sector. However, the quality and cost-effectiveness of teaching and learning in the sector are increasingly under the microscope. There has long been concern that traditional curricula, delivered and assessed in traditional ways, promote a surface approach to learning rather than a deep or even a strategic approach (Entwistle, 1992). Teaching quality assessment exercises consistently result in criticism of departments for failing to promote the development of transferable skills in their students (Barnett, 1992; Ellis, 1993). At the same time, increased student numbers coupled with reduced resources have often resulted in larger class sizes, thus encouraging a reversion to a traditional lecturing style of delivery and a reduction in small group and tutorial contact – in short, less interactive teaching and learning.

The dual requirement to improve teaching quality while 'doing more with less' has recently increased interest in peer tutoring in higher and further education. However, it would be unwise to seize upon peer tutoring as a universal, undifferentiated and instant panacea. Different formats of peer tutoring have been the subject of research of differing quantity and quality, with various outcomes.

Definitions and Typology

Peer tutoring is a very old practice, traceable back at least as far as the ancient Greeks. Archaic definitions of peer tutoring perceived the peer tutor as a surrogate teacher, in a linear model of the transmission of knowledge, from teacher to tutor to tutee. Later, it was realized that the peer tutoring interaction was qualitatively different from that between a teacher and a student, and involved different advantages and disadvantages.

At this point of development, a definition might have been: 'more able students helping less able students to learn in cooperative working pairs or small groups carefully organized by a professional teacher'. However, as development and research in different formats of peer tutoring proceeded apace in more recent years, it became clear that peer tutoring is not necessarily only about transmission from the more able and experienced (who already have the knowledge and skills) to the less able (who have yet to acquire them). As peer tutoring has developed, defining it has become more difficult, and a current definition seems so broad as to be rather bland: 'people from similar social groupings who are not professional teachers helping each other to learn and learning themselves by teaching'. However, this definition does include reference to the gains accruing from the tutoring process to the tutor – increasingly, peer tutoring projects target gains for both tutors and tutees.

Peer tutoring is characterized by specific role taking: at any point someone has the job of tutor while the other(s) are in role as tutee(s). Peer tutoring typically has high focus on curriculum content. Projects usually also outline quite specific procedures for interaction, in which the participants are likely to have training which is specific or generic or both. In addition, their interaction may be guided by the provision of structured materials, among which a degree of student choice may be available.

A typology of peer tutoring could include ten dimensions:

1. *Curriculum content* – which may be knowledge or skills oriented, or a combination. The scope of peer tutoring is very wide and projects are reported in the literature in virtually every imaginable subject.
2. *Contact constellation* – some projects operate with one tutor working with a group of tutees, but the size of group can vary from two to 30 or more. Sometimes two tutors take a group of tutees together. Less traditional, and more intensive, is peer tutoring in pairs (dyads).
3. *Year of study* – tutors and tutees may be from the same or different years of study.
4. *Ability* – while many projects operate on a cross-ability basis (even if they are same-year), there is increasing interest in same-ability tutoring (where the tutor has superior mastery of only a very small portion of the curriculum, or a pair are of equal ability but working towards a shared, deeper and hopefully correct understanding).
5. *Role continuity* – especially in same-ability tutoring, the roles of tutor and tutee need not be permanent. Structured switching of roles at strategic moments (reciprocal tutoring) can have the advantage of involving greater novelty and a wider boost to self-esteem, in that all participants get to be tutors.
6. *Place* – peer tutoring may vary enormously in location of operation.
7. *Time* – peer tutoring may be scheduled in regular class contact time, outside of this, or in a combination of both, depending on the extent to which it is substitutional or supplementary.
8. *Tutee characteristics* – projects may be for all students or a targeted subgroup, eg the especially able or gifted, those considered at risk of under-achievement, failure or drop-out, and those from ethnic, religious and other minorities.
9. *Tutor characteristics* – the traditional assumption was that tutors should be the 'best students' (ie, those most like the professional teachers). However, very large differentials in ability can prove under-stimulating for the tutor. If tutors are students who are merely average (or even less), both tutor and tutee should find some cognitive challenge in their joint activities (eg, Fantuzzo *et al.*, 1989). Although tutee gain may not be so great, the aggregate gain of both

combined may be greater. Many projects in schools have deployed students with learning and behaviour difficulties as tutors, to the benefit of the tutors themselves (Ashman and Elkins, 1990; Scruggs and Osguthorpe, 1986).

10. *Objectives* – projects may target intellectual gains, formal academic achievement, affective and attitudinal gains, social and emotional gains, self-image and self-concept gains, or any combination. Organizational objectives might include reducing drop-out, increasing access, etc.

Theoretical Advantages of Peer Tutoring

The cognitive processes involved in peer tutoring have been explored by various writers over the years, many of whom emphasized the value of the inherent verbalization and questioning (eg, Bargh and Schul, 1980; Durling and Schick, 1976; Foot, Shute *et al.*, 1990; Forman, 1994; Gartner *et al.*, 1971; Webb, 1982). A neo-Piagetian interpretation of individual development through the cognitive conflict and challenge involved in many forms of peer assisted learning is offered by Doise and Mugny (1984). However, peer tutoring is more fully understood through the social interactionist (or socio-cultural or social constructivist) view of cognitive development. Supported (or 'scaffolded') exploration through social and cognitive interaction with a more experienced peer in relation to a task of a level of difficulty within the tutee's 'zone of proximal development' remains a theoretical cornerstone of peer assisted learning (Vygotsky, 1978). This theme has been further developed by Rogoff (1990) under the label of 'apprenticeship in thinking'.

Peer tutoring is often promoted on the grounds that, for the tutors, it is 'learning by teaching'. This view is expanded in the old saying, 'to teach is to learn twice'. Sternberg's (1985) theory of intelligent performance identifies components which might be enhanced during peer tutoring (Hartman, 1990): the meta-cognitive skills of planning, monitoring and evaluating and the associated use of declarative, procedural and contextual knowledge; and the cognitive processes of perceiving, differentiating, selecting, storing, inferring, applying, combining, justifying and responding. Just preparing to be a peer tutor has been proposed to enhance cognitive processing in the tutor – by increasing attention to and motivation for the task, and necessitating review of existing knowledge and skills. Consequently, existing knowledge is transformed by reorganization, involving new associations and a new integration. The act of tutoring itself involves further cognitive challenge, particularly with respect to simplification, clarification and exemplification.

An excellent study by Annis (1983) compared three randomly allocated groups of students: one which merely read the material to be studied, one which read the material in the expectation of having to teach it to a peer, and a third which read the material with the expectation of teaching it to a peer and then actually carried this out. On a 48 item test of both specific and general competence, the 'read only' group gained less than the 'read to teach' group which in turn gained less than the 'read and teach' group. The tutors gained more than the tutees. A similar study by Benware and Deci (1984) compared the relative effectiveness of reading to learn for a test and reading for learning to teach a peer. Subjects were randomly assigned to conditions and the outcome measure was a 24 item test of both rote memory and conceptual understanding. While both groups performed equally well on rote learning, the 'learn to teach' group performed better on higher order conceptual understanding, and on a questionnaire regarding motivation and learning perceived their experience as more active and interesting.

Many other advantages have been claimed for peer tutoring and related forms of peer assisted learning (eg, Greenwood *et al.*, 1990). Pedagogical advantages for the tutee include more active, interactive and participative learning, immediate feedback, swift prompting, lowered anxiety with correspondingly higher self-disclosure, and greater student ownership of the learning process. The pupil/teacher ratio is much reduced and engaged time on task increased. Opportunities to respond are high, and opportunities to make errors and be corrected similarly high. In addition to immediate cognitive gains, improved retention, greater meta-cognitive awareness and better application of knowledge and skills to new situations have been claimed. Motivational and attitudinal gains can include greater commitment, self-esteem, self-confidence and empathy with others. Much of this links with work on self-efficacy and motivated learning (Schunk, 1987), leading to the self-regulation of learning and performance (Schunk and Zimmermann, 1994). Modelling and attributional feedback are important here – perhaps peer tutoring can go some way towards combating the dependency culture associated with superficial learning. From a social psychological viewpoint, social isolation might be reduced, the functionality of the subject modelled, and aspirations raised, while combating any excess of individualistic competition between students. Moust and Schmidt (1994a) found that students felt peer tutors were better than staff tutors at understanding their problems, were more interested in their lives and personalities, and were less authoritarian, yet more focused on assessment. Economic advantages might include the possibility of teaching more students more effectively, freeing staff time for other purposes. Politically, peer tutoring delegates the management of learning to the learners in a democratic way, seeks to empower students rather than de-skill them by dependency on imitation of a master culture, and might reduce student dissatisfaction and unrest.

Peer tutoring can have disadvantages, however (Greenwood *et al.*, 1990). Establishing it does consume organizational time in designing and effecting appropriate peer selection and matching, and it may also necessitate some adaptation to curriculum materials. Certainly the requirements for training students in teaching and learning skills are greater, although it can be argued that peer tutoring merely serves to bring to the surface needs that traditional teaching tends to overlook. All these may involve increased costs in the short term, with a view to reduced costs and/or greater effectiveness in the medium and long term. The quality of tutoring from a peer tutor may be a good deal inferior to that from a professional teacher (although this should not be assumed), and the need for monitoring and quality control cannot be overstated. This also significantly consumes time and resources. Likewise, the tutor's mastery of the content of tutoring is likely to be less than that of a professional teacher, so curriculum content coverage in peer tutoring may be much more variable. For these reasons, project coordinators may experiment initially with peer tutoring for consolidation and practice, rather than the first learning of new material, utilizing it on a small scale with suitable topics.

Research on Peer Tutoring in Schools

A recent review (Topping, 1992) identified 28 previous reviews and meta-analyses of research on peer tutoring, mostly in schools. Sharpley and Sharpley (1981) conducted a meta-analysis of 82 studies in schools, reporting substantial cognitive gains for both tutees and tutors. Same-age tutoring appeared as effective as cross-age tutoring, and training of tutors significantly improved eventual outcomes. Cohen *et al.*, (1982) discovered 500 titles relating to tutoring. In 65 studies with control groups, tutored students out-performed controls in 45. There was again evidence that tutor training produced larger sizes of experimental effect. Highly structured tutoring was also associated with larger effect sizes. There was evidence that peer tutoring improved tutee attitudes in class, as well as tutee self-concept. In 38 control group studies measuring tutor achievement, tutors out-performed controls in 33. Improved tutor attitudes and self-concept were also reported.

There is thus substantial evidence that peer tutoring is effective in schools. Beyond this, relative cost-effectiveness may also be considered. Levine *et al.*, (1987) conducted a cost-effectiveness analysis of four different interventions designed to improve reading and mathematics in primary schools (elementary schools) in the USA: computer-assisted learning, reducing class size, lengthening the school day, and cross-age peer tutoring. The most cost-effective intervention (peer tutoring) was four times more cost-effective than the least. The least cost-effective was reducing class size. While evidence concerning peer tutoring in schools can certainly not be automatically generalized into higher and further education, there is considerable food for thought in these findings. A wider recent review of various forms of peer assisted learning in schools is available in Topping and Ehly (1997).

Peer Tutoring in Higher Education – Previous Reviews

Previous reviews and surveys of peer tutoring in higher and further education include those of Cornwall (1979), Goldschmid and Goldschmid (1976), Lawson (1989), Lee (1988), Maxwell (1990), Moore-West *et al.* (1990) and Whitman (1988). All of these are interesting, but the earlier papers were completed at a time when most of the literature was descriptive in nature. The Goldschmids' own empirical work (1976) was well before its time in this respect. Cornwall (1979) offered a wide ranging overview of the field, including advice on organization and problem-solving. In a survey of 93 colleges, Lee (1988) made a comparative analysis of seven different kinds of programmes targeted on increasing retention and reducing student drop-out. Programmes involving peers as resources showed up particularly well. The most expensive programmes were not more effective than cheaper ones and size of institution was not a factor in retention and drop-out rates. Peer tutoring and peer counselling both showed good cost-effectiveness, while traditional remedial programmes proved very cost-ineffective. Lawson (1989) surveyed 19 colleges and universities in Canada identified as having peer assisted learning programmes. Peer tutoring was found to be more common than peer counselling. Detailed descriptions of goals, selection, training, logistics and methods for evaluation of programmes are given, but little hard data on comparative effectiveness and cost-effectiveness. Peer assisted learning programmes in United States medical schools were surveyed by Moore-West *et al.* (1990). Of 127 colleges in an association, 62 replied, and of these 47 had peer tutoring programmes, while 40 had 'advising programmes' and 13 had 'peer assessment programmes'.

Cross-year Small-group Tutoring

In this review of the more recent substantive literature on different forms of peer tutoring, the format most like surrogate professional teaching will be considered first. This is where upper year undergraduates (or postgraduates) act as tutors to lower year undergraduates, each tutor dealing with a small group of tutees simultaneously. The literature search revealed 18 studies of note (American River College, 1993; Arneman and Prosser, 1993; Bobko, 1984; Button *et al.*, 1990; Cone, 1988; House and Wohlt, 1990; Johansen *et al.*, 1992, Johnston, 1993; Lidren *et al.*, 1991; Longuevan and Shoemaker, 1991; McDonnell, 1994; Mallatrat, 1994; Meredith and Schmitz, 1986; Moody and McCrae, 1994; Moust and Schmidt, 1992, 1994b; Moust *et al.*, 1989; Schmidt *et al.*, 1994). Many of these gathered only subjective feedback outcome data. Of 11 studies doing this, nine reported very positive outcomes, one noted outcomes as good as those from teaching by professional faculty, and one reported less good outcomes than for professional faculty. Three studies reported reduced drop-out in association with such tutoring. Five studies reported improved academic achievement, another four reported academic achievement as good as that from professional teaching and one reported achievement slightly but significantly worse than that. Much of the research is not of the highest quality, but good quality studies (eg, American River College, 1993 and Lidren *et al.*, 1991) do clearly demonstrate improved academic achievement.

In Bobko's (1984) study, the peer tutors had groups of 25 tutees for 12 hours per week. Course grades did not show a significant improvement over previous years, but previous groups may not have been comparable. Interviews with tutees yielded many reports of increased confidence and less anxiety, while tutors reported improvements in their knowledge and ability to communicate. Meredith and Schmitz (1986) reported a study involving many subjective ratings, and although some favoured peer tutoring compared to faculty tutoring, others indicated the opposite, and a great many were not significantly different. A mixed method project reported by Cone (1988) involved rotating recitation and testing between same-year peers with coaching and testing by cross-year peer teaching assistants. Tutoring objectives and materials were highly structured. Outcomes on test were markedly higher than normal expectations, but the lack of proper control groups and the absence of information about assignation to groups limits the conclusions that might be drawn.

A comparative study by Moust *et al.* (1989) in law included process measures that indicated that student tutor behaviours were very similar to those of professional faculty. Nevertheless, on outcome test scores the faculty tutored students scored higher than those tutored by peers. Button *et al.* (1990) reported cross-year tutoring (which they termed 'proctoring') in mechanical engineering and computing in relation to specific design projects. The subjective feedback from the vast majority of tutors and tutees was very positive. House and Wohlt (1990) compared achievement outcomes on grade point averages (GPAs) for peer tutored and non-tutored students. Male peer tutored students achieved higher GPAs than non-tutored, but female tutees did not. The subjects were self-selected into groups and the outcome measure was very general and probably insensitive to small-scale intervention effects. Student drop-out also improved. A better quality study by Lidren *et al.* (1991) used randomized control groups and compared outcomes for peer tutored groups of six with groups of 20. Both groups performed better academically in terms of examination results and positive subjective feedback than non-tutored students. The smaller peer tutored groups yielded better outcomes than the larger ones.

Longuevan and Shoemaker (1991) deployed upper year students and clerical staff as volunteer tutors. The tutors were required to attend the same lectures as the tutees prior to giving tutorial assistance. This tutoring programme charged a fee to tutees and 10–15 per cent of undergraduates in the institution participated. There was some evidence that larger amounts of tutoring resulted in higher GPAs, although the size of difference was small and its significance not easy to establish. Johansen *et al.* (1992) reported subjective feedback, with tutees mostly satisfied but tutors rather anxious. Arneman and Prosser (1993) studied peer tutoring in dentistry in Australia. Subjective feedback indicated confidence gains in tutors and tutees. Johnston (1993) deployed trainee teachers as tutors for economic students in 'micro-learning groups' of four. Although subjective feedback was very positive, the examination and test results of participants and non-participants were not very different.

American River College (1993) deployed 24 paid 'learning assistants' for three hours per week with groups of two to six tutees. Tutees' subjective feedback was very positive, and tutors felt their own knowledge of their subject improved. Most strikingly however, although tutees had lower general GPAs than non-tutored students, they scored as well or better than them in tutored subjects. In the area of computer science, McDonnell (1994) researched tutoring by third-year students of small groups of up to four second-year students, and reported very positive subjective feedback. Moody and McCrae (1994) reported on cross-year tutoring in groups of six to 14 in law. Subjective feedback from tutors was positive. Mallatrat (1994) targeted reduced drop-out rate for a peer tutoring project in computing. Half the students utilized the scheme, a quarter regularly. Tutees reported finding the experience supportive and achieved improved grades compared to previous cohorts of students. Seven students reported that peer tutoring had been the critical factor in preventing them from leaving the course, and other subjective feedback was positive.

Moust and Schmidt (1992, 1994b) found student tutored and staff tutored groups gained equally in achievement during an eight-week problem-based law course. Schmidt *et al.* (1994) compared the achievement of 334 peer tutored and 400 faculty tutored groups in a problem-based health sciences course. Overall, the latter achieved slightly but significantly better, but peer tutoring was equally beneficial in the first year of the course.

The Personalized System of Instruction

Fred Keller is credited with the 'invention' of the Personalized System of Instruction (PSI), which is also called the 'Keller system'. In 1968 he described the procedure, which is based upon programmed learning material, through which each student proceeds at their own pace with the goal of mastering each step. The peer tutor's involvement is largely as a checker, tester and recorder, to ensure tutee mastery. In 1977 Robin and Heselton compared training PSI tutors interactively with training by a written handbook only. The direct training produced higher quality tutoring behaviour, but no difference in tutee outcomes. Davis (1978) discussed the components of the tutoring role in PSI, and queried whether the tutors benefited more than the tutees. The most substantial review of the effectiveness of PSI was produced by Kulik *et al.* (1979), who meta-analysed 75 controlled studies. Of 61 studies evaluating in terms of class marks, 48 found PSI to give superior results. Of 20 studies scrutinizing variation in achievement in the target group, 18 found PSI was associated with reduced variability. Sixty-one studies considered final examination performance and 57 of these found PSI tutees superior.

Eleven studies also considered student subjective rating of teaching quality, ten of these finding that PSI students gave more favourable ratings. Eight studies also measured delayed retention of the material learnt, and all found PSI students superior. PSI was found to be effective across the whole ability range. It raised the final examination score of a typical student in a typical class from the fiftieth to the seventieth percentile. Effects were even more striking on delayed examination and these differences were more pronounced on essay than on multiple-choice examinations. PSI effects were evident in studies with both good and less good research designs. Despite this very convincing evidence, Sherman (1992) noted that PSI use reached a plateau and speculated that computer-aided learning may be currently more fashionable because it is less threatening to teachers.

Supplemental Instruction

Another well known 'brand name', Supplemental Instruction (SI), aims to reduce drop-out rate and usually targets high risk courses rather than high risk students. It is often used in courses with new and difficult content, a predominance of lectures and low rates of interactive teaching, and where assessment and monitoring are relatively infrequent. It operates on a cross-age basis with one 'leader' working with several tutees. Originated at the University Missouri at Kansas City (UMKC) in 1975, it has come to be offered to almost half of the first-year students in its host institution. Over 300 institutions have been trained to use SI in the USA and more than 15 institutions now use SI or some variant in the UK. Leaders are trained to 'model, advise and facilitate' rather than directly address curriculum content. They have always previously completed the same course as the tutee, and usually again attend the tutees' lectures.

Martin and Arendale (1990) report a controlled study of SI at UMKC. The drop-out rate halved, the average course grade was 0.5 to 1.0 higher and graduation outcomes were 12.4 per cent higher. The National Centre for Supplemental Instruction (1994) reviewed evidence for the effectiveness of SI from UMKC and other universities in the USA. UMKC data from 14 successive academic years, involving 295 courses and 11,855 SI participants, indicated statistically significant differences in grades for participants compared to non-participants, even when initial (pre-SI) academic performance was controlled. There was widespread evidence of effectiveness across the whole ability range. SI participation was also associated with higher re-enrolment and graduation rates. Similar data were reported from 146 other institutions, involving 2875 courses and 298,629 SI participants. (See also Martin and Arendale, 1992; Martin *et al.*, 1983).

Kenney and Kallison (1994) report two studies of SI in mathematics courses, using comparable participant and non-participant groups. One study found significant differences favouring the SI group, the other found no difference. In both studies there was evidence of low-ability students responding disproportionately well to SI. Bridgham and Scarborough (1992) used a regression model to predict medical students' expected final outcomes from their entry level, finding a subsequent statistically significant 'over-achievement' for SI participants. Average SI effect size was between one-third and one-half of a standard deviation in final test scores.

Research in the UK was reported by Bidgood (1994), Healy (1994), Rust (1993), Rust and Wallace (1994), Rye *et al.* (1999) and Wallace (1993). Wallace (1993) reported that levels of attendance at SI sessions were correlated with final course marks. However, further details were lacking. Rust (1993) reported that the course-work marks of SI tutees were on average 5 per cent higher if they had attended two or more sessions, although the SI tutees were far from being model students. This improvement was modest and again details were lacking.

Healy (1994) reported improved performance in annual examination results of SI students as well as reductions in drop-out rates, coupled with enhanced communication and other transferable skills and a deeper understanding of the principles of the curriculum area in question (engineering). However, as the groups were self-selected, comparability was doubtful, and no control group was used. Healy (1994) noted the need for longer-term follow up of SI effects. More persuasively, Bidgood (1994) reported that end-of-year course-work and examination marks in two successive years of a computer science course at Kingston University were statistically significantly better for SI participants than for non-participants with equivalent entry qualifications and start-of-year marks. SI students did not figure in failure or resit lists.

It has been claimed that SI in the UK has also demonstrated improved grades for SI leaders compared to non-participants, as well as gains in self-confidence and communication skills, but details of the data are difficult to find. In the USA SI leaders are usually paid, whereas this is much less frequent in the UK. A related development is the establishment of faculty-wide cross-year small-group 'student supported learning', with many of the features of SI but much more focus on gains for the tutors, who are unpaid but receive credits in a course accreditation transfer scheme for their participation (Topping, Simpson *et al.*, 1997).

Same-year Dyadic Fixed-role Tutoring

More innovative (and perhaps easier to organize) is tutoring between pairs (dyads) in the same year of study, ie at the same point in the course, where one member retains the role of tutor throughout. Seven studies, some of considerable age, have focused on achievement gains resulting from this practice. The classic studies by Annis (1983) and Benware and Deci (1984) referred to earlier were examples of this format. Rosen *et al.* (1977) worked with same gender pairs in which the tutors were either more, less or equally competent than the tutees. Also, for half of the participants, roles were reciprocated halfway through the project. Subjects received only 20 minutes of training and 48 out of 90 pairs did not supply full data. Outcome measures included 20 item pre- and post-tests and satisfaction questionnaires. There was some evidence the changing role from tutee to tutor was associated with an improvement in achievement. There was also an indication that pairing with someone of greater or equal ability was associated with a greater achievement.

Fremouw and Feindler (1978) studied the effectiveness of dyadic same-year tutoring in contrast with that of tutorials in groups of nine led by a professional faculty member. The peer tutors were given some additional content training. Two control groups were used, one given equal attention of a different sort and another a non-participant waiting list group. The peer tutored group achieved outcomes as good as the professionally tutored group. A study in Esperanto teaching was reported by McKellar (1986). Tutors were trained in new material and study guides were provided to support the tutoring. High accountability was inbuilt, since post-test tutor and tutee scores were combined as a performance indicator. The researchers found that the more tutors gave information, the higher was the tutor score and combined tutor and tutee score. High scores were also associated with the tutee asking for clarification and asking for the main points to recall. However, where tutors gave wrong information, this was associated with reduced scores for both tutor and tutee. The tutor simply asking if the tutee understood was also associated with poorer scores.

Two studies in Edinburgh are reported by Falchikov (1990). One study allocated participants randomly to tutor/tutee and study alone conditions, but found no significant differences in achievement between these conditions. Although some tutors reported subjective perceptions that they had gained more from tutoring than they would have done from independent study, some tutees reported lacking confidence in their tutors. As in the Rosen *et al.* (1977) study, it appears that random allocation can create its own problems. In the second study, following tutoring some participants became tutees again while some became tutors. Although there was less global satisfaction at role repetition, some tutees expressed more confidence in their tutors. No significant differences in achievement were found as a function of role repetition or non-repetition, but attrition at post-test was high.

In summary, most of the studies of dyadic same-year fixed-role peer tutoring have not compared the procedure to an alternative procedure, but considered organizational variations within the procedure and their relationship to outcomes. However, one study (Fremouw and Feindler, 1978) showed this format of peer tutoring to be as effective as small group tutoring by a professional, two studies that it was more effective than independent study, but one study found no difference. The literature demonstrates the side-effects of random allocation to conditions and the potential problem of 'the blind leading the blind'.

Same-year Dyadic Reciprocal Peer Tutoring

Although this format might be considered even more innovative than same-year dyadic fixed-role tutoring, the first relevant study dates back to 1976. Although there is relatively little work in the area, some is of high quality. Goldschmid and Goldschmid (1976) used dyadic reciprocal peer tutoring in an undergraduate psychology course of 250 students. They compared outcomes for three groups: one involved in a seminar with faculty, one pursuing independent study, and the third involved in peer tutoring. The peer tutoring group did the best of the three on an unexpected post-test and they rated their learning experiences more positively.

More recently, John Fantuzzo and his colleagues have reported a series of high quality studies of reciprocal peer tutoring (RPT), consistently showing that it results in greater achievement, greater satisfaction and less feeling of stress in comparison to other treatment and control groups. Fantuzzo *et al.* (1989) allocated psychology students randomly to three conditions: reciprocal peer tutoring, questioning only, and placebo control. The RPT group reciprocated roles within each session, creating tests for each other before the session, administering them to each other, scoring them, discussing the outcome and coaching their partner as necessary. The questions-only group created the tests alone but never administered them – they studied to give the test. This group also saw the questions generated by the RPT pairs. In the placebo condition, students met and watched instructional videos with the same curricular content and answered the questions on the videos. On examination scores, all three groups gained, but the RPT group did significantly better than the other two groups, which were not significantly different from each other. Student satisfaction was significantly improved and distress indicators significantly reduced for the RPT but not the other groups. Subsequently, Fantuzzo, Riggio *et al.* (1989) conducted a component analysis to attempt to determine what elements of RPT were implicated in its effectiveness. One hundred and twenty-five students were allocated to five conditions: a dyadic peer tutoring group with a structured interaction process, a dyadic unstructured contact group involving general discussion related to upcoming exam topics, an independent unstructured condition in which individuals had to submit a short essay on upcoming examination topics, an independent structured learning condition similar to the 'questions-only condition' in the previous study, and a no treatment control group. The researchers found that dyadic interaction was associated with gains in achievement on pre-post tests, and a higher degree of structure was also associated with better outcomes. They also found that structured methods were associated with better scores on student stress inventories. Their conclusion was that it was not merely pairing but structured exchange which was effective.

Riggio *et al.* (1991) sought to replicate the study but with more diverse students in a different setting. The RPT group showed significantly higher achievement scores than the other groups, and there was generally a significant main effect for dyadic conditions, but not for structure. However, structure did yield better scores on two out of three stress inventories. Satisfaction ratings for the RPT group were significantly higher than those of the other groups. Thus compared to the previous study, dyadic factors showed less impact on stress and structure factors less impact on achievement. Riggio *et al.* (1991) note that the subjects were from a 'commuter' college who were not already well socialized with each other.

In the UK, all 45 students in a year-long undergraduate calculus class were involved in same-year dyadic peer tutoring (Topping *et al.*, 1996), the 12 one-hour peer sessions substituting for traditional lectures. Degree examination results in calculus were significantly better for the experimental group than for the previous (comparison) year, especially for students who were not maths majors, but the year cohorts were non-equivalent in some respects. Structured subjective feedback from the students suggested that peer tutoring had improved their transferable skills in a number of areas. Similarly, a project with 125 undergraduates in a year-long class in mathematical economics was reported by Topping, Hill *et al.* (1997). Final degree assessment results for the experimental group were in general not statistically significantly different from those of the previous (comparison) year. However, subjective feedback from the students indicated that peer tutoring had improved their transferable skills in a number of areas. Furthermore, students who regularly attended the peer tutoring sessions obtained significantly better degree assessment outcomes, and gave significantly better feedback about improved transferable skills, than those who did not. Additionally, student drop-out rates were lower in the experimental than in the comparison year.

Dyadic Cross-year Fixed-role Peer Tutoring

This format is reported in four studies, three from Australia. Schaffer *et al.* (1990) analysed the exam results of a cohort of students, some of whom had participated in a peer tutoring programme. There was a positive relationship between degree of participation in tutoring and examination results. However, no control groups were used and no demonstration of causality is evident. A study by Black (1993) focuses on ethnic minority group tutees in nursing and midwifery, and claims 'higher than expected' pass rates, but lacks sufficient detail to enable this to be verified. Loh (1993) deployed paid peer tutors in a course for anatomy for nurses with a previous high failure rate. Subsequently the peer tutoring participant failure rate was less than the non-participant rate, but no information was given about assignment to groups. Subjective feedback was positive however, tutees reporting feeling more confident. Quintrell and Westwood (1994) paired newly arrived international students with host national students, expecting twice monthly contact during the year. Tutees showed more positive attitudes than a comparison group matched for course of enrolment, but not significantly better academic performance. Many of these studies appear to suffer from problems of self-selection to groups and consequent non-comparability.

Same-year Group Tutoring

Four studies have considered same-year group tutoring, often in the format of rotating presentations by individual students to the peer group. Unfortunately, only one of these reported achievement outcomes. Autonomous student study groups were established by Beach (1960), who measured achievement gains with pre- and post-tests. Results indicated that extroverts did better in peer tutoring than did introverts, the introverts gaining equally in traditional lectures. The study raised questions regarding interactions between teaching and learning methodologies and student personality or learning style. Fineman (1981) reported on rotational presentations to the peer group by members of a group of 12 students of organizational behaviour. Peer assessment on peer brainstormed criteria was included. The subjective evaluation by the participants was positive. Similarly, Hendelman and Boss (1986) found rotating presentations to groups to yield positive subjective feedback from the students. The tutees reported that peer tutoring was as effective as faculty tutoring, and the tutors that peer tutoring was more effective than faculty tutoring. A course in computer-aided engineering design was the focus of a study by Magin and Churches (1993), occasioned in part by a lack of sufficient access to hardware. Those students who had had access to machines tutored those who had not had such access, over a four-week period. Subjective feedback indicated the tutees found the tutoring as or more effective than tutoring by faculty.

Peer Assisted Writing

Within the traditional higher education system, written output is often used as a vehicle for assessment of the individual, and collaborative writing can be problematic to assess. However, in recent years there has been greater interest in writing as a device for improving learning and thinking, coupled with the advocacy of 'writing across the curriculum', 'writing centres' and 'collaborative writing' (Gere, 1987; Olson, 1984). Rizzolo (1982) describes the use of peer tutors in a writing centre, also staffed by English faculty. The tutors were paid and trained through internship. It was noted that tutoring in writing had to be more than merely proof-reading. The tutees rated their peer tutors very highly on subjective feedback. Similarly, Bell (1983) emphasized the role of peer tutors in a writing centre in promoting confidence and encouraging new students to view writing more as a process and less as a product. More substantial data were offered by O'Donnell *et al.* (1985), who compared randomly assigned cooperative writing and writing-alone conditions. The writing of the 36 students was assessed for communicative quality. The cooperative writers did better on the initial post-test and on transference to a further individual writing task.

Holladay (1989, 1990) reports on the use of peer tutors in a 'writing across the curriculum' programme at Monroe Community College. Seventy-six per cent of tutees found their tutors helpful or very helpful, faculty felt the quality of papers improved in tutored classes versus non-tutored classes, and all the tutors felt their own writing had improved as a result of tutoring. This programme continued in subsequent years with even better results. A study by Levine (1990) also yielded very positive subjective feedback. The experimental class improved in meeting deadlines and the failure rate reduced from 35 to 3 per cent. However, grades and exam results were very similar for experimental and comparison groups, although comparability is unclear. Students who had tutoring in writing from faculty and peers were compared by Oley (1992) with those who had tutoring from peers only or faculty only. Many of the participants had been identified as weak writers, and some received help voluntarily and some on a compulsory basis. Assignations to conditions was random. Those who received peer tutoring subsequently attained higher grades than those who did not.

Louth, McAllister and McAllister (1993) assigned freshman composition students randomly to three conditions: some students wrote in a traditional independent manner, others wrote (partially) interactively although producing individual written products, while a third group wrote wholly interactively producing a joint product. The independent writing group, which scored higher than the other two groups at pre-test, did not improve during the project, while both collaborative conditions improved their performance, although the statistical significance of this was debatable. The use of mixed-ability writing groups of four students in geography is reported by Hay (1993), who emphasized the importance of writing as a transferable skill which is vocationally valued. In groups, the students reviewed their essay assignments, read each others' writing and made written reviews of each others' work, with a rotating chair person. Hay noted that it was possible to do the reading actually in the group sessions to avoid any possibility of plagiarism. Two groups gave subjective feedback: in one 65 per cent were positive and in the other 80 per cent. Problems included that peers were insufficiently critical and that errors were not always detected. Ninety per cent felt that the writing group should continue. The cooperative writing did not necessarily save faculty time on marking, as monitoring the group process occupied some time. A wider discussion of the role of peer assessment in written assignments in higher education will be found in Topping (1997), and a wider discussion of peer assisted writing in schools in Sutherland and Topping (1997).

In summary, of nine studies on peer assisted writing, five give only subjective feedback, but this is generally very positive. Four studies give data on gains in writing competence and of these, two good quality studies show tutee gains, one shows no statistically significant difference and a third shows some tutee gains of equivocal status. Other improvements include raised deadline attainment rates, reduced failure rates, and self-report of improved writing in the tutors.

Peer Assisted Distance Learning

In distance learning feedback and support from any peer group is problematic. Attempts to build this in by way of occasional summer schools are little more than a token gesture, and the loneliness of the long-distance learner is a widespread phenomenon. Distance learning is also fundamentally difficult to research, and the quantity and quality of evidence on the role of peer support in this process limited. Amundsen and Barnard (1989) worked with bank employees studying accounting and business administration.

One set met in peer support groups, a second had peer support groups and also distance learning on study skills, while a third had both of these and also a nominated mentor who was a previous graduate of the programme. A fourth group was a control condition. Outcome measures included assignment grades, final exam scores, final degree grades and subjective self-assessments. However, the study groups were formed inevitably on a geographic basis, and were thus self-selected and of doubtful comparability. Furthermore, the degree of conformity to the intended process was in doubt and some subjects were excluded from the analysis. Virtually no significant differences were found between the groups. However, the authors are to be commended for a brave effort in a difficult area.

A programme for audio-teleconferencing as a part of continuing education for nurses was developed in Australia by Hart (1990). The topics varied from week to week and were suggested by the participants. Each tele-conference involved between six and 12 nurses. The majority of participants were women and the author discusses whether females need or seek group support more than males. Subjective feedback from the participants was reported, but the response rate was only 34 per cent. This paper does include a good discussion of practical problems involved. In summary, although there is some weak evidence that building-in peer contact is liked by some participants in distance learning, there seems to be little satisfactory evidence that it increases student achievement. Further research in this area is certainly needed.

Summary and Conclusion

Peer tutoring is already widely used in further and higher education, in a variety of different forms. Surveys suggest several hundred institutions deploy this interactive method of teaching and learning. Of course, the existence of one small pilot project at one time in an institution does not constitute peer tutoring on a large scale across the curriculum that is quality controlled and embedded within the organizational culture. Of the different formats and methods, PSI and SI have most nearly approached the latter scenario.

A considerable amount is already known about the effectiveness of peer tutoring in further and higher education. Cross-year small-group tutoring, the format least disparate from traditional methods, can work well. Studies of achievement gains almost all indicate outcomes as good as or better than group tutoring by faculty, and student subjective feedback is generally very positive. PSI has been widely used and evaluated in the US. Two-thirds of studies found PSI involvement associated with higher class marks and 93 per cent of studies found PSI associated with higher final examination performance, compared to control groups. PSI also improved longer-term retention of the material learnt. SI adopts a very different model of operation and has become more popular outside the USA than PSI. There is very substantial and persuasive evidence from the USA of impact on course grades, graduation outcomes and drop-out rates. Research in the UK is improving in quality and also demonstrating positive outcomes.

Same-year dyadic fixed-role tutoring has been the subject of several studies over the years, research of mixed quality yielding mixed results. However, two good quality studies found improved achievement from this format, while three others found achievement the same as with faculty teaching.

Five out of six studies of same-year dyadic reciprocal tutoring have demonstrated increased attainment. There was also evidence of reduced student stress and improved transferable skills. The degree of structure in the programme was positively related to outcomes. Dyadic cross-year fixed-role tutoring has been the subject of three studies of poor quality. Same-year group tutoring has yielded positive subjective feedback in four studies, but no harder evidence on achievement outcomes.

Nine studies of peer assisted writing have shown generally favourable outcomes in terms of subjective feedback. Gains in writing competence were shown in two or three of the four studies examining this, despite the inherent difficulty of this kind of research. There is little evidence that peer assistance in distance learning improves achievement outcomes, but this area is even more difficult to research.

In summary, three methods of peer tutoring in further and higher education have already been widely used, have been demonstrated to be effective, and merit wider use in practice – these are cross-year small-group tutoring, PSI and SI. Same-year dyadic reciprocal tutoring has been demonstrated to be effective, but has been little used, and merits much wider deployment. Same-year dyadic fixed-role tutoring and peer assisted writing have shown considerable but not necessarily consistent promise and should be the focus of continuing experimentation and more research of better quality. In three areas there are barely the beginnings of a satisfactory body of evaluation research: dyadic cross-year fixed-role tutoring, same-year group tutoring and peer assisted distance learning.

It is essential that subsequent research strives to achieve adequate quality in design and execution, preferably including control groups or comparison groups that are truly comparable, and addresses issues of achievement gain and parameters of successful course completion as well as subjective participant feedback. If achievement gains can be demonstrated that go beyond the narrow confines of the institutional assessment system and endure in the longer term, so much the better. This implies that impact upon wider cognitive abilities and transferable skills should also be measured.

However, peer tutoring is usually a relatively small component of a wide range of teaching and learning strategies deployed in higher education, so the extent to which it is realistic to expect associated gains to be measurable, widespread, maintained and generalized is debatable.

The support of the Scottish Higher Education Funding Council is gratefully acknowledged.

Address for correspondence: Dr Keith Topping, Centre for Paired Learning, Psychology Department, University of Dundee, Dundee DD1 4HN. Tel. 01382 223181 ext 4628. Secretary 4622/3/4. Fax 01382 229993. e-mail k.j.topping@dundee.ac.uk or cpl@dundee.ac.uk

PART C: EMBEDDING TUTORING IN THE SYSTEM: ACCREDITATION AND QUALITY ASSURANCE

Chapter 5

QUALITY ASSURANCE THROUGH THE ACCREDITATION OF STUDENT TUTORING AND STUDENT MANAGEMENT OF TUTORING

Jim Wood

One large project is reviewed, using accreditation to enhance and reward student tutor commitment, to recognize its validity within undergraduate degree course programmes and to provide sustainable funding. In a further initiative, experienced student tutors manage groups of new student tutors, gaining academic credit and valuable workplace experience that can increase their employability.

Introduction

Student tutoring involves the systematic and sustained support for pupils in schools by undergraduate students from a local (relative to the school) university. The model adopted by the majority of student tutoring programmes based in universities and colleges in the UK is for students to work alongside teachers, helping pupils with their work and telling them what it is like to go to university. In a typical placement, a student visits the school one morning or afternoon each week for about ten weeks.

Following the first International Conference on Tutoring and Mentoring sponsored by British Petroleum in 1995, identification of 'weak links in the chain' resulted in three main aims for the Tyneside and Northumberland Students into Schools Project (henceforth referred to as the 'Project') based in Newcastle upon Tyne, England:

1. To ensure student commitment to 'quality tutoring'.
2. To maintain effective contact with student tutors once they have begun tutoring.
3. To develop sustainable funding mechanisms.

Beginning with a brief description of the history of the Project, this chapter describes how the Project has attempted to achieve these aims through the introduction of an accreditation system that helps students to improve their contribution to the work of the school, develops their transferable personal skills and allows them to progress from tutoring to helping other students tutor to a high standard. It is recognized that some of the processes and outcomes have a particular national, regional, or university dimension, but that there will also be areas where general principles may be apparent.

The Tyneside and Northumberland Students into Schools Project: The University of Newcastle upon Tyne and The University of Northumbria

History of the project

In 1991 a small BP grant supported a pilot programme in which engineering foundation year students from the University of Newcastle tutored in four local secondary schools as an optional part of the communications strand of their industrial and design studies, managed by their course director.

In 1993, following further support from a Community Service Volunteers (CSV) grant based on donations from two charitable foundations and in partnership with Tyneside Training and Enterprise Council (TEC), the opportunity to tutor was offered to any student from either the University of Newcastle or the University of Northumbria with the appointment of a full-time project manager. In 1995, Northumberland TEC became involved with the Project as a partner with student tutoring addressing some of the issues in their 'Aiming High' strategy.

Training and Enterprise Councils (TECs)

TECs were the result of a White Paper in 1988 which identified a lack of skills as a significant barrier to growth and outlined a new approach to training that would establish a training and enterprise framework to meet Britain's key employment needs and increase national competitiveness. Each TEC is focused upon maximizing benefit for local people which means a commitment to working in partnership with a range of other organizations at the local level. (Source of information: Tyneside TEC, 1997.)

Project aims

A low regional rate of progression to higher education, particularly in science and engineering subjects, was a concern of both universities and TECs. In 1990, for example, 45 per cent of 16-year-old pupils in Tyneside schools continued in post-compulsory education compared with 53 per cent overall in England and Wales (Tyneside TEC, 1997). This indicated a need to raise the aspirations of pupils in local schools, with one strategy identified as using undergraduate students as positive role-models in local schools. In addition, the universities wanted to offer more of their students the opportunity to broaden their experience and develop transferable skills through participating in a community service that would benefit all the participants.

Outcomes

The Project has become one of the largest individual student tutoring programmes in the UK with 380 students tutoring in 130 schools and colleges in 1996/97. Although initially the Project focus was on mathematics, science and technology in secondary schools, students now tutor in schools (including schools for children with special educational needs) that cover the entire age range and support subjects across the whole curriculum (see Tables 5.1 and 5.2).

In 1996/97, 37 per cent of students expressed some interest in using tutoring to gain experience in teaching. For accredited students the figure is 28 per cent and for purely voluntary students 48 per cent. Of 113 students completing end-of-tutoring evaluation questionnaires (to April), 35 per cent said they were more likely to consider teaching as a career as a result of tutoring and 17 per cent said they were less likely. These figures are generally consistent with figures from 1995/96.

Table 5.1 Summary of numbers of student tutors and schools receiving tutors 1996/97

	Primary 4–11 years	*Middle 9–13*	*Secondary 11–18*	*Special 4–18*	*Further education*	*Total*
Students	139	70	142	18	11	380
Schools	58	24	38	8	4	132

Table 5.2 Summary of numbers of student tutors involved relative to Project targets

Outcome in relation to Project targets	*91/92*	*92/93*	*93/94*	*94/95*	*95/96*	*96/97*
Target number of student tutors	N/A	N/A	200	400	400	400
Actual number of student tutors			272	403	396	380
Newcastle engineering foundation year	48	35	96	68	54	23
Percentage of students accredited directly for tutoring by Project	100	100	40	37	52	59
Number of schools receiving student tuors	4	5	65	89	120	132
Percentage of students tutoring in secondary schools (including middle schools)	100	100	81	73	70	63
Percentage of students tutoring maths, science or technology (all schools)	100	100	70	60	51	45
Percentage of students tutoring maths, science or technology (secondary/middle schools only)	100	100	52	48	40	30

In 1996/97, over half the students in the Tyneside and Northumberland Project will receive academic credit for their tutoring through a coherent accreditation system that has been specifically designed to develop students' personal transferable skills, otherwise known as core skills or key skills. In addition, 20 experienced student tutors have completed or are completing a degree course module in which they are given responsibility for managing a group of student tutors using National Vocational Qualification (NVQ) management standards as the basis for their work and which could result in the award of a vocational unit or units in addition to the mark given as part of the degree-course assessment. Details of the accreditation for tutoring and management of tutoring are given in later sections.

National Vocational Qualifications (NVQs)

The 1985 White Paper, *Education and Training for Young People* led to the 'Review of Vocational Qualifications' in 1986. This set the criteria for NVQs and led to the establishment of the National Council for Vocational Qualifications which called for a national framework of qualifications based on national standards of competence. In 1995, it was estimated that 87 per cent of the UK workforce had access to vocational qualifications, with one million (4 per cent) having these qualifications and at least twice that number working towards them (Beaumont, 1995: 8).

Student tutoring research findings

In research and evaluation papers commissioned by CSV Learning Together in 1995, Topping and Hill reviewed much of the literature concerning gains for tutors and tutees and concluded that the current situation was characterized by serendipitous gains for some coupled with considerable inequality of opportunity, and recommended attention be given to monitoring and quality control of the process of tutoring (Topping and Hill, 1995). Other contributions to the work on gains in pupils' aspirations, for example Ellsbury *et al.* (1995), found residual gains for certain groups, eg previously low-aspiring 16-year-old pupils; and with regard to intentions to continue in education post-16 for 13 to 15-year-old pupils, particularly those with a parent who had been to university. These 'marginal benefits' replicated similar findings by Campbell (1995) and elsewhere eg, Jones (1989). Wilson (1995) reported gains for student tutors when compared with a matched control group in problem-solving, communication and self-management, but not teamwork, dealing with people or finding and organizing information skills.

Topping and Hill (1995) also reported gains in students' cognitive and transferable skills but also that some students had reported significantly lower ratings for some transferable skills after tutoring when compared with pre-tutoring. Topping and Hill (1995: 23) also comment on subjective evaluation by teachers that indicate that over half report lessons easier to handle with student tutors, about 50–75 per cent find lessons more enjoyable and well over half (42–80 per cent) feel the pupils learn more, but there is considerable variation in tutee perception of whether lessons are more interesting or enjoyable (30–80 per cent).

Goodlad and Hirst (1989: 56) sought to establish peer tutoring within learning theories, suggesting that tutors develop personal adequacy and a sense of vocation in a perceived adult role as well as learning by reviewing. However, it was noted that affective changes may only occur while intervention (tutoring) is taking place and are not transferred – the tutoring may simply increase the time on task (1989: 88). Further consideration of the distinction between engaged time and exposure time is highlighted by Kennedy (1990: 71).

Anecdotal evidence within the Tyneside and Northumberland Project from students, teachers and pupils suggests that there is a perception of gains having been made by the participants. Some illustrative examples are given below.

Teachers:
'The student provided a very positive adult male role-model for pupils which is essential in our context as an inner-urban primary school.'

'Lindsay allowed me to utilize a wide range of teaching strategies with ease and confidence and she made a great impact on most pupils in the group if not all judging by responses.'

'To work alongside undergraduates quickly makes pupils realize that they are really no different to them and talking to them reinforces that. To an ambitious inner-city school with little tradition of higher education take-up this is a crucial factor.'

Pupils:
'Gill has helped me with my work and now I have more brains.'

'I think there should be more student tutors in lessons because they give a fresh insight and are very keen and confident. I hope the university will do more schemes like this one.'

'I've learnt that it isn't really like going to school. You do your own thing and aren't told what to do by teachers. I think I would probably like to go there.'

Students:
'Most pupils see me as a friend and it is quite satisfying when they stop to talk to you in town. I have enjoyed working with pupils who were maybe less fortunate than myself.'

'I've had to think how I actually do things before I can explain it to the children.'

'I enjoyed the challenge of tutoring and feel my adaptability and communication skills improved greatly.'

Given the wealth of positive subjective evidence of the value of student tutoring and the difficulty of 'measuring' objective gains attributable to the tutoring within a multivariate environment and with limited opportunities for comparison with any 'control' groups, the emphasis in the Project has been to concentrate on promoting 'quality tutoring'. Research within the Project on how to identify a potentially 'good' student tutor and what criteria should be used to evaluate 'quality tutoring' has focused on the core skills shown in Table 5.3, identified as employer-defined requirements in most graduate jobs. The research findings have been integrated into the accreditation process for student tutors.

Table 5.3 How tutoring can develop students' core skills

Core skill	*Generic tutoring (voluntary)*	*Accredited tutoring (value added)*
Communication	negotiation of role contact with pupils	oral presentation written report
Teamwork	with teachers and other adults with groups of pupils	reporting developing role contact with Project staff
Problem-solving	making it work better overcoming difficulties	part of reflective diary reporting outcomes
Initiative	self-confidence making decisions	action planning special projects
Planning and organizing	reliability time management	number of visits structure of report
Adaptability	reacting to new situations taking a proactive approach	creativity and innovation versatile learning

The 'core skills' identified here are taken from the University of Newcastle Careers Advisory Board document of February 1995 (*Skills Employers Look for in Their Graduate Recruits*) and should be regarded as inter-connected rather than independent elements.

Quality assurance in student tutoring

Assurance of quality tutoring is provided through:

- initial visits to schools by Project staff;
- information provided to schools in the form of newsletters and reports that give examples of best practice;
- emphasis during the training of student tutors on the role of a student tutor and how to reflect on and evaluate a learning experience (all student tutors undertake two, two-hour training sessions before tutoring with an additional session for accredited students that describes the assessment process);
- the use of a detailed logbook for students, a compulsory part of the accreditation, designed to develop good practice;
- support for accredited students in the form of meetings organized by student managers, who are the first point of contact for their student tutors (non-assessed voluntary students are asked to contact Project staff for advice and guidance);
- support for the placement by visits from Project staff, including students taking the management module (see below under 'Student management of tutoring').

Accreditation of student tutoring

Accreditation for student tutoring in the form of a mark awarded as part of a degree course has been developed in several programmes in the UK (eg, Glamorgan, Manchester, Sunderland, Thames Valley) and abroad, eg, New Zealand by Jones (reported in Goodlad, 1995a: 191), the STAR programme in Australia, although there has been little published information in this field. In many cases, only one university department has been involved. This makes the administration, assessment, moderating and staffing of the work relatively straightforward when compared with a more generic piece of work offered across departments.

In the first two years of the Tyneside and Northumberland Project, from 1993 to 1995, the opportunity to tutor for credit was limited to students from a small number of courses. In many cases, students who joined the Project as purely voluntary student tutors at the start of the academic year expressed difficulty in continuing to 'give up' one half-day each week once their academic workload increased. This was particularly the case for science and engineering students. In 1995/96, modularized or unitized courses were adopted to a large extent in both the universities, and within this framework it was possible to offer tutoring for academic credit to a larger number of students. Over 200 students in 1995/96 and 220 in 1996/97 have been accredited for tutoring. This compares with numbers of non-assessed volunteers of 200 and 160 for the same periods.

The University of Northumbria offers tutoring as a free elective unit worth ten credit points at both level one and level two, equivalent to one-twelfth of a year's work on a degree course. The University of Newcastle offers similar stage one and stage two optional modules, a voluntary half-module in 'communications' in chemical and process engineering and an optional module in the engineering foundation year. In both universities, the assessment procedures are carried out by Project staff with the modules administered and moderated within the respective education departments. In general, students complete the tutoring module within one semester (half-year).

On the basis of pilot work in 1991–93 with the engineering foundation year students and work done in other tutoring programmes, and improved through feedback and evaluation in subsequent years, the accreditation system currently in operation has been developed to include many features that are intended to develop quality tutoring. In particular, students are expected to become reflective practitioners, evaluating what they consider to be the most important aspects of the contribution they have made and identifying the areas in which they feel this could be improved. The students are asked to indicate, after discussion with the class teacher where appropriate, how and why they feel they can contribute more to the work of the pupils, reporting subsequently on the outcomes of proposed action. The theoretical basis for experiential learning can be traced through many writers and is discussed in more detail below ('Assessment components for student tutoring'). Students tutoring on a purely voluntary basis are encouraged to maintain a reflective diary but there is no compulsion on them to do so.

University internal funding transfer mechanisms for work done by Project staff within this framework have been developed. In 1995/96, the first year of operating this system, £17,000 out of a total Project budget of £54,000 was provided through internal university funding. This proportion may rise to over 40 per cent of the budget in 1996/97, although the exact level of funding per accredited student has yet to be firmly established in one of the universities. The interrelationship between the extra time and level of staffing needed to accommodate the assessment of tutoring and the amount of funding 'generated' by the accreditation is complex and should be a factor when any similar programme is considering introducing accreditation.

There are some perceived disadvantages for students who tutor for credit rather than purely as volunteers. These include the diminished value of tutoring as a completely extracurricular activity, the perceptions of extra 'pressure' on the quality of their tutoring, considerations of equable assessment, and what action needs to be taken if the placement does not run smoothly. Where students have completed sufficient visits but 'failed' the unit, they are asked to resubmit as many assessment components as is necessary to enable them to be credited with a pass which will allow their degree progression. Students who have not completed sufficient visits are asked to do this and then resubmit work.

The experience to date has indicated that, on balance, the additional time available to a student choosing a tutoring module ie, there is one less module from elsewhere, and the focus on self-assessment and personal development are considered to outweigh the negative features. Within the universities, there are considerations with regard to funding transfer which have an impact on whether or not courses will allow their students to tutor for credit. Students currently have the option of tutoring on a purely voluntary, non-assessed basis if they choose to do so or if they are not permitted to tutor for credit due to the nature of their course or degree regulations.

Assessment components for student tutoring

The three components of the accreditation system are a formative logbook (including personal action plan), a summative formal written report and a summative oral presentation. The weighting and requirements of these components varies slightly for the two different levels as follows:

level one	logbook 30 per cent	oral 20 per cent	report (2000–3000 words) 50 per cent
level two	logbook 40 per cent	oral 20 per cent	report (500 words) 40 per cent

The students generate evidence of their contribution and development, with pupil and teacher comments as well as observation by Project staff used to corroborate any claims made. All procedures and the criteria for assessment are made clear to the students in the form of a booklet they receive during the training sessions and at a subsequent briefing session part-way through the tutoring. The assessment criteria were initially based on examples of good practice from other similar projects as well as criteria used in the education departments of the two universities and have been modified through evaluation within the Project. At the end of the process, the students receive detailed feedback from Project staff on their performance, which helps them to identify their strengths and weaknesses.

Tutoring logbook

Student tutors write a reflective personal diary that is structured to ensure that they complete a learning cycle (Dennison and Kirk, 1990; Kolb, 1984; Mumford, 1980), based on the following processes:

- analyse and evaluate the work done by selecting critical incidents and examples;
- focus on their contribution to pupils' learning and what they themselves have learned, drawing on relevant theory where possible;
- develop and justify action plans and include evidence of outcomes;
- articulate evidence of personal qualities (core skills) they have demonstrated while tutoring.

Note that these processes represent the elements of an approach to experiential learning for students based on doing, reviewing, analysing/evaluating and action planning in all aspects of the tutoring. The reflective diary establishes a learning situation whereby the students can themselves extract the maximum benefit from the tutoring (Boud *et al.*, 1985: 36), using regular target-setting and monitoring (Stephenson *et al.*, 1993: 173) as part of the process. Central to the process is the interaction between the process (the cycle), the individual (learning style) and the environment (which style is encouraged by task and content) (Mumford, 1980: 67).

Student tutoring logsheet

(In practice, an A4-sized document; see Figure 5.1.) The assessment of the logbook is based on the quantity and quality of evidence, including progression and continuity between the different sections of the logbook. Students are asked to make ten visits to the school with one logsheet completed per visit. Students can supplement their tutoring with involvement in student shadowing or other activities coordinated by the Project and the University Education Liaison Officers, and can replace up to three school visits with such activities. Students are also expected to write and review a brief personal action plan in weeks one, five and ten, indicating their aims and objectives.

Oral presentation

Students present a five- to ten-minute summary of their experience which is assessed for communication (organization and presentation) and content (breadth and depth). The work is peer-assessed by other student tutors. Marks awarded by students are used to guide Project staff who are the principal markers, and comments made by students are passed on as feedback to other student tutors.

Name: ______________________ Date: _________ Sheet number: ☐

Contribution to Class and Successful Outcomes (including evidence of understanding shown by pupils and outcomes of Forward Planning/Action on Difficulties from previous visits)

Difficulties Encountered/Areas to Improve
Proposed Action on Difficulties/Improvements (including the justification for your chosen course of action)

Personal Quality	Evidence from tutoring

Summary of Critical Issues and Forward Planning	Action points for next visit

Figure 5.1 Student tutoring logsheet

Formal written report

Students are asked to produce a well-presented and coherently organized summative account of their experiences, drawing together the various strands of the logbook and analysing and critically evaluating the outcomes. Credit is given for integrating first-hand experience into wider contexts and relevant theories, making valid generalizations supported by examples from tutoring, evidence of a proactive role in contributing to learning and developing relationships with pupils and teacher(s), and making an evaluation of the benefits of the tutoring to all the participants.

The summative components encourage an holistic appraisal of the experience which complements the sequential (serialist) nature of the tutoring and logbook reporting. The range of processes involved helps promote the versatile learning approach associated with a deep level of understanding (Entwistle and Ramsden, 1983: 42, 106) and reinforces 'learning through teaching'. Extrinsically motivated students are encouraged to achieve high marks through adopting procedures associated with 'quality tutoring'.

Teacher involvement

Some student tutoring programmes include an assessment mark given by the teacher. However, it was felt that because of the large number of schools involved in the Tyneside and Northumberland Project, from infant schools to colleges of further education and including special schools, the assessment process should focus on the students' reporting of their work and should not include a subjective mark given by the teacher.

The use of self-reporting to 'measure' the quality of what is essentially a practical (or vocational) experience presents a point for discussion. For example, in the case of a student who did not perform well in the classroom but who wrote a good reflective journal and/or summative report, it could be argued it would be unfair for the teacher to award a mark which reflects to a considerable extent the role the teacher defined for the student within their classroom. Several schools say that they have always received 'good students' from the Project, when it is clear that they actually get the most from whoever is placed there.

The tutoring is monitored through a visit to the placement by Project staff and by means of an informal, short evaluation of the placement by the teacher. It is not the intention to exclude teachers from this process and they have the opportunity to be involved at any stage. Receiving a student tutor therefore involves minimal extra work for the teacher whether the student tutor is accredited or purely voluntary. This further emphasizes the distinction between student tutors and students who are training to be teachers. Feedback from teachers in the Project steering group suggests that they recognize a greater level of commitment in most cases from those student tutors who are seeking to be accredited.

Student management of tutoring

Project staffing

Maintaining effective contact with a large number of students recruited from a wide range of courses across two universities was a problem for a permanent staff comprising one full-time coordinator and one part-time secretary, the position in 1993. Since 1994, following discussion with coordinators from other student tutoring projects, one or two graduate students have been employed each year on a fixed-term contract to share the workload. In 1996/97, the Project is staffed at a similar level although the role of these assistant coordinators is changing as a result of the introduction of student managers.

Several students who completed the tutoring module expressed interest in undertaking another accredited module with the Project because they felt they had benefited from the whole process. Degree regulations do not allow students to repeat a module. Other tutoring schemes (eg, Edinburgh, Pimlico) use student volunteers to help run the programmes.

Student managers

Using the job description of the assistant coordinators as a basis, in the second semester in 1995/96 in the University of Northumbria (and in Newcastle from September 1996) a ten-credit level-two degree course module in the management of student tutoring was made available to undergraduate students who had tutored previously. To date, all student managers have previously completed the tutoring module although the criteria for acceptance on the management module is that a student should have 'tutored to a satisfactory standard in the Tyneside and Northumberland Project or other student tutoring programme'. Working under the direction and guidance of Project staff each student manager is given some responsibility for supervising a small group of between six and ten student tutors with three main areas of responsibility:

1. liaison with Project staff and other student managers, coordinating student shadowing and organizing student involvement in special projects;

2. contributing to the induction and training of student tutors and organizing support meetings and a mid-tutoring seminar for students in their own group;
3. visiting students on placement.

Accreditation of the management of student tutoring

The accreditation process is based on student managers collecting evidence of their competence in each of these areas of work using criteria indicated in NVQ supervisory management standards. In particular, the principal focus currently is the competencies described in Unit five which has three elements of planning, evaluating, and giving feedback. The new Management Charter Initiative standards, published in April 1997, offer a more appropriate framework for the work, with four of the new units covering the work of the student managers as currently described. Evidence of competence can also be demonstrated through working in collaboration with Project staff in any aspect of the work of the Project. Student managers are expected to plan their workload across the semester, working on the basis that a module should comprise 80–100 hours of work.

Using a system similar to that which they will have experienced in being accredited for tutoring, the assessment components are

1. a portfolio of evidence generated by the student in the form of plans, contact notes, letters, evaluation sheets, personal reports, witness statements and other documentation as well as observation of performance by Project staff (and others);
2. a summative written test of underpinning knowledge and understanding gained through work done, comprising short answers to questions based on Project aims and procedures and longer responses to questions that simulate hypothetical student tutoring situations in which the student managers indicate how they might respond;
3. a summative written report comprising a detailed summary of the work done by the student manager and the student tutors in their group that should also include references to the evidence they have presented in their portfolio and the management standards. It is recognized that the term 'portfolio' as used above is not strictly appropriate and it is intended that further development of the module will lead to a single assessed outcome for student managers that is a genuine NVQ portfolio ie, as a claim for competence.

Dual certification

Through using learning outcomes based on NVQ performance criteria it is possible to award a degree course mark for the module and by cross-referencing with performance criteria it may be possible to construct the report as a claim for competence for a unit in NVQ supervisory management. At this stage of development, there is doubt whether the student managers can be said to be working in an authentic role as a manager and there are funding implications for the award of an NVQ unit or units through an external awarding body. In practice, the process the student managers follow exposes them to competence-based assessment within the relevant national framework and, in addition, their portfolio can be retrospectively considered as evidence of prior learning in any future management position in which this might be appropriate. The Department for Education and Employment Higher Education Projects Work-based Learning Briefing Paper, February 1996, discusses this issue in detail and highlights the 'advantages in encouraging greater independence and in developing greater awareness of the learning which takes place in the work place' and that 'even if a student did not achieve an NVQ or units towards an NVQ, familiarity with the system might be advantageous in the current competitive graduate labour market.'

The system of assessment for student managers is being constantly reviewed and is becoming more manageable and user-friendly for students who it is recognized are asked to cope with competence-based acquisition of evidence from the start of the module with no prior experience. The management standards are used as a development tool as well as an assessment framework, with competence in management developed and demonstrated rather than assumed. Student managers report that, by the end of the module, they understand the NVQ process, have developed their skills in a wide range of areas and recognize their aptitude for progression into employment in a management role. Anecdotal evidence suggests that undertaking a module that explicitly involves NVQ has been a considerable advantage when applying for jobs and placements, with several student managers reporting that they had been told that it was this experience that had got them an interview.

Summary and Forward Planning

'We'll take as many student tutors as you want to send as long as they are good ones.' This quote from a teacher in one of the schools receiving student tutors from the Project is particularly illuminating and is at the heart of the development of systems designed to ensure that student tutors contribute as much as possible to their placement. One evaluative measure which can be applied to the Project is the willingness of participants to continue their involvement, with evidence of positive outcomes in the growth in numbers of schools and of students accredited for tutoring. When asked, 'How did you find out about tutoring?', 24 per cent of 1996/97 students responded, 'From a friend', the largest individual figure chosen from seven categories (40 per cent of purely voluntary students were recruited in this way).

Research suggests that student tutoring can be most effective when used in conjunction with other strategies for raising aspirations. In 1995, 55 per cent of Tyneside 16-year-old pupils continued in education compared with 67 per cent nationally (Tyneside TEC, 1997). This is seen as an indication of the continuing need to support programmes that are trying to address the issue of low progression rates rather than a measure of the success or otherwise of any one programme in isolation. It is clear from the involvement of 17-year-old pupils in student shadowing visits to the universities that finance is a major factor in whether or not they are considering going on to higher education. In the UK there is regular newspaper reporting of the impact of reductions in student grants and the increase of student loans, resulting in average debts per student in 1996 of £1,982 (Barclays Bank, reported in *The Guardian*, 6 July 1996).

The introduction of a systematic accreditation process for student tutoring that generates funding has been successful in securing the future of the Project for the academic year 1997/98. The use of student managers has provided a vital link between Project staff and student tutors that can ensure that any problems with any aspect of the tutoring can be dealt with quickly and less formally. Students who tutor for credit engage in a process that encourages them to adopt approaches associated with versatile learning and become more aware of the development of their personal transferable skills.

In the longer term, it may be possible to devolve considerable parts of the student tutoring process into departments in the universities, with experienced student tutors recruiting, training and supporting new student tutors within an accreditation system that can evolve to include criteria that the department wishes to highlight. The role of a central coordinating 'agency' in such a system is unclear, although the introduction of electronic communication networks offers a range of new possibilities such as using bulletin boards to manage the placement process.

Like several other student tutoring programmes, the Tyneside and Northumberland Project is looking to use links with other organizations such as Education Business Partnerships, local education authorities and voluntary organizations to find ways to embed the tutoring process into a wider framework of activity.

Address for correspondence: Jim Wood, Project Manager, Tyneside and Northumberland Students into Schools Project, Joseph Cowen House, St Thomas Street, Newcastle upon Tyne NE1 7RU. e-mail SIS@ncl.ac.uk

Chapter 6

ESTABLISHING STUDENT TUTORING WITHIN A HIGHER EDUCATION CURRICULUM THROUGH THE THEME OF PERSONAL AND PROFESSIONAL DEVELOPMENT

Danny Saunders and Ray Kingdon

The design and validation of a free-floating student tutoring module is discussed in relation to the theme of personal and professional development at the University of Glamorgan. Student tutoring, where students help school teachers in the classroom, is usually an extramural and voluntary activity. In this chapter it is argued that, while tutoring should always be voluntary, it may also on occasions be included within the higher education curriculum. Seven reasons are given for such inclusion, these being, permanence, skills development, consistency of quality, curriculum flexibility, focus, external credibility and demand from students based on feedback. A variety of issues are identified, including the challenges of assessing student tutoring and strategies for recruiting and selecting students.

A Personal and Professional Development Theme

The theme of personal and professional development (PPD) encourages transferable and personal skills and competencies that are associated with effective performance within a variety of life-situations. Curricula incorporating such skills and competencies have developed out of recent initiatives dedicated to the pursuit of 'capability' (Craig and Martin, 1986; Stephenson and Weil, 1992) and 'enterprise' (Department of Employment, 1994) within higher education, recognizing that the enabling value of courses or modules is crucial for the successful preparation of future graduates for a variety of professional careers.

Providing Support for Traditional and Non-traditional Students

Skills development is important to the self-identity of each individual learner (Thorley, 1994), and these are especially important considerations now that lifelong learning (see, for example, the Carnegie Inquiry, 1993; Uden, 1994) is becoming a major feature of learning in higher education institutions (HEIs). Within this context higher education has been made more accessible for non-traditional students who may be resuming their learning after some time away from the classroom, who may have alternative qualifications to the standard university entry profile, and who do not therefore resemble the conventional intake of school-leavers.

Vocational Relevance

Recent initiatives in the UK underline the importance of recognizing vocational standards and transferability, and emphasize the vocational value of personal development throughout all educational sectors. These include:

- the introduction of core and common skills in awards from bodies such as the Business and Technology Education Council, the Royal Society of Arts, and City & Guilds;
- the extension of National Vocational Qualifications (NVQS) to levels 4 and 5 (ie, into higher education); the emergence of General National Vocational Qualifications (GNVQS) and vocational A-levels;
- the introduction of the National Record of Achievement in the post-16 sector;
- and the specification of National Education and Training Targets.

All serve to emphasize the vocational value of personal development throughout all educational sectors. The National Council for Vocational

Qualifications is actively defining, through the establishment of an array of lead bodies, competence frameworks for various occupational groupings. These developments emerge in part from a widespread concern about the unsuitability of UK graduates to many work environments once employment is secured after leaving higher education. This is in part a criticism of career choice and planning by undergraduates, but it is also a consequence of limited employment opportunities and underemployment. Another criticism has to be levelled at conventional higher education programmes of study which fail to address those essential skills that employers most value once specialist graduates are in post and have typically gravitated towards management responsibilities:

> 'More and more these days we find that if we promote specialists, the absolute specialist, the one-discipline person who cannot deal with people, we get an immediate response. That person sorts out all the specialists and then comes up against a brick wall that he or she cannot deal with people, or take a relaxed view, or accept that the more open, participative management structures that are relevant today do work.'
>
> (Employer, cited in Cowie and Ruddock, 1988)

Such disappointment has led to the identification of 'core', 'common' or 'personal' skills by employers – and the generation of assorted checklists which have been introduced in schools and colleges as well as universities (see Table 6.1).

Accredited Modular Provision

Many HEIs have now developed compatible credit accumulation and transfer frameworks that allow for student mobility between institutions, and that offer greater flexibility for course design and mixed modes of study. This has had a major impact on the design and implementation of a personal and development curriculum. A common development has been the conversion of courses spanning one or more years into shorter discrete modules or units that have a consistent number of credits attached to them at designated levels of undergraduate study (see Moon and Reynolds, 1996). The outcome has been the creation of an increased variety of awards and the opportunity for more varied learning experiences.

In some HEIs students are encouraged to complete one or more subsidiary modules that are relatively distanced from their programme of studies, and that are offered on a free-floating basis. Of crucial importance is the linking of such optional modules with personal development, study skills, and learning strategies; they can also be offered across an entire institution while being centrally located rather than attached to a particularly department or faculty. At the University of Glamorgan, for example, a module is based on a set number of credits for learning time (to include preparation of coursework and revision for examinations); each module carries a notional 120 hours of learning time within a 15-week semester and leads to a total of 12 credit points, the equivalent of one-tenth of a student's total credits for a level of study.

Confederation of British Industry

Values and integrity
Effective communication
Applications of numeracy
Applications of technology
Understanding of work
Personal and interpersonal skills

National Curriculum Council (Core)

Communication
Problem-solving
Positive attitudes to change
Personal
Numeracy
Information technology
Modern language competence

NCVQ Core Skills

Communication
Application of number
Application of technology

In addition:
Problem-solving
Personal skills

Department for Education and Employment

Communication
Numeracy
Personal relations
Familiarity with technology
Familiarity with systems
Familiarity with changing working and social contexts (including modern languages and overseas)

Business & Technology Education Council

Managing and developing self
Working with and relating to others
Communicating
Managing tasks and solving problems
Applying numeracy
Applying technology
Applying design and creativity

Figure 6.1 'Common skills' as viewed by five sources (after COIC)

The Student Tutoring Module

The Student Tutoring module at the University of Glamorgan is a 'free-floating' option for students. All undergraduate modules are designated at levels 1, 2 or 3, indicating, respectively, introductory, intermediary or advanced study. The student tutoring module is located at level 2 because it demands some sophisticated analysis, reflection and insight based on previous experience, and because it prepares students for career choice and subsequent applications for employment that are typical of the final year experience. If this module were set at level 3, its completion would be too late to help students choose and apply for specific employment opportunities. Figure 6.1 provides details of the validated module at the University of Glamorgan.

Student tutoring has been well documented (Goodlad and Hirst, 1989, 1990; Hughes, 1992; Hughes and Metcalf, 1994; Potter, 1995; Topping, 1988). It is defined in terms of students from colleges and universities helping pupils in local schools on a sustained and systematic basis, under the direction and supervision of teachers (Goodlad, 1995a). The activity began with the Pimlico Connection at Imperial College London and later expanded into such projects as STIMULUS at Cambridge University (Beardon, 1990), the Tutor Outreach Programme in Scotland (Ogg, 1992), and Student Tutoring Wales (Wilson and Saunders, 1994). It is widely regarded as a successful student-pupil-teacher tripartite initiative that develops students' cognitive and transferable skills, raises pupils' aspirations and awareness of higher educational opportunities, and provides teachers with extra support and resources (see Topping, 1990, 1992, for thorough reviews). The ultimate aim of student tutoring is that of providing positive role models for underachieving pupils who then become more aware of higher educational pathways and opportunities.

Student tutoring resembles other initiatives through which people are supported in their learning. One example is supplemental instruction (Rust and Wallace, 1994), where undergraduates help other undergraduates. Another is proctoring, where final year undergraduates help first and second years (and which is an assessed activity that contributes to a final award – see Button *et al.*, 1987). With tutoring in schools, a voluntary and extramural student involvement has not enjoyed a formal position within the undergraduate curriculum. Some might argue that this is an essential feature of tutoring, which relies on the goodwill and altruism of learners within higher education. Furthermore, its extramural and voluntary status becomes a self-selection method that ensures that only the motivated students help others to learn, thereby raising the overall quality of tutors who help in the classroom,

Level: 2	Credit rating: 12	Semester: A or B
Learning time (student hours per week):	Supervised: 2	Directed: 3 Undirected: 3
Prerequisites:	120 Level I Credits	

Aim:

To explore communication, problem-solving, and self-appraisal skills associated with a live work situation, and to experiment with a variety of educational methods associated with classroom-based teaching and learning.

Introduction:

The module involves visiting a school or college in order to assist teachers in the classroom. The main focus will be on activities associated with a part of the curriculum that higher education students are familiar with and confident about. In so doing, students will engage in small and large group tutoring which can include 1:1 discussion, active listening, and debating, demonstrating, advising, assessing, and the delivery of at least one 20-minute presentation to pupils.

At all times the higher education student will be observed and guided by the qualified teacher, and that person will also contribute towards the assessment of the student. Support workshops and seminars at the University of Glamorgan will help to develop confidence and interest in the development of a range of skills including interpersonal communication, creative problem-solving, synectic reasoning, cooperative groupwork, self-assessment, and public speaking.

A series of lecturers will introduce educational theories and practice to students in order to encourage critical debate about classroom-based activity and observations, and to provide a basis for reflection about self, pupil, teacher, and lecturer-based assessment of higher education students.

Targeted transferable and personal skills:

- cooperative groupwork
- gathering feedback
- oral presentations
- leadership
- numerical/literary analysis
- listening and questioning
- negotiating.

Figure 6.2 The validated syllabus

In this chapter it is emphasized that the voluntary status of tutoring should be preserved at all costs: the consequences of forcing students into tutoring via a compulsory curriculum element would be too serious for pupils and teachers within the schools. However, this discussion also argues that the higher education curriculum should offer an opportunity for student tutoring to be an accredited experience that is formally assessed and that contributes to an academic award.

Seven reasons are provided for locating student tutoring within the higher education curriculum, and these are based on the last four years of experiences at the University of Glamorgan in Wales which has successfully encouraged tutoring as an extramural activity:

- permanence
- skills development
- consistency of quality
- curriculum flexibility
- focus
- external credibility
- student feedback.

Permanence

As an extramural activity student tutoring is located at the periphery of the curriculum and does not attract core funding from fees or core revenue. It is therefore an obvious potential casualty when cutbacks are made. By contrast, tutoring formally incorporated into a course or programme of academic study necessitates core funding.

Skills development

Various organizations and professional groups have published lists of skills and competencies that help to improve vocational awareness amongst undergraduates (see Table 6.1), and these have percolated into the curricula. Specific courses that develop core skills can therefore provide a suitable location for student tutoring as a vehicle for developing some employment-related skills. With extramural tutoring a particular problem is the involvement of students who have very demanding programmes in engineering and science. In effect, their crowded schedules preclude extramural activities because there is little free time. In recent years a variety of professional bodies have emphasized the value of including core skills development within the undergraduate curriculum, and this has helped with the inclusion of activities such as tutoring within engineering and science students' study programme.

Consistency of quality

In many cases extramural programmes rely on the goodwill of the organizer as well as of the student tutors and the participants themselves. To give two examples: a student society may take on this organizational responsibility within the Students' Union (which in itself can raise problems of academic credibility); in other cases a member of staff may be seconded by an Enterprise or Education Development Initiative to lift-off a student tutoring programme. Often these are successful ventures, but worst-case scenarios should be borne in mind. Problems may emerge when a change of staffing and leadership occurs, and this can have serious external consequences. Teachers and pupils may be disappointed when they compare one group of tutors with another, or when there is an unexpected breakdown of communication. The emerging lack of confidence in the consistency and quality of the programme will pose problems for future student tutors, Many of these difficulties are minimized when tutoring becomes a part of the curriculum, because the activity is then subject to the usual quality assurance procedures and systems. This includes monitoring and collecting student feedback, external examining, continuity of staffing, and the validation and periodic review of the programme.

Curriculum flexibility

Recent moves towards a widespread credit and accumulation transfer scheme (CATS) (Robertson, 1994) have led to the award of academic credits for discrete amounts of learning associated with modules or units within the higher (and further) education sector. This has led to an increase in choice via a more flexible curriculum (see Brown and Saunders, 1995a), which encourages the development of more subject combinations as well as new curriculum areas. Modularization and CATS frameworks allow for the creation of student tutoring modules that can be offered on a free-floating basis to all students, regardless of their academic location. Furthermore, modularization has encouraged many programmes of study to include 'curriculum windows' that allow students to occasionally engage in a completely different and new form of learning activity.

Focus

Student tutoring as an extramural activity attracts students into the school classroom, and it may be intrinsically rewarding for its own sake as an enjoyable experience which is a welcome release from academic analysis. The converse may also be the case on occasions: the absence of a curriculum that is formally assessed has the disadvantage of not motivating students in terms of analysing their tutoring experiences and reflecting about abilities and skills that are either developing or need to be strengthened. The exclusion of tutoring from the curriculum prevents students from making the most of this as a learning experience.

External credibility

Some student tutors plan to apply for teacher training courses in their undergraduate final year, but test the water first by tutoring during the year before they apply for places on Postgraduate Certificate in Education programmes. Others want to have evidence of their transferable skills development when applying for more wide-ranging employment. Extramural tutoring can lead to a certificate on completion of a set number of classroom visits: while this is useful evidence for employers and in line with moves towards updating certification within the National Record of Achievement (Saunders, 1992b), it has added credibility when a specified number of academic credits at a given level within higher education are clearly stated on any certificate or diploma awarded to students.

Student feedback

A series of debriefing discussions at the University of Glamorgan noted a recurring comment from student tutors: the lack of recognition of tutoring as part of students' courses. Many students value the academic challenges associated with explaining a subject or discipline to pupils, and are simply frustrated by this activity not being an accredited experience. Such qualitative comment becomes even more poignant when statements are made about student tutoring being one of the most valuable learning experiences in higher education – as has been stated by a variety of students within the Students Tutoring Wales Initiative (Saunders and Kingdon, 1994).

All of these reasons have combined towards the creation of a student tutoring module at the University of Glamorgan, which has been piloted by 65 level 2 (second year) students from such diverse backgrounds as mathematics, law, humanities, and business studies. The remainder of this chapter charts the development of the module and associated assessment and delivery strategies. A fundamental concern has been to locate student tutoring within the previously defined context of personal and professional development, rather than to produce excellent student tutors *per se*: it is this feature which distinguishes a student tutoring module from the usual teacher training programme.

Theoretical Perspectives

The location of personal, professional and transferable skills programmes within the curriculum continues to be debated, especially in relation to the embedding of such initiatives as Enterprise in Higher Education. The main concern is with 'bolt-on' programmes that are isolated and detached from the main curriculum. In some cases this can generalize to the lecturing staff who deliver transferable skills modules, and who are not perceived as a main part of the course team. In other instances a separate unit, centre or department may be a central resource that then delivers transferable skills programmes across an entire institution. Much depends on specific institutional contacts as regards the best policy and strategy for transferable skills education. At the University of Glamorgan the student tutoring module selects tutoring as a vehicle for the development of personal and professional skills as opposed to simply singling out specific skills and competencies as the module's declared reason for existence. This decision is based partly on feedback from academic staff who have experience of running 'transferable skills' modules that do not appeal to students because of their perceived frivolity, vagueness, and fragmentation – despite later realizations about the importance and relevance of such skills when students are applying for jobs.

A second recurring comment from students and staff concerns the atheoretical status of skills and competence based modules, which are seen by some (see Barnett, 1994) as being more akin to training than higher education. While this debate continues, such criticism has been taken very seriously. In part, the decision to select such a theme as tutoring in a local school has helped to provide a context for the development of skills and competencies. With such contextualization the introduction of applied theoretical issues is inevitable, and in some instances the challenge for academic staff will be that of reminding learners that personal and professional development is the focus rather than getting too involved in the minutiae of a specific activity.

The major theoretical input for the module, however, is devoted to personal and professional development itself. At one level this involves asking students to reflect about the training versus education debate mentioned previously. At a more personal level, however, the focus is on definitions of learning, learning styles, motivation and stages or phases of personal development in higher education. The following theoretical themes become crucial for analysis and critical reflection:

- experiential and active learning (Kolb, 1984)
- deep and surface learning (Entwistle and Ramsden, 1983)
- dualistic and relativistic reasoning (Perry, 1970)
- self-actualization (Maslow, 1954)
- changing personal constructs (Rogers, 1961, 1983).

A common assessment objective is the successful application of theory to practical activities that develop specific skills and competencies.

Delivery

A free-floating module creates a logistical problem when it comes to the timetabling of workshops for all students from any Department, and necessitates the use of flexible learning materials. The delivery of the module therefore involves scheduled workshops and meetings for groups of student tutors, in addition to schools visits (organized by the local Education and Business Partnership which is closely linked with the local Training and Enterprise Council), and the use of a tutoring resource pack that gives details of background development, theoretical perspectives, profiles and inventories.

The pack contains a study plan, summarized in Figure 6.2. It can be seen that the module begins with briefing sessions and preparatory workshops which introduce students to basic skills and methods associated with classroom context. During the first phase of the module, students are also introduced to the notion of portfolio collection, and the development of action plans that identify relevant evidence that has to be collected for later inclusion within the portfolio. At the same time students are allocated to schools and encouraged to complete a preliminary administration visit where they meet the teacher they will be working with.

During the middle phase of the student tutoring module, students complete a minimum of ten half-day visits to a particular school in order to help teachers within the classroom; those students are then invited to attend interim progress and debriefing sessions at the University of Glamorgan.

Towards the end of the module, workshops are scheduled to confirm final assessment criteria associated with the portfolio and the personal journal, including an overall narrative based on the development of student tutoring skills. Furthermore, inventories are completed to help students measure the extent to which skills have been developed and possible weaknesses have been turned into strengths. Such development is demonstrated through later comparisons with earlier baselines established through the completion of exactly the same questionnaires and rating scales at the outset of the module.

Week	*Activity/Learning*
1.	Briefing, introductions, enrolment with Mid Glamorgan Education and Business Partnership.
2.	Read through section A, making notes. Attend support workshop on assessment criteria and keeping a journal. Open your personal journal and record initial impressions and observations. Start baselines.
3.	Read through section C of booklet, making notes; continue with support workshops, complete baseline self-assessment inventories and summarise in journal. Tutoring administration visit – initial impressions to be entered in journal.
4.	Read through section B of booklet, making notes; begin tutoring and record observations in journal, collect evidence of tutoring activity where possible.
5.–8.	Continue with tutoring and update journal, continue with evidence collection for portfolio, re-read section C of booklet, arrange interim tutorial meeting.
9.	Continue tutoring and updating of journal, attend support workshop on giving a presentation and preparing a final portfolio, ask teachers for feedback where possible, plan collection of feedback from children/pupils.
10.	Finish tutoring, update journal, attend support workshop and summarise evidence for inclusion in the portfolio, plan presentation using some of portfolio as well as section B chapter from the booklet 'Giving Presentations'.
11.	Give presentation at the University, prepare final portfolio, reassess using inventories and compare with earlier baselines; return once again to section C of the booklet and write an overview for the module based on your personal and professional development since beginning tutoring.
12.	Finishing touches to portfolio, which will include personal journal and any evidence of tutoring activity along with teacher and if possible pupil feedback.
13.	Hand in the portfolio.

Figure 6.3 Suggested study plan

The module concludes with a presentation within the University of Glamorgan to an audience that includes academic staff and other student tutors; this is followed by a formal submission of the portfolio.

Discussion

The challenge of assessment

The location of student tutoring within a formal higher education curriculum necessitates assessment. The inevitable challenge is that personal and professional skills associated with tutoring in schools are not assessed validly by traditional unseen examinations or essays. To make matters more complicated, processes of self- and peer assessment actually contribute to personal development. The same observation applies to the subsequent planning of learning programmes based on learning agreements with academic staff and/or employers, thereby demonstrating how weaknesses have been converted into competencies and even strengths:

> 'there have been a number of curricular assessments in the last few years which could have quite major implications for traditional assessment practices if they are adopted on a wider scale. Work-based learning schemes, "active learning projects", the greater prominence of supported self study including use of computer-aided tools and courseware, records of achievement, students' contracts, and the projects supported under the Enterprise in Higher Education programme are all examples. These initiatives are raising doubts about over-reliance on the essay assignment and the unseen examination. In the context of these and other developments it is argued that students should take responsibility for their own learning and for its assessment.'
>
> (Atkins *et al.*, 1993:9)

In recent years the advancement of the accreditation of prior learning (APL), of prior experiential learning (APEL), and the assessment of portfolios of evidence compiled by candidates has proved to be very popular – three examples being the Management Charter Initiative, the promotion by the Training and Development Lead Body of training programmes which lead to the D32/33/34/35/36 assessor awards, and the very innovative Personal and Professional Development course designed by the Open University. Helpful assessment guidelines have been produced by the Learning From Experience Trust (Evans, 1993) for the assessment of portfolios and the formulation of learning contracts based on work-based learning.

The crucial reminder when it comes to the assessment of student tutoring concerns the need to monitor, analyse and reflect about the development of skills and abilities rather than the achievement of universally predefined standards and targets associated with student tutoring. In the very extreme, it is possible for a 'poor' student tutor (ie, somebody who is not good at helping teachers and pupils in the classroom) to achieve a high grade – provided that the individual critically reflects and analyses the reasons for why his or her performance was not as good as that of other tutors, or simply not as good as the individual hoped it would be. Such a possibility may trade skills of self-reflection against those associated with classroom tutoring. The implications of this have to be considered in relation to the learning objectives and outcomes for the module: a personal and professional development theme emphasizes self-reflection, and so this has to be an assessment priority over and above the practical demonstration of tutoring skills,

The emphasis on personal development underlines the importance of action planning, the targets defined by the individual student tutors, and the revision of those targets as the tutoring placement progresses. Furthermore, a variety of evidence is to be collected to prove that targets have been met, or to explain why they were not feasible goals in the first place. For these reasons, the most suitable vehicles for assessment within the University of Glamorgan pilot were deemed at the outset to be a portfolio of evidence, and a presentation based on that portfolio. The portfolio pack has to include:

- a personal development log or journal
- a reflective overview of no more than 1500 words
- a summary of teacher feedback.

Student tutors along with three members of staff also generated examples of additional evidence for inclusion within the portfolio, by way of workshop activity that ensured agreement about assessment criteria (see Figure 6.2, weeks 2, 3 and 10) for portfolios and presentations. Such evidence has included:

- inventories and profiles
- graphs and spreadsheets
- pupil and teacher feedback audio-video tapes
- handouts, displays, posters, slides and photographs
- simulations, games, activities and case studies.

This list includes inventories and profiles which can be used to monitor personal and professional development (see Thorley, 1994). A central assessment strategy therefore involves the establishment of baselines that are self- and peer assessed and that allow student tutors to make comparative judgements about progress via the repeated use of the same inventories and profiles at the end of the module. In this way the development of skills and competencies can be monitored in a highly structured way.

The first two cohorts

Sixty-five students were assessed over two semesters by way of a short presentation (20 per cent of marks) and a portfolio (80 per cent of marks). Presentations and portfolios referred to an average of ten school visits per student tutor.

The presentations took place over three-week periods (at the end of the semester) to give the students some flexibility in their timetabling. The audience for each presentation was between five to ten students and staff. Most of the presentations involved the use of a projector, handouts and/or display materials. Five presentations also incorporated video clips.

The presentations were of an exceptionally high standard in general, typically lasting 15 minutes followed by five minutes for questions and discussions.

The portfolios contained the students' logs of their visits (the suggested page format involving three columns entitled: date, description and reflection), evidence of their work within the classroom, feedback from the teachers(s) and pupils, and a reflective essay on their tutoring experience (with a word limit of 1500). The students were introduced (in the third lecture/workshop) to some of the learning and development theories and asked to relate what they found in the classroom and their own learning experience to this theoretical groundwork. At the start of the module each student was given a 'Portfolio Starter' – a short booklet of self-assessment questionnaires on transferable and study skills. The purpose of these two booklets was to provide students with a possible means of showing personal development.

All but four portfolios were received on time from the students. The majority of the portfolios contained full logs of the tutoring sessions (with reflective comments), copious evidence of work and feedback from teachers. The essays described much reflection and an appreciation of the development issues. There were, however, very few attempts to relate the classroom and the student's own learning to any of the current theoretical frameworks, for example Kolb's learning cycle. At the end of the first semester of operation, a book of notes based on selected readings was compiled by staff to provide a learning resource that summarized a variety of theoretical approaches to the analysis of personal and professional development. This was used by student tutors in the second semester of operation, and staff agreed that there was a marked improvement in students' attempts to integrate personal experience within theoretical frameworks for learning,

The majority of the students used the module as a taster for the teaching profession. In their reflective essays many of these thoughts were articulated. Eighty per cent contained explicit reference to career plans, for example:

> 'Considering teaching as a career.'
> 'Now I know it is a career (teaching) that I could not pursue.'
> 'As I continued to reflect on how good I thought I would be as a mathematics teacher.'
> 'The net result is that I am now seriously considering teaching as a career after my time at university.'

Favourable student responses were also recorded for module organization (80 per cent satisfied), workshop support (90 per cent satisfied), and contact with staff (90 per cent satisfied).

Final Concerns

The piloting of assessed modules in student tutoring has exposed a wide range of challenges. Assessment strategies have been discussed in some detail, but an important further query concerns cases of referral where portfolios are insufficient and there is little or no evidence in support of personal and professional development. In most traditionally assessed modules students have the same right to resit examinations and resubmit coursework as a second attempt. The same principle applies to a module in student tutoring although difficulties may emerge when additional school visits have to be completed prior to the resubmission of a portfolio of evidence or a second presentation to an audience within an HEI. It is therefore crucial at the outset of the module that students are clear about the paramount importance of collecting evidence throughout the original tutoring placements, and the need to keep an up-to-date journal or log. Provided that such evidence has been collected in the first place, and a record of experiences has been completed, such material can be reworked after referral without students having to undertake repeat placement visits.

A second concern is with the recruitment and selection of tutors from within an HEI. At the University of Glamorgan all scheme leaders were informed of the module, with contact names and telephone numbers being supplied. There is always the possibility, however, of a free-floating and open module attracting thousands of students: the administrative workloads associated with placing very large numbers of undergraduates in schools necessitates the stipulation of a maximum number of enrolments for each semester. A key question now emerges: what criteria should be used for selecting students who want to register for student tutoring?

A variety of strategies can be used for selection and recruitment, ranging from a 'first come-first served' policy through to in-depth interviews which identify those students who would most benefit from tutoring, in order to advance their personal and professional development. It can even be argued that such a module is of maximum value to those students who have the most ground to cover when it comes to learning about themselves and developing a variety of skills. In this sense the natural communicators and the most confident and creative people should be placed at the bottom of a waiting list for student tutoring! At this point the organizers of student tutoring modules face a dilemma: are their loyalties with the undergraduate students, or are they with the pupils and teachers in schools? The latter would prefer the good communicators, and it is essential that pupils are actually helped with their learning. One solution may be to develop a parallel student tutoring activity which allows undergraduates to help teachers prepare learning materials rather than actually tutor in the classroom. This would allow a wider range of student tutoring activity and it would give teachers and coordinators a contingency strategy should problems emerge in the actual classroom. The preparation of learning materials, however, requires a completely different set of skills and competencies as linked with personal and professional development.

At the University of Glamorgan these are currently hypothetical issues, although the challenges of over-recruitment have been anticipated through the design and validation of other personal and professional development modules. If student tutoring is 'full' another module that targets the same or similar transferable skills can be chosen from a list that includes community project work, career planning, outdoor education, and study skills.

A third and final concern is with the essentially mercenary atmosphere associated with student tutoring which earns reward through academic credits. Some would argue that one of the core features of tutoring is its altruistic context, and the importance of encouraging students to help other people rather than to think only of themselves. This is admittedly a strong argument, although readers are reminded that at no point has this discussion advocated a position where student tutoring replaces extramural and voluntary activity. Particularly problematic, too, is the inevitable confusion caused in schools when two groups of students (those who are completing a student tutoring module, and those who are not interested in assessment and academic credit) work with the same teachers. To minimize this possibility, it is recommended that separate schools are used for placing students who are enrolled on a student tutoring module, and placing those who are tutoring as an extramural activity,

In this chapter we have outlined the development of a curriculum that promotes students' personal and professional development through tutoring in schools. A variety of issues have been reviewed, especially based on experiences of working with students over two semesters of operation. While concerns have been listed, we view student tutoring as a beneficial and valuable activity where it might even be said that our students are our best ambassadors for higher education. We conclude by referring to a Welsh verb: *dysgu*. This means to learn and to teach. It is an ideal for our student tutoring initiative – *Dysgu yng Nghymru*: teaching and learning in Wales!

The authors would like to thank BP for their kind sponsorship of the Student Tutoring *Dysgu* project, and the Mid Glamorgan Education and Business Partnership for their help in coordinating school placements for University of Glamorgan students.

Address for correspondence: Professor Danny Saunders, University of Glamorgan, Prifysgol Morgannwg, Pontypridd, Mid Glamorgan, Wales CF37 1DL. Tel. 01443 480480. Fax 01443 480558.

PART D: HELP FOR TRANSITIONAL STUDENTS

Chapter 7

EVALUATION RESEARCH FINDINGS OF THE PRE-UNIVERSITY PROJECT ON TRANSITION AND STUDENT MENTORING INTO UNIVERSITY

Jane Hofmeister

The University of Amsterdam has implemented a Crossover programme to motivate pre-university students, especially those school populations from a non-academic background, to attend higher education. The programme's four themes are: developing one's possibilities and investing in one's future, choosing a course of study and a profession, studying at the university, and life at the university. University professors and school teachers in cooperation with student mentors and tutors are involved in this career guidance education programme. This chapter describes the first evaluation research findings among the pre-university students from this programme who now attend the University of Amsterdam.

This chapter summarizes the findings of a three-year evaluation of the pre-university project from its start into university. This evaluation is held at the end of the school term every year among the participating *Voorbereidend Wetenschappelijk Onderwijs* (VWO) or pre-university and first-year students, their tutors and mentors. It focuses on the aims of the pre-university project: improving the motivation of VWO students for university studies, increasing their understanding of the requirements implied by university education, improving social and learning skills (eg, optimizing their valuation of their own capacities) and improving the way VWO students are being taken care of in their first academic year.

The major finding in the evaluation was that the students of the project compared to the regular students have better performances with respect to their rates of drop-out or study switching and progress.

Easing the Passage

The University of Amsterdam (UvA) and a number of schools intend to improve the link-up between the pre-university educational sector, VWO and the university by developing a more intensive collaboration with each other. Apart from efficiency considerations and the wish to increase the number of students entering higher education, this university and the participating schools also take justice aspects into consideration, especially in their effort to increase the numbers of migrant students as well as to improve their performance, since it has been found that a lot of qualified school-leavers do not opt for a university education, thus failing to take advantage of the opportunities that their VWO diploma offers them to continue their education at university level. A large number of this group come from less-educated and non-academic circles, including a substantial percentage of ethnic minorities. Though the number of VWO students among these groups is growing, many are still daunted by the prospect of going to university. On the other side of the spectrum, VWO students from more highly educated and academic circles are not automatically at an advantage. Experience shows that they are often wrong-footed by too rosy a picture of university and student life.

Another effort of the university is to reduce the rate of drop-outs in the first academic year, due to students switching to another course of study, mainly because the first one was chosen for the wrong reasons. One of the concerns of the university is to improve student counselling and tutoring, refining its system of registering students' progress based on monitoring of their performance.

Collaboration between the university and VWO schools seemed also to be fruitful in adjusting to the restructuring requirements to which the Dutch government recently subjected upper secondary education. Both government and university are responsible, and dependent on each other, for the students' career outcomes.

The contribution of the UvA in this project is substantial as some 60 professors from all its 14 faculties are working closely together with their counterparts, over 150, in VWO schools to provide the VWO students with an education programme involving orientation, experience and reflection.

The Crossover Programme, VWO–University of Amsterdam

The primary aim of the programme is to reduce any obstacles – especially social barriers – that may impede a smooth transition to higher education and in particular the university.

Many students, including a substantial percentage of ethnic minority students, experience difficulties due to purely cultural factors when entering the university. Therefore a major concern of the university is to deal with students' motivation in opting for university studies, the social dimensions of study, the learning attitudes, and the learning skills required by higher education. In this area the Crossover programme has been developed for students who attend the fifth and sixth grade of VWO schools and for those students in their first university year.

There are four themes for the VWO sector:

1. *Developing my possibilities and investing in my future.* This theme provides an orientation into one's possibilities of attending higher education. It includes questions such as: 'What are people's motives in opting for higher education, in general?', 'What are my own motives?' and 'What would be the implications of other options in organizing my own life?' This theme should increase VWO students' motivation for higher education.
2. *My choice of study subject and its professions.* This theme deals with choosing a study subject and the relations between study subject and professional perspectives (career opportunities). The theme should increase students' knowledge of the various branches of study and professions and improve their motivation for a particular course of study. The intention is to give students real insight into their chosen study subject.
3. *Studying at the university.* Studying as a day-to-day activity is about what specific kinds of learning attitudes and learning skills are required by higher education. What is the difference between studying at the university and being a VWO student? Which is the best way to prepare oneself for becoming a university student? This theme is to increase students' knowledge and experience of the social and

learning skills required by university study.

4. *Life at university, a tag-along day*. Studying at university not only implies acquiring knowledge. One also needs specific attitudes and social skills to be able to function well as a university student, in a tutorial or chapter and also in communicating with fellow students, housing mates, lecturers, advisers and counsellors. This theme is handled in the sixth grade and these VWO students may spend a day accompanying a university student, often one of the student mentors who studies the subject of their choice. In this way the VWO students can become more familiar with various aspects of university life and studies.

Upon students' entrance to the UvA, the programme is continued with those students whose schools have participated since the students' fifth grade.

The fifth theme of the Crossover programme, started for the first time in September 1995, is focused on the relation between their VWO learning experiences, including those of the Crossover programme, and their applicability in university. The sub-themes refer to their degree of success, social and socio-economic factors (income, ethnic background, work, committee/administrative activities) and their views on university education (facilities, relations with professors/fellow students, tutorials, study progress, study skills, etc). They are also asked to comment on and evaluate their future study progress. These survey-like questions provide the university with some of the necessary data for its student monitoring system.

Characteristic of this Crossover programme is the students' guidance in their transition from VWO to university education. It is a career education programme in which students orientate themselves to, and collect information about, studying and the professions. It started in 1993, and in 1995 the university dealt with its first cohort (cohort 1993) of this project.

Orientation, experience and reflection are the key concepts in this career education crossover programme. Orientation and reflection take place at school, whereas VWO students experience the theme-based issues at the university by paying a visit to it. All the faculties or specific subject departments organize a special programme covering those issues.

The career advising and planning process is given full attention by careful fostering of elements like VWO students' self-concept, their educational/occupational knowledge and identification of realistic alternatives, the influence of other people, and decision-making knowledge. As part of the programme VWO students pay visits to the university to undergo realistic study experiences like lectures, tutorials/chapters, laboratory sessions. During these visits university students are their mentors. Mentoring is focused on broadening students' views of the social aspects of the subject and student's daily life at and outside the university, and on helping them to cope with any conflicts that arise.

The Mentor Project VWO-UvA

The mentoring contacts with students regarding the aims of the Crossover programme aroused a great deal of enthusiasm, so an additional project called the 'VWO-UvA Mentor Project' was started officially in 1996. For this project it was decided to deploy on a regular basis students as mentors at the participating schools too. The student mentor programme had to be fitted into the timetable of the Crossover programme. In the first year this mentor project is confined to six schools only, and, if successful will be extended to all of the participating schools.

Over 60 student mentors from a range of studies are now fully involved in the programme inside as well as outside the schools. They act as models for the VWO students, using their own experiences as the basic working material to provide them with guidance and answer any questions they might have.

The schools where student mentors are being deployed generally have students, either ethnic or non-ethnic minority, who do not see a university education as a natural progression from secondary school, as virtually no one in their immediate surroundings has preceded them. They have no one to ask other than their teachers or counsellor at school. If they complete their VWO successfully and decide to go to university, they often have no idea of what awaits them. Some of them switch study subject and are faced with delays, others drop out; only the most determined persist to the end.

How the student mentors are used depends on the arrangements made between the school and the student mentors. One option is for the student mentors to be assigned to a small number of VWO students, in which case the mentors will act as the intermediary between the VWO student and the university for all aspects included in the Crossover programme. To be able to convey the correct information the student mentors must form a clear picture of their own education, particularly of the first year. They must have a thorough knowledge of the various graduation subjects and career opportunities. In addition, the student mentors must be capable of explaining the specific skills necessary to complete a course of study successfully and the differences between studying at a university and at a school.

Here the beneficial effects work two ways: by reflecting on their own experiences when passing from the VWO to the university, the student mentors may gain a better understanding of their own choices. This self-reflection may help the student mentors with the further progress of their study.

Beforehand all student mentors were screened by means of personal interview and received appropriate training as well as an instruction manual. Evaluation will take place several times a year, both with the student mentors and the coordinators of the particpating schools.

Methods of Evaluation and Data Resources

The execution of the programme is evaluated every year and by the end of the school year 1996 the first cycle (fifth and sixth grade secondary education and first academic year) of the three years' programme was finished for those who started in 1993. The schools continue the project every year with a new group of fifth grade VWO students.

The evaluation is carried out by means of a survey among university professors, pre-university teachers and, of course, their students. Data are acquired from observations, evaluation consultations, and written questionnaires for teachers and students. The students' questionnaire mostly consists of evaluation questions concerning the programme and questions about the teaching effects experienced by the students. These students' evaluations are presented here, because they are the primary concern of interest.

Programme evaluation

Evaluations of the programme's themes and sub-themes have been marked on a scale from 1 to 10 by fifth grade VWO students (see Table 7.1). Note that in the Netherlands marks from 1 to 5 are insufficient. Information was obtained from 645 students (fifth year VWO) from 19 schools.

The VWO students still appreciate the programme; 80 per cent gave a sufficient mark. The visits to the university are also positively marked; over the years the visits have been marked highly by 80 per cent of the VWO students.

The schools and the university also consider the visits to be embedded in an extensive school programme which has to be part of the regular educational curriculum and to which several school subjects and teachers should contribute. The students' evaluations show that they are also quite positive about the school's contribution to the programme: 75 per cent marked it higher than 6.

Table 7.1 Crossover programme themes and sub-themes, 1993 to 1996, evaluated by fifth-year VWO students. N = 645

Programme themes	*1993/94* %	*1994/95* %	*1995/96* %
Programme 5-VWO			
– mark 7 or higher	51	61	65
– mark 6	31	29	23
– insufficient marks	16	10	12
Option first visit			
– mark 7 or higher	47	55	48
– mark 6	21	25	28
– insufficient marks	22	20	24
Option second visit			
– mark 7 or higher	47	54	70
– mark 6	17	26	15
– insufficient marks	23	20	15
School programme's contribution			
– mark 7 or higher	34	41	47
– mark 6	36	37	32
– insufficient marks	26	22	21
Contribution UvA professors			
– mark 7 or higher	51	54	55
– mark 6	24	30	29
– insufficient marks	22	16	16

The VWO students appreciated the contribution paid by the university and some were even very enthusiastic about it (marks like 9 and 10); 80 per cent marked it higher than 6. All in all, it seems that university professors, tutors and mentors adapt well to VWO students' questions.

Effects on learning

The VWO students were also asked about the effects of the scheme on their learning; do they now know more about what studying means, what a university is, which skills are required and for which study they can opt in the future and why? These results, evaluated on a scale from 1 to 4, are presented in Table 7.2.

Table 7.2 Crossover learning effects, 1993 to 1996, evaluated by fifth year VWO students. N = 645

Learning effects	*1993/94* %	*1994/95* %	*1995/96* %
What studying means			
1 do not know	6	10	12
2 know a little	45	47	45
3 know quite some more	41	39	39
4 now know a great deal more	7	5	4
What a university is like			
1 do not know	9	8	9
2 know a little	28	34	34
3 know quite some more	50	47	49
4 now know a great deal more	13	12	8
Which skills are required			
1 do not know	12	13	13
2 know a little	45	40	36
3 know quite some more	34	40	42
4 now know a great deal more	9	8	9
Which subject to study			
1 do not know	40	42	37
2 know a little	23	24	22
3 know quite some more	15	16	20
4 now know a great deal more	21	17	21

There are no remarkable evaluation differences over the past three years. If students indicate learning effects with 'now know a great deal more', the conclusion may be drawn that the effects on their learning can be ascribed to the programme.

The evaluation results show a high score (over 57 per cent) on 'what the university is'; over 51 per cent now know a great deal more about 'which skills are required'. The effects on their learning with respect to options for study are fewer. It appears that the programme succeeds in offering the VWO students a realistic image of the university. The effects on learning indicated by the students correspond to those noted by their teachers. Also according to the teachers, students now know better what a university is, what studying means, and what is required from students.

Every year when the programme starts at the beginning of the school year, VWO students are asked for which study they intend to opt; in 1993, 47 per cent of the students did not know but at the end of that school year this number dropped to 28 per cent. Both their preference for colleges for higher vocational education and for universities increased in that period. The preference for universities increased from 36 to 47 per cent: (in 1996 these percentages were 52 to 56 per cent).

The Cohort of 1993

In 1995, 31 per cent of VWO students (N=159) on the Crossover programme began to study at the UvA. This first group who started in 1993 is called 'cohort 1993'. This cohort 1993 has been monitored next to the other students who enrolled at UvA from other schools in 1995.

A range of questions, personal interviews and written questionnaires were put to all of them. The survey is one of a number held among all first-year students. The questions are focused on:

- Which factors and mechanisms influence the progress of the students' studies?
- How can the students' insight into these mechanisms and factors be increased, thus enabling them to change their study patterns?
- Can differences be established between ethnic majority and minority students?
- Which (policy) measures can be taken, on the basis of this information and any differences between these student groups, to improve the educational quality to positively influence the study patterns of the students and to prevent drop-outs and delays as much as possible?
- Will changes in secondary education alter the factors that influence drop-outs and delays? Can effective measures be taken to obviate these possible effects?
- Which factors inhibit and stimulate students in the pursuit of their studies? What motivates their decisions to continue, switch or stop their studies? What role is played by the various backgrounds of the students?

Another survey, conducted first among all first-year students and a selection of graduation students, documents a number of 'objective' characteristics in the process.

From both surveys it appeared that students of the 1993 cohort seem more successful with respect to their chosen study subject as their rate of switchers/drop-outs is 8 per cent compared to 22 per cent of the remaining first-year fellow students. With respect to students' progress, 83 per cent of the 1993 cohort succeeded in achieving students' progress standard against 68 per cent of the remaining first-year fellow students. These positive results may well be attributable to the Crossover programme activities.

Summary

Collaboration between schools and universities in a so-called network is increasingly regarded as an important means for modernizing education in The Netherlands. The Crossover Project VWO-UvA is a kind of network which seems to provide a programme appropriate to the upper secondary schools' new curriculum decreed by the Dutch government. This career education programme, either chosen as modular or centrally instructed, has now become part of the compulsory curriculum for the VWO students. Hence there is a national demand for the Crossover programme VWO-UvA, which now will be rewritten for purposes of all upper secondary schools and higher education. This also means that the other national universities are forced to provide schools in their regions with similar Crossover programme activities in the introduction of reforms with respect to VWO students' careers in higher education, in the upper grades of secondary education.

As the Crossover project method implies an intensive collaboration between the VWO schools and the university, ties will be strengthened between the university and its environment, not only with respect to the implementation of the programme, but also as partners who feel responsible for their students' careers. Both school teachers and university professors work together on constructing a new educational programme. They will be given the opportunity to take a good look behind the scenes of each others' institutions. Some of them are officially involved in the so-called VWO-UvA Inspection Programme. The character of the inspection commission in the Crossover programme involves reciprocal visits for advice and consultations. At the same time university professors learn a lot about their future students, of whom they seemed to lack sufficient knowledge when the programme started. The student mentors take part in the relationship between VWO students and university professors. In the Crossover programme both have to convey the necessary information on university education and life at university. But no matter how involved professors may be, they can never fully place themselves in the students' shoes. Student mentors act as intermediaries between the VWO students and the university for all aspects of the programme.

Address for correspondence: Jane Hofmeister, coordinator Aansluiting VWO-UvA, Department of Expertise Centre of Academic Affairs, University of Amsterdam, POB 19268, 1000 GG Amsterdam. Tel. +31 20 5252492. Fax +31 20 5252136. e-mail jhofmeister@bdu.uva.nl

PART E: MEETING NATIONAL NEEDS

Chapter 8

THE SCIENCE/TECHNOLOGY AWARENESS RAISING (STAR) PROGRAMME: A PARTNERSHIP IN RAISING PARTICIPATION THROUGH PEER TUTORING

Russell Elsegood, Judith MacCallum, Ruth Hickey and Bruce Jeffreys

The Science/Technology Awareness Raising (STAR) Peer Tutoring Programme is a partnership between BP Australia, Murdoch University and schools in Perth, Western Australia.

STAR's aims are to:

- *tackle the drift away from science and technology (S&T) by students at all levels*
- *address issues of equity – to motivate girls and students from educationally-disadvantaged backgrounds, and to raise their aspirations for further study in S&T*
- *better prepare school-leavers for the often difficult transition to university (or further study) and to help reduce the wasteful and potentially tragic attrition in the first year*
- *provide a programme that stimulates university students, helps them develop generic/transferable work skills and improves their employability*
- *involve the university, its staff and students, in a worthwhile community service*

- *establish an ongoing partnership between the university, schools and industry sponsors/mentors.*

Building long-term partnerships is fundamental to the success and future growth of any peer tutoring or mentoring programme – but particularly so when the programme is cross-institutional, cross-age, and seeks to achieve a given goal in the face of complex challenges.

The STAR Peer Tutoring Programme, sponsored by BP Australia and based at Murdoch University in Western Australia, was founded to raise students' aspirations for study and a career in science and technology (S&T), at a time when high school and university students' preferences for science were, at best, stable if not declining. It also seeks to help address university drop-out rates. The attrition rate among first-year students in Western Australia's four state (public) universities in 1996 was 24 per cent.

STAR has sought to address these challenges using the talents and resources of a wide range of 'partnerships': partnerships within the university; between the university and schools, and between the education sector and the corporate/employer sector. Those involved with the Programme recognize that the partners must be in 'for the long haul'. There is no 'quick fix' remedy.

There are six 'Ps' in the STAR Programme: partners, principles, process, progress, performance and potential.

Partners

STAR has actively sought and fostered partnerships with a wide range of key players in the fields of science and technology, building on the director's 20 years' experience in developing contacts within S&T industries and professional organizations, and with relevant government ministers and departments. The Programme's advisory panel, which meets regularly, is widely representative of the STAR partners. It includes a senior government S&T adviser; industry representatives (both administrative and those involved in R&D); schools; the Science Teachers' Association; the WA Education Department; the chief executive of the state's premier science and technology education centre – The Scitech Discovery Centre; university scientists; and peer tutors.

Government

At the government level, the STAR Programme contributed to Western Australia's first Science and Technology Policy, launched in April 1997. The

Policy contains a commitment to fund extension of STAR to regional schools – a major undertaking, given that Western Australia is ten times the area of the UK.

Close association with senior Education Department staff has helped merge the STAR Programme's aims with the Department's educational strategies in science. As a result, the Programme has been integrated into 18 metropolitan high schools over the past three years. And, to complement the Department's initiative to improve primary science and technology studies, STAR tutors were introduced into upper primary school classes (Grades 4–7) this year.

Industry/government employers

To effect a positive change in students' attitude to science, to raise their aspirations for further study in S&T, and to counter the perception that S&T offers few job or career prospects, the Programme is progressively involving employer mentors from a wide range of industries and government agencies, as well as university academic mentors. Tutors and tutees have the opportunity to see and discuss contemporary S&T with these mentors, and to receive first-hand information about the 'world of work'.

An innovative, dynamic economy demands new combinations of skills within a diversifying labour market. Therefore, employer partners are encouraged to recognize that programmes such as STAR are not merely employment services, matching graduates to established career paths. Equally, tutors and the tutees are encouraged to think more laterally about potential job and career opportunities in S&T, rather than be driven by expectations that reflect career opportunities that, more than likely, will be outdated by the time they graduate.

Field trips to industrial R&D sites and special half-day and full-day field trips/laboratory sessions at the university campus help to reinforce the school students' knowledge of S&T in a practical/vocational context. For many students from STAR's priority area – Perth's industrial suburbs – these campus visits are the first time they have set foot inside a university.

The visiting students get a feel for the campus life and environment, through mixing with the peer tutors on their 'patch', meeting academic staff, and using facilities and equipment not available to them in school.

With the help and support of STAR's coordinator, and working closely with classroom teachers, peer tutors help organize and run excursions to industry sites and the university campus. Opportunities to interact with employer mentors has helped several STAR tutors and some tutees secure summer vacation jobs with various partner industries.

Enthusiastic and articulate scientists and technologists – mentors drawn from both the university and industry sectors – add another dimension to the positive role model image presented by the STAR peer tutors, helping dispel negative, stereotypical perceptions about science and scientists.

STAR is the university link in a special partnership with the Kwinana Industries Council (KIC), representing 24 of WA's major secondary industries in an area between Murdoch's two campuses. In partnership with the KIC, STAR and a local Technical and Further Education (TAFE) college have organized a community forum to develop practical strategies to help students make a successful transition from school to further education and the workforce.

Peer tutors

University science students are key partners in the STAR enterprise. To foster this partnership, the director and coordinator encourage the tutors to offer ideas for improving the Programme (and specifically their role in it); to suggest special projects or initiatives that they want to try. For example, STAR tutors have assisted in running an after-school science club (with special research projects on weekends); provided extra, one-on-one tuition for a blind student; presented a special series of lessons on mining (which was the student's major, but freely acknowledged by the teacher as outside his own experience and expertise); and helped coordinate the rehabilitation of a wetland on a school campus as a student project.

STAR tutors meet regularly with the coordinator (individually and in small groups) and are encouraged to offer feedback on the Programme. Refresher training courses and social functions provide tutors with opportunities to meet and talk informally about experiences in schools that differ markedly in size, teaching style, academic performance and socio-economic environment.

Annually, all tutors are surveyed by questionnaire and asked for their frank (anonymous) assessment of STAR. Over the past three years their views have 'fine-tuned' the Programme.

For its part STAR offers tutors the opportunity to develop valuable workplace skills in communication, teamwork and problem-solving, as well as building self-confidence, self-esteem and interpersonal skills. Through fostering good relations with industry/government partners, STAR is progressively developing avenues for peer tutors to find work relevant to their science qualifications on mine sites and in industrial, government and the university's R&D centres.

Former STAR tutors have said that when successfully applying for jobs they have found employers' interview panels to be curious about the Programme, very positive about its aims and impressed with the relevant experience it has afforded.

Campus partners

The Programme has a strong commitment to equity in educational opportunity and has concentrated much of its effort and resources in Perth's South-West Metropolitan Region where there is, traditionally, an extremely low, post-secondary participation rate and high youth unemployment. STAR works closely with the university's equity staff and complements much of their effort in schools in this region. STAR tutors are involved in an equity programme in which Year 11 (16-year-old) students spend three days on campus 'shadowing' university students in lectures, tutorials and laboratory sessions.

Several initiatives have been taken to more fully integrate the Programme into the university's organization and structure. Under an agreement negotiated with the Vice Chancellor, the university provides a dollar-for-dollar matching grant (to a maximum of $20,000AUD) to STAR for every dollar the director raises from non-university sources. This performance-based funding was secured for 1997 and is subject to annual review.

STAR also has cooperated with Murdoch's School of Education to offer a special unit in science communication. This initiative is described below.

As a member of the Science Division's public relations committee, the director works closely with academics in coordinating STAR's activities with the Division's promotional initiatives. STAR has co-sponsored special lectures (for high school students) and public seminars (for industry and community leaders) on S&T.

Through inter-campus cooperation STAR helped launch a second S&T peer tutoring programme in Perth and, under a Fellowship agreement with Murdoch University, BP Australia employs the Programme's Director half-time to promote peer tutoring and mentoring nationally. Following recent heavy fee increases for science and engineering courses, and a subsequent drop in science enrolments in states other than Western Australia, senior university faculty in three states have invited STAR's help in launching similar programmes.

As part of this programme to take tutoring and mentoring nation-wide, the STAR team (in collaboration with BP's John Hughes) sponsored a workshop on students as tutors and mentors for representatives from 20 Australian and New Zealand universities and colleges.

Schools

School partnerships are developed through link teachers, whose enthusiasm and initiative have been central to the Programme's acceptance. The link teachers are the point of regular contact between STAR, the school administration and the classroom teachers, and help maximize the tutors' time in classrooms and laboratories.

Apart from day-to-day contact between the coordinator and the link teachers, twice-yearly forums have been instituted to give teachers, STAR staff and the School of Education's Science Communication unit coordinators the chance to exchange views.

School staff have involved STAR peer tutors in special projects sponsored by various government agencies and industries. Through partnerships forged between Western Australia's Environmental Protection Authority (EPA), STAR and link teachers, peer tutors will coordinate high school students in air quality monitoring as part of the EPA's Airwatch project. STAR tutors drawn from Murdoch's mineral science programme are helping launch a new Year 11 and 12 course in mining at Kent Street Senior High School. The new course, unique in Australia, has backing from WA's $11AUD billion a year mining industry, whose member companies provide practical, mine-site experience for the students. As part of this programme, a STAR tutor has accompanied Kent Street students on a fly-in/fly-out work experience programme at a mine 800 km north east of Perth. Murdoch's mineral scientists are academic mentors in this programme.

Principles for Partnerships

STAR has employed a short list of key principles in building and maintaining partnerships.

Adhering to these key 'partnership principles' can, and often does, lead to unexpected, but surprisingly rewarding initiatives, the BP/Murdoch link being a classic case. Before teaming up through the WA science summer school and STAR, Murdoch University had not had any ongoing relationship with BP Kwinana – though the refinery is one of WA's longest-established and biggest industries. As a direct result of the successful partnership, BP Kwinana has since set up several joint industry/university projects, including a four-year programme monitoring the unique lifecycle, behaviour and environment of dolphins in Cockburn Sound – one of Australia's busiest harbours.

The principles STAR has found most useful for establishing partnerships are:

- when seeking support, think of it as a long-term relationship;
- treat your partner(s) well all the time, not just when you are seeking help or money;
- be creative, be willing to adapt and try to find common ground with present and potential partners;
- don't ignore your neighbours when seeking partners. Neighbours (schools and corporations) very likely have more in common with you and the local community than anyone else. Like your own organization, they want to be seen as serving the community as a good neighbour;
- corporate sponsors are very often keener to invest in projects for youth than in other programmes. After all, the future of young people in their community is vital to the corporation's future – as potential customers, and their future workforce.

Process – the Launch of STAR

STAR evolved from a strategy launched by Murdoch scientists in the mid-1980s to help reverse the decline in student enrolments in science at both secondary and university level. The keystone of the strategy was a residential science summer school launched in 1989. Industries in the immediate neighbourhood of the campus, including the BP Kwinana refinery, and federal and state government agencies welcomed the WA science summer school (WASSS) proposal.

The successful introduction of peer tutors in the WASSS from 1991 played a central role in developing the STAR Programme. Each year between 25 to 30 former WASSS students, the majority of them young women, vie for the six peer tutor positions at the school, and female students constitute the majority of the 60 peer tutors regularly working in STAR. Early discussions with education leaders and teachers about peer tutoring revealed a degree of scepticism about 'another new scheme to stimulate students'. There were warnings about how some teenagers would respond to the presence of university students in their classes. Nevertheless, the enthusiasm of a small group of principals and teachers provided encouragement to press on. There was no lack of enthusiasm from university students canvassed as potential peer tutors.

There was a clear onus on the education *and* the industry sectors to work in partnership to ensure that:

- talented students – male and female of all backgrounds – and those who influence them, were aware of the skills, training and education requirements in modern science and technology;
- students, parents, teachers and careers advisers were better informed about new and challenging jobs and careers constantly emerging in S&T; and
- schools, industry and universities were more in tune with each others' needs, expectations and limitations.

Surveys of prospective university students provided evidence that peer influence, if not overt pressure, was a factor in the decision-making processes of many Australian teenagers. There also was strong anecdotal evidence that peers could influence where school-leavers chose to continue their studies – or whether they continued their education. STAR's proponents were, therefore, acutely aware that the Programme had to establish early credibility in the commitment of the peer tutors and their ability to be positive role models in the fields of science and technology.

The science summer school provided the experienced peer tutors for the STAR Peer Tutoring Programme when it was launched in February 1994. Backed by a three-year sponsorship agreement with BP Australia, a small pilot programme was planned with six tutors in three schools for the first year, with gradual expansion both within Western Australia and (hopefully) nationally.

Announcements by the Federal Department of Education rather broadened thinking and expectations. On Christmas Eve, 1993, STAR was awarded the first of two $100,000AUD National Priority Reserve Fund grants, which allowed a full-time coordinator to be appointed to the Programme and for 30 peer tutors to be assigned to ten schools in the first year.

Recruiting peer tutors was not a problem. Word-of-mouth recommendation from tutors was and continues to be most effective in recruitment. But rapid expansion strained the Programme's ability to provide adequate training before placing tutors. The practice of teaming new tutors with trained, experienced tutors, first introduced as a stop-gap measure, proved very successful and now complements the formal training and refresher courses for all STAR tutors.

As personal recommendation proved successful in recruiting new tutors, so teachers working with STAR tutors proved equally effective in introducing new schools to the Programme. At the end of the first year STAR had its full quota of schools and peer tutors – and a waiting list of schools.

As of April 1997 the Programme has more than 60 peer tutors at any one time working regularly in 18 high schools and two primary schools.

Progress

The Australian Government's National Priority grants carried a proviso that STAR should concentrate its resources in an area of low post-secondary participation and high youth unemployment. The needs of students in such areas were already identified as a STAR priority and, although it has partner schools in other suburbs, the Programme has placed its emphasis and resources in those schools in a region embracing Perth's heavy industries.

Murdoch University's Tertiary Options Programme (TOP) – an equity programme targeting this area since the late 1980s – showed that few students aspired to continue their education beyond the minimum time in high school. Absenteeism is a chronic problem, with a high percentage of upper school students reportedly missing each day and with peer group pressure perceived as a powerful influence to abandon study for the surf, video games or the 'dole' queue. Many students are from families with little knowledge of, let alone experience with, education beyond the second or third year of high school. Most families in the region have lived comfortably on traditional trades jobs in heavy industry and, until the recession of the 1980s, most teenagers expected to follow in their parents' footsteps.

It is a quantum leap for students from this area to consider a university education, let alone to raise their aspirations for high-tech S&T careers. But Murdoch University has since planned and will open a second campus in this region in mid-1997.

After consultation with industries in the area the university has introduced programmes in instrumentation and control engineering and software engineering for the new campus – both fields replacing some traditional work in the region's heavy industries. But many students from traditional blue-collar/trade backgrounds (whose families are in the second generation of long-term unemployment created by the impact of new technology) do not see these high-tech courses as offering them new options for further study and employment, despite the fact that each year Australia 'head-hunts' suitably-qualified engineers from abroad.

For STAR peer tutors to offer advice on making a successful transition from school to university, it is important that they should have successfully negotiated first-year university study and experienced campus life. Therefore, tutors have been recruited from second-year onwards. But with the introduction of tutoring/mentoring in primary schools, first-year students are being given the opportunity to join the Programme.

All prospective tutors attend a half-day initial training programme that includes sessions on classroom etiquette (teacher/tutor/student relationships); questioning techniques, basic communication skills and common problems they may encounter. Progressively, informal refresher sessions have been introduced to allow tutors to exchange experiences, provide feedback and update their knowledge.

Academic Credit for Tutoring

In 1996 a unit of study for academic credit, Peer Tutoring in Science, was introduced through Murdoch's School of Education. The move, prompted by STAR's success, provides academic support for peer tutors who want to understand more about the tutoring process.

The unit has an on-campus component (two hour-long seminars per week over ten weeks of the semester) conducted by three lecturers, and the off-campus component (peer tutoring half-a-day per week in a school) organized through STAR. The lecturers, whose expertise and experience cover a broad range of science, science education, educational psychology and school teaching, developed the unit collaboratively after discussions with the STAR director and coordinator. The STAR coordinator supervises the initial training of peer tutors, arranges and oversees their placement in schools, and acts as the interface between the university, the school and teachers. This division of roles is mainly due to funding arrangements, the unit being financed through regular university allocations for teaching, and STAR financed largely through sponsorship.

Enrolment in the unit remains optional for STAR tutors, but students enrolling in the unit for credit must also sign up for STAR. Twenty-one students enrolled for credit in 1996, and 28 in 1997.

The unit's aims are strongly linked to the aims of STAR, with an emphasis on supporting peer tutors in the schools, improving the effectiveness of their tutoring, and developing their personal and professional communication skills. The unit integrates substantive knowledge and peer tutoring experience, and engages tutors in reflecting on their experiences. These experiences and skills are systematically linked to more general areas of science communication beyond peer tutoring.

The unit was developed around three themes: peer tutoring, communicating science, and learning in science.

Peer tutoring

Definitions of peer tutoring; the investigation of tutoring issues, such as learning through interaction and the benefits to thinking and learning of sharing ideas, listening to others' views, and refining your own views;

cooperative group development and group skills, the roles that people take in groups such as 'initiator' or 'challenger'; and changes in group dynamics over time, with people establishing routines, expectancies, and ways of operating.

Communicating science

Community views of science as the provider of both good and bad aspects of our society; stereotypical views of scientists, and how these are continued in the media; and a study of public perceptions of gene technology, and how scientists work to change such views.

Learning in science

Alternative frameworks, misunderstandings and misconceptions in science, and how resistant these are to change; appropriate ways to use questions to draw out a person's knowledge and how questions could support others to learn, not just be shown to be wrong; how science textbooks may inhibit or hinder learning; how expectations of society of schools and educational institutions influence our views of the roles of teachers, students and tutors.

Opportunities for tutors to interact and provide continuing mutual support have been enhanced through the unit's weekly, workshop-style seminars. Issues are discussed in small groups and placed in the realistic and immediate context of classroom tutoring experience.

Each tutor is required to keep a 'reflective journal'. General observations on their classroom experiences are supplemented by closer focus on a student or a small group of students, and on specific episodes relating to the themes of the unit. Journal entries maintain the anonymity of the school, teachers and students.

While it is stressed that the skills of reflection are valuable life skills and can be used to self-evaluate and improve effectiveness in many personal and professional settings, tutors have had mixed reactions to the idea of a reflective journal. Some have found it very difficult to move away from the traditional science writing style to the more individualized and subjective journal style. Initially, journal entries tended to be a critique of the school system and science teaching. But by sharing journal extracts and discussing what can be included in a journal of this type, tutors have gradually developed reflective skills.

The journals are also a resource for assessment. The unit has four components of assessment: three, short reflective written assignments based on learning journals (50 per cent); seminar participation (10 per cent); link teacher evaluation of effectiveness in peer tutoring (pass/fail); and an examination (40 per cent).

The 30 hours of tutoring in schools is evaluated by the teacher, rating the tutor's success in eight items, including 'ability to develop a positive working relationship with students', 'explaining concepts in a manner students understand' and 'ability to develop an effective working relationship with the teacher'.

Financial constraints and the logistics of viewing many tutors, all with different days at different schools spread over the Perth area, prevented a formal evaluation of the classroom tutoring, and a 'once off' assessment was unlikely to be a reliable or satisfactory way to gauge each tutor's success in their role. Therefore, it was decided that teachers should evaluate tutors on a 'pass' or 'fail' basis only, as formal allocation of percentage points may not be equitable. This limits pressure on the teacher to evaluate – distinguishing the peer tutor who is there to help the teacher, from the 'trainee teacher' who requires formal assessment of their contribution.

Initially, because of concerns about providing insurance cover for peer tutors while 'on the job', they were signed to contracts and paid an hourly rate plus travelling expenses. Changes to the university's insurance now provide cover for student volunteers involved in authorized university projects, and the Programme now relies on a mix of students who are volunteers or undertaking the special unit in science communication. All tutors remain eligible for travel expenses – not unreasonable given that some schools in the STAR Programme are more than 35 kilometres from the campus.

The peer tutor selection and training process has earned high praise from teachers and high school students. The following, from a senior science teacher at Kolbe Catholic College, Rockingham, is typical of teachers' comments:

> '(STAR) is an excellent programme where all participants benefit, including the teachers. The peer tutors are very enthusiastic and helpful which suggests a good screening process.'

In promoting the Programme, and in the selection and training process, it is continually emphasized that there are key benefits for the peer tutors. Depending on their initiative and commitment they can acquire or improve their self-confidence, and hone 'transferable' skills – important attributes which enhance (but do not guarantee) employability. Peer tutors cite acquisition (or improvement) of these skills as an important reason for being involved in STAR.

The Programme is most successful in schools where the director and coordinator jointly and personally brief the science department staff. The director explains the background and philosophy behind the establishment of STAR, and the advantages of long-term partnerships being forged between the schools, universities and industry; while the coordinator explains day-to-day involvement in recruiting and training peer tutors, rostering them to schools and providing the link between schools and the university.

Through discussions with the principal and/or science department head, a link teacher is designated at each school, and all day-to-day contact between the Programme and the school is then maintained through this one person.

The STAR coordinator and the link teacher negotiate a programme that matches the school's priorities with suitably-qualified tutors. Factors considered when placing tutors are:

- the subject to be tutored – eg, chemistry, biology, lower school general science;
- the subject level – from this year tutors can be assigned to help students aged from 9 (fourth grade primary) to 17 (fifth year high school);
- how well tutors' university timetables match with the school timetable;
- whether the student wishes to tutor at his or her former school;
- special needs/requests – for example, one school had a special need for tutors in computing; another wanted a tutor to help with science students for whom English was their second language; and
- the distance the tutor is required to travel to the school.

In some cases special requests come from the peer tutors, some tutors preferring to work with young students; others preferring working with upper high school students (aged 16 and 17). One tutor found her niche in one-on-one tutoring for students with disabilities.

STAR tutors are recruited from the physical sciences, biological sciences, environmental science, computer science, mathematics and even veterinary studies, and there are very few occasions when the coordinator and link teacher cannot achieve a match. Most tutors are quite flexible and can move between science classes and laboratories and, in many cases, between subjects.

Tutors complain if they are not being used to the optimum, and teachers giving a test or a 'chalk and talk' session are encouraged to offer the services of the tutor to another colleague who can use the tutor to better effect. Regular contact between the coordinator, teachers and the peer tutors monitors day-to-day performance and helps to establish the best practice for integrating peer tutors into classrooms. Informal contact has proved best in establishing a strong rapport with the peer tutors, and this style of contact is now being extended to informal meetings with teachers at both the schools and on campus. Apart from providing valuable and frank feedback for STAR, these meetings enable the teachers to network their ideas and experiences with other teachers, university academic staff and industry mentors. One immediate benefit is that field trips, campus visits and special academic briefings can be conveniently arranged.

Teachers new to the Programme can be concerned about the extra time needed to integrate peer tutors into their lessons; whether there will be extra work in 'assessing' the peer tutors; whether the tutors will have the motivation and ability to help their students; and whether the presence of such young people as tutors might be a disruption to classroom discipline.

With experience, many of these concerns can now be anticipated and allayed through informal discussions. But the quality, training and commitment of the STAR peer tutors and the cooperation of the link teachers have, to a very large degree, avoided problems. Clearly defining the status and role of the peer tutors also has been important in the implementation and acceptance of the Programme.

At the outset it is made clear to teachers (and to the students volunteering to be tutors) that:

- peer tutors are not trainee teachers and that, while feedback on volunteer tutors' performance is useful and appreciated, it is not a prerequisite for involvement in the STAR Programme (where students undertaking tutoring for credit are involved, teachers are advised of this in advance); and
- tutors always work under direct supervision of the teacher who, at all times, retains responsibility for discipline in the classroom. This reinforces the teacher's authority, while allowing the peer tutor/student relationship to comfortably develop at a different, less formal level.

But, as schools have become more comfortable with and confident of the abilities of 'their' peer tutors it has become necessary, on occasions, to remind them about the role and responsibilities of peer tutors. In some cases where a classroom teacher has been absent and a non-science relief teacher has been assigned to the class, peer tutors have run the lessons. While this is a great fillip for the morale of the individual, and has more than answered questions of whether STAR tutors have motivation and ability, it is not a role nor responsibility that the Programme encourages: (a) because it puts extra pressure on tutors who are already heavily committed in their own studies, and (b) there is a risk that their relationship and value as peer mentors and role models for the students will be eroded – as they can come to be seen as another teacher/authority figure.

Tutors' hours are set at half a day (maximum four hours) a week, and they are counselled, regularly, not to over-extend themselves. If peer tutoring begins to affect their own studies they are advised to drop out of STAR. Nevertheless, peer tutors (some of whom are now in their third year with the Programme) show a remarkable ability to juggle commitments to 'their' students and their own study workload. For example, because of the demands of their course, veterinary students have little or no time available for tutoring during the school week, so two veterinary students are tutoring in special school projects on Saturday and Sunday mornings.

While advisory panel meetings are the formal avenue for communication with the Programme's key partners, the director maintains regular, informal contact with the wider network of STAR corporate, government and educational partners, including relevant Federal and State government ministers, corporate executives, bureaucrats and academics.

Performance

Quality assurance processes are now a fact of life for Australian universities and assessment by regular survey is an integral part of the STAR Programme. Apart from the informal feedback from teachers, high school students and peer tutors, surveys by questionnaire are conducted annually.

Over the past three years more than 70 teachers' and approximately 1000 students' responses have been received in the surveys. More than 90 per cent of teachers want STAR peer tutors in their classes. More than 80 per cent of the high school students say they want peer tutors in their classes – many asking for peer tutors in subjects other than science. And there is an overwhelming, positive response from the peer tutors, with most opting to continue well beyond the minimum one semester. These experienced tutors, all volunteers, are trainers and mentors for new students joining the Programme. Data are also being gathered from peer tutors and teachers for the ongoing evaluation and revision of the unit. The lecturers and STAR personnel regularly discuss the progress of the unit during the semester.

University course preferences of Year 12 students from STAR schools that joined in the founding year of the Programme have been analysed to gauge the desire for science studies at Murdoch University. Preferences for science courses at Murdoch have begun to increase, but given the relatively low base number of students from STAR schools currently applying for university places – let alone S&T courses – the welcome increase must only be taken as a possible indication of the impact of the STAR Programme upon participating schools. The Programme acknowledges that to assume or credit any one factor for the result is too simplistic an analysis, given the relatively short time that STAR has been operating.

Potential

STAR is using both e-mail and the Internet to stay in touch with its local and global network. The next step is to use the Internet to provide 'interactive' peer tutoring/mentoring to students in Western Australia's rural regions. Research is continuing to maximize the 'personal' interface between tutors and tutees via the Internet. Current thinking is that regular contact via e-mail will be supplemented with once-a-semester visits by tutors to 'their' remote schools.

A STAR Programme service gives Internet access to Murdoch's R&D projects. WEBSTER (the acronym stands for WEB – the World Wide Web – Science/Technology Education Resource) was initially developed as a resource for science teachers and students, but is being revamped to widen its accessibility and relevance.

STAR recognizes that information technology is a means to strengthen links between schools and the university; consequently, some schools have been granted Internet access via Murdoch University's dial-up facilities, and e-mail accounts issued to some teachers involved with STAR. And STAR plans to add an on-line newsletter to its web-site, networking peer tutoring and mentoring programmes in the South-East Asia region.

Recent partnership arrangements will enable STAR peer tutors to work as demonstrators/guides in Western Australia's Science Museum – the Scitech Discovery Centre – and to join the Scitech 'Roadshow', which visits towns throughout the state. These arrangements will enable peer tutors to further develop their role as effective science communicators.

STAR's future depends on the imagination and vitality of the Programme's partners, and their commitment to providing a better, more well-rounded educational experience for school and university students.

Address for correspondence: Russell Elsegood, BP Fellow in Tutoring and Mentoring and Director STAR Programme, Murdoch University, South Street, Murdoch, Western Australia 6150. Tel. 61 9 360 2491. Fax 61 9 310 4233. e-mail elsegood@central.murdoch.edu.au

Chapter 9

THE PSYCHOLOGY TUTORIAL PROGRAMME AT WITS UNIVERSITY: THE ROLE OF STUDENT TUTORS IN SUPPORTING LARGE GROUP TEACHING

Charles Potter, Moira de Groot, Peter Fridjhon, Claudia Landsman, Ceasar Pirs, Michael Pitman, Meira Puterman and Megan Virtue

This chapter highlights the increasing involvement of student tutors in tutorials which has taken place over the past four years in the psychology department at the University of the Witwatersrand, Johannesburg. This has enabled the department to offer weekly tutorials to all its first- and second-year students.

The training of senior students as tutors in the department has given additional dimensions to the teaching and learning environment in a university department where large group teaching has traditionally been the norm. This chapter outlines how the tutorial curriculum in the psychology department has evolved, and describes how postgraduate students have been trained as tutors at departmental level, as well as how tutorials have been organized at both first- and second-year levels. Some indications of the success of tutorials, and the relationship between attendance at tutorials and pass rates, are also provided.

Background

At the end of 1992, faced with an increasing diversity in its first-year student body, the Faculty of Arts and the Academic Support Programme at Wits university initiated a tutorial development programme in four departments. This focused on the training of postgraduate students as tutors, as well as the development of methodologies for tutorial development (Potter 1993, 1995, 1996; Potter *et al.*, 1993; Taylor, 1995). The number of participating departments in the faculty escalated rapidly. By the end of 1994, 17 departments were involved in the programme. Some 310 postgraduate students had been given a central training programme providing an orientation to issues involved in the planning and evaluation of tutoring, supported by weekly meetings at departmental level focused on tutorial development. During 1995, a number of the participating departments (including psychology) provided their own orientation as well as ongoing training and support programmes for student tutors, while centralized training was provided for those departments which were not yet in a position to do so. In 1996, the central training programme was then phased out.

This chapter focuses on the tutorial programmes using student tutors that have been developed over the past four years in the department of psychology, which draws the majority of its students from the faculty of arts, but also teaches students from the faculties of health sciences, science, education, and commerce. There are over 800 students on first-year psychology courses, and approximately half this number at second-year level. At this time, postgraduate students are involved in providing tutorial support to all our first- and second-year students, and also assist in providing academic support tutorials to meet the needs of educationally underprepared students.

In a department where large-group teaching has traditionally been the norm, student-led tutorials now play an increasingly important role in providing face-to-face contact with students, in mediating concepts which may require detailed explanation and application, and in identifying students who may require additional academic support. Weekly meetings focusing on tutorial development have taken place over the past four years, involving student tutors and academic staff in each of the tutorial programmes described in this chapter. These meetings have focused on planning and evaluation of tutorials, and have provided initial orientation as well as ongoing training to the postgraduate students who tutor in the department.

In terms of this organizational model, between 60 and 70 tutorials are provided each week in small groups, to between 1100 and 1200 undergraduate students. The tutorial programmes are developed cooperatively by staff and the postgraduate student tutors, who have in many cases become involved in curriculum and materials development through the process of planning and evaluation conducted at weekly tutors' meetings.

The tutorial programmes described in this chapter may thus have relevance to others who are also faced with large student numbers and an increasingly diverse student body. Tutorial programmes developed jointly by lecturing staff and student tutors have particular relevance where universities face diminishing budgets at the same time as admitting increasing number of students drawn from a variety of educational and cultural backgrounds. This is the situation faced by the majority of South African universities at present. In the psychology department, which forms part of a large inner-city university environment, we have found that student-led tutorials can make a very positive contribution to supporting large-group teaching. However, it is the degree of lecturing staff involvement in working with the student tutors in ongoing tutor training and in curriculum development that has been the key to developing successful tutorial programmes in our particular context.

Tutorial Programmes at First-year Level

The psychology department at Wits has a full-time coordinator of tutorial programmes, and also employs three other full-time tutors who work at the first-year level. Two of these full-time tutors are employed to service the needs of the mainstream students, drawn from the faculties of arts, science, commerce and education, while the other full-time tutor services the needs of students in the health sciences stream, drawn from the faculty of medicine and dentistry.

In addition to these four academic staff members, 14 postgraduate students, who are registered for Honours or Masters degrees in psychology, are involved as tutors. Based on these human resources, the department has been able to provide tutorial support to all its first-year students. It has also been able to implement various levels of tutorial assistance to students experiencing difficulties with making the transition from school to university, or experiencing difficulties with lectures or course content.

The department currently provides a two-tier tutorial curriculum at first-year level. The first tier involves all the students taking the first-year course. In 1996 there were 24 mainstream tutorial groups which met weekly, catering for the needs of 572 students registered for first-year psychology through the faculties of arts, science, commerce and education. An additional 174 students registered for first-year psychology through the faculty of medicine and dentistry, whose tutorials were organized in six additional tutorial groups.

The department has also provided academic support tutorials which cater for the needs of underprepared students in each of these first-year streams. This second tier (referred to as 'Academic development tutorials') involves those students who voluntarily elect to join the academic development programme, which offers additional weekly tutorials as well as personalized academic support. In 1996, 62 mainstream first-year students were involved in academic development tutorials, and 30 first-year students in the health sciences stream.

This implies that all students taking first-year psychology courses attend at least one tutorial per week, and some students attend two tutorials per week (ie, one mainstream and one academic development tutorial). Logistically this involves providing over 40 first-year tutorials per week, each of which needs to be individually planned and evaluated. Without the contribution of senior students as tutors, this degree of tutorial support would be impossible.

The mainstream tutorial programme

All mainstream first-year students are offered weekly tutorials within fairly small groups (tutorial group size is generally 20–25 students). The tutorial curriculum is planned by the lecturing staff to cover the entire academic year and to include a range of different learning experiences for students.

Skills such as essay writing, preparing for tests, strategies for answering multiple-choice questions, applying theories of psychology in 'real-life' situations, and developing a critical perspective on psychology, are built into the tutorials from the beginning of the year. The aim of each week's tutorial is to allow for the development of skills within the framework of course content. Group exercises and activities are thus designed which complement and reinforce the focus of the lecture programme.

In 1996, three full-time tutors were involved in implementing the programme, supported by nine psychology Honours students, each of whom ran two tutorials per week. The focus and plan for each tutorial was devised by the lecturing staff and then relayed to the senior student tutors during a weekly meeting. This was found to be the best way of ensuring consistency across the 24 mainstream tutorials run every week. This model of implementation, based on cooperative planning and evaluation of tutorials through a process involving academic staff and student tutors, has been continued in 1997.

The health sciences tutorial programme

The 'Psychology for the health sciences' tutorial stream was initiated at the beginning of 1996. Eleven tutorials were implemented per week by a full-time tutor supported by five postgraduate student tutors for the 174 undergraduate students registered in this stream. In addition, two academic tutorials were implemented every week for educationally underprepared students.

The tutorial curriculum was developed in consultation with the lecturing staff, the course coordinator and the first-year tutorial coordinator. Empowerment, skills development and the ability to apply psychological concepts to the self were the main aims of the programme. The aim was that students should be able to apply psychological concepts to themselves. This was stressed as it was considered important that medical professionals be self-aware for the sake of their patients as well as for themselves.

Using the framework of the tutorial curriculum developed in 1996, this teaching model has been implemented again in 1997. Each week the student tutors are provided with a number of options on a similar theme. In the weekly meeting, each tutor then decides how he or she wishes to structure the tutorial session (eg, group discussion, panel discussion, debates or individual exercises), which option or combination of options will be presented in the tutorial, as well as the teaching aids that will be used. Implementation and observation of process and outcomes then take place, followed by reflection and evaluation, as the basis for further planning.

Academic development tutorials

Academic development (AD) tutorials are provided for psychology students registered in both the mainstream and the health sciences stream. Students in both these streams voluntarily choose to enlist for the programme, which aims to develop the academic skills of students who, because of inadequate school backgrounds, are underprepared for university-level study.

In 1996, the programme involved a number of small tutorial groups of between eight and 12 students, and also involved one group of 45 students, taught by a team of five student tutors led by an academic staff member. A curriculum of tutorial activities supported by teaching materials was developed, based on the areas of the first-year curriculum with which the students experience difficulty. Tutorials were then organized around this materials base, involving plenary sessions as well as small-group work.

This model has now been implemented for a number of years. A deliberate attempt has been made to involve as many black student tutors as possible, as the majority of the first-year students in the academic development tutorial programme are black. To date, all the student tutors involved in the programme have themselves been 'graduates' of the first-year academic development programme. We make this known to the first-year students, which appears to have an enormous impact on motivation.

The other advantage of using black student tutors in this context has been their ability to move from English to vernacular in cases where first-year students' English has not been adequate to assimilate a particular concept. It has been interesting to observe that discussion during the tutorials has shifted from language to language, as the need arises. This is certainly an asset which neither the full-time tutors nor white student tutors have been able to bring to the situation.

Tutorial Programmes at Second-year Level

Tutorials to support the introductory research design and analysis (RDA1) course

At second-year level, student-led tutorials are provided to support the introductory Research Design and Analysis (RDA1) course, which is compulsory for all undergraduate students wishing to major in psychology. The course was initiated in 1992. Many students experienced difficulties with the statistical, research design and psychometric concepts covered in lectures, as well as their applications. As a result, the course had a very high failure rate in its first two years of operation (35 per cent and 29 per cent in 1992 and 1993 respectively), and in 1994 voluntary tutorials were introduced to supplement lectures. These were implemented by postgraduate students who had taken the course in previous years, working under the supervision of the course coordinator.

In 1996, 24 tutorials were organized every week for the entire second-year intake of 332 students. These were taught by ten student tutors, drawn from the Honours programme and from the third year. Similar numbers of undergraduate students and student tutors are also involved in the programme this year.

As the basis for planning and implementing the RDA tutorial programme, we have undertaken research-based teaching within a cooperative action research framework (Davidoff and Van den Berg, 1990; Ebbutt, 1985; Elliot, 1978a and b; 1981; Graves and Graves, 1985; Hustler *et al.*, 1986; Slavin, 1985; Stenhouse, 1975, 1980, 1981, 1983; Street, 1986).

Weekly tutors' meetings are based on a cyclical process of planning, implementation, observation of the process of tutorials both by the tutor and a tutorial supervisor, and reflection on teaching. Each tutor reports verbally to the group and shares experiences and problems. Suggestions are then made by the group as to alternative strategies for coping with difficulties, and activities for the next week's tutorial.

This process of cooperative action research has involved both lecturers and student tutors, providing an ongoing focus on tutor training as well as on curriculum development. This has been effective both for quality control as well as for ensuring the ongoing relevance of what is taught and how it is taught.

Activities and materials have been developed to provide a structure for tutorials, focusing on application of concepts covered in the lecture programme. These include tutorial exercises and worksheets, linked to a tutors' manual that provides suggestions as to how to introduce particular aspects of the curriculum.

Tutorials to support the advanced research design and analysis (RDA2) course

The RDA2 course is also a second-year course, taught in the second semester of the year to a selected group (1995 N = 44; 1996 N = 69) of psychology students who have achieved a mark of 60 per cent or more in their RDA1 exams. Four of the components of the course (advanced statistics, advanced research design, advanced psychometrics and qualitative methods) are lecture-based, while the fifth course component is a research design project concerned with small-group work involving student syndicates.

Based on positive evaluation of tutorials supporting large-group teaching in the RDA1 course (Virtue and Terre Blanche, 1995), tutorials led by senior students were also introduced to support lectures in RDA2 in 1995 and 1996. In 1995, these focused on one component of the course only (advanced research design), while in 1996 the focus of tutorials was broadened to include all course components. As with the introductory RDA course, weekly tutors' meetings have been integral to the development of the programme. Time has been set aside for regular contact between lecturing staff and the tutors, to facilitate the planning, implementation and evaluation of tutorials. A structured curriculum of activities and materials has been developed, based on cooperative action research involving analysis of students' work, observation of tutorials, and evaluation at weekly meetings between tutors and lecturing staff.

SI tutorials

In addition to the RDA tutorial programmes, supplemental instruction (SI) tutorials were introduced in 1995 to support other courses in the second-year curriculum. This tutorial programme was, however, discontinued at the end of 1995, as the response of the students to the SI tutorials was negative, and attendance at tutorials poor. Some of the possible reasons for the failure of this programme are highlighted in the following section.

Evaluation

The first-year tutorial programmes

Evaluation of the first-year tutorial programmes has been based on observation of tutorials linked to ongoing reflection at weekly tutors' meetings, as well as qualitative data from student and lecturer evaluations. The indications from these data are that first-year tutorials have been generally well received by the students. Attendance has been good and overall, the response of the students has been encouraging. Academic development tutorials have also been positively evaluated by the student and well attended.

We have found, however, that the quality of student-led tutorials has varied. One of the reasons for this is the sheer size of the programme, and the fact that support required by students varies, reflecting the diversity of our first-year intake. There is wide variation in the quality of the previous schooling received by first-year students, with the result that their needs, as well as their preparedness for university study, differ widely. Some students have difficulties with one course component but not with another, or with one type of assignment and not with another. Other students have great difficulties in adjusting to the level of university work, and to the language and concepts used in lectures, and thus require intensive academic support.

All first-year students are required by the department to attend at least one tutorial a week. As attendance at tutorials is compulsory in both the mainstream and health sciences tutorial programmes, the influence of tutorial attendance on pass rates is difficult to disaggregate.

With respect to academic development tutorials that are voluntary, tutorial attendance has been found to be a predictor of academic performance (Schochet, 1986). In our department, the aim is that increasing number of educationally disadvantaged students entering our first-year courses should attend academic development tutorials regularly and voluntarily, and that the pass rate of this group should approximate that of students from more advantaged backgrounds.

In 1996, attendance at academic development tutorials was high, and they were well rated by the students. The pass rate of mainstream students attending academic development tutorials was 77 per cent, which compared favourably with the other mainstream students, of whom 83 per cent passed the first-year course. The pass rate for the health sciences students attending academic development tutorials was 97 per cent, which also compared favourably with the 99 per cent pass rate of other first-year psychology students in the health sciences stream.

Based on positive student ratings, high attendance at tutorials, and pass rates which approximate overall first-year results, the evidence would suggest that the first-year academic development tutorials are well supported by the student body, are considered useful by the undergraduate student body, and are currently meeting their aims.

The second-year tutorial programmes

Improvement in student pass rates after the introduction of tutorials

At second-year level, where tutorials have been introduced to support particular courses, we have been able to use an element of time series analysis in our evaluation design, based on analysis of pass rates before and after the introduction of tutorials in support of lectures in these courses. In addition, evaluation of the second-year tutorial programmes has been based on attendance records, student ratings, minute chapters (short written student evaluations at the end of lectures and tutorials) and interviews with students.

In the RDA1 course, in particular, there has been a marked improvement in pass rates after the introduction of tutorials. In 1992, when the course was first introduced, the pass rate was 65 per cent. Interviews with students indicated that many had found the course content difficult and that, in addition to the high failure rate, large numbers of students had dropped out. Attempts were made to improve the presentation of the course in 1993, and the pass rate improved to 71 per cent.

Many more students wrote the final examination in 1993 compared to 1992, reflecting a lower drop-out rate, as well as a considerable proportion of students who were repeating the course. While the pass rate improved, overall the 1993 distribution was not significantly different to that obtained in 1992 (chi-square = 3,3 (4); not significant).

Student-led tutorials were introduced to support large-group lecturing in 1994, and the pass rate improved to 86 per cent. The higher pass rate was associated with positive student evaluations of the tutorial programme, as will be evident from the following extracts, drawn from the 1994 evaluation of the course:

> '1994 saw the increase in the proportion of students achieving first, upper second and second class passes. Those obtaining a third class pass have decreased. The proportion of students failing the course was reduced by more than half. Course content and lecturers were kept constant from 1993 to 1994 increasing the likelihood that this noticeable improvement is due to the introduction of the tutorials system.
>
> 'At the end of the term students who had attended tutorials were asked to evaluate their experience of the tutorial programme. The students who completed the questionnaire had attended between two and ten tutorials. The median attendance was six tutorials; six students had attended six tutorials and six other students had attended ten tutorials. Three students attended a total of seven tutorials, three a total of four tutorials and four a total of two, three, eight and nine times respectively...
>
> 'Students found that tutorials helped them to understand general concepts necessary for the application of statistics to psychological data. Many of them reported that the individual attention which the tutorial system provided made a significant difference to their mastery of course material and provided a vital supplement to large-scale lectures.'
>
> (Virtue and Terre Blanche, 1995, 25–6)

The 1994 distribution of marks was significantly different to that obtained in 1993 (chi-square = 36,31 (4); p<,001). The change in failure rates was the major contributor to the significant change observed. The higher pass rates for the course were maintained in both 1995 and 1996, with some variation within the distributions of marks, particularly in students who were unable to attend lectures due to timetable clashes.

The 1995 distribution of marks was significantly different from that obtained in 1994 (chi-square = 45,36 (4); p<,001), this difference being related to a higher failure rate, as well far fewer students obtaining second class passes, and far more students obtaining third class passes than had occurred in 1994. These changes were associated with a raising of the standard of the psychometrics section of the course, which was taught in a problem-based way. The 1996 distribution and that of 1995 were similar (chi-square = 6,75 (4); not significant).

Twenty-six students were admitted to the course in 1996, but were unable to attend lectures due to timetabling problems. Additional tutorials were provided, but the majority of these students failed. The distribution of marks for this group was markedly different to that of students attending both lectures and tutorials (chi-square = 16,18 (4); p<,005), suggesting that both lectures and tutorials are necessary for students to benefit from the course.

Analysis of the marks for the course from 1992 to the present indicates that a major shift in pass rates took place with the introduction of tutorials in 1994, and that the higher pass rates have been maintained at around the 80 per cent level, with some fluctuations from year to year due to changes in lecturing staff and course content. The distributions of marks obtained in 1995 and 1996 are similar, and are significantly different from those obtained prior to the introduction of tutorials (comparison of 1993 and 1995 distributions: (chi-square = 26,67 (4); p 001).

Overall, the evidence would suggest the value of student-led tutorials in supporting large-group teaching in this second-year course, and would also suggest that attendance at tutorials has an impact on pass rates. However, it is clear from analysis of the 1996 results that tutorials are an adjunct to lectures, and are not able to replace them.

Attendance at tutorials and student pass rates

Voluntary tutorials were introduced to support the research design section of the RDA2 course in 1995. This was done on a trial basis, with five voluntary additional tutorials being given at lunch-time. They were run by the course lecturer and focused on application of concepts covered in lectures in practical exercises.

The relationship between attendance at these tutorials and pass rates was a direct one. Of 44 students taking the course, 22 achieved first or upper second class passes in the research design section of the examination. There were three second class passes and seven third class passes. Twelve students failed. Examining these data against attendance records for the five tutorials, there was a direct correspondence (point-biserial correlation of 1,00; $p<,0000$) between those students who attended tutorials and those who passed. There was also a high correlation between number of tutorials attended and marks obtained for this section of the course ($r =,88$; $p<,0000$).

While the motivation of students is clearly a possible confounding influence which could have affected these results (more motivated students being the ones who would attend voluntary tutorials at lunch-times), minute chapters and interviews with students attending tutorials indicated that they found the tutorials valuable in clarifying concepts they had covered in lectures. In 1996, the decision was thus taken to increase the number of tutorials from five to 14, and to broaden their focus to cover all components of the RDA2 course. Tutorials would be run weekly, focusing on concepts as well as their applications in research problems based on articles drawn from the literature. In terms of increased numbers of students taking the course, five tutorial groups would be formed, tutored by the senior students who had worked in the RDA1 tutorial programme in the first semester of the year.

Attendance at these tutorials was very high, and student ratings were positive, both in terms of the materials provided in support of lectures, as well as in terms of the value of working through practical examples in tutorials. As nearly all students attended tutorials regularly, and as all students were provided with the tutorial materials which they could then work through in their own time, the effects of tutorials on pass rates are difficult to disaggregate. However, there was an upward shift in marks in 1996.

In 1996, the large 'tail' of students failing the research design section of the course in 1995 was eliminated, the whole distribution of marks shifting upwards (chi-square = 20,15 (10); $p<,05$). There were a number of changes associated with the 1996 tutorial programme which did not occur in 1995. These included the breaking up of students into smaller groups tutored by senior students as opposed to the lecturer, and the provision of extensive printed notes and tutorial exercises to all students, which formed the basis of the tutorial curriculum and were very positively evaluated by the students. The course content was, however, unchanged, and on this basis it is probably reasonable to attribute the increase in pass rates in the research design section of the course to the influence of the tutorial programme.

With respect to the RDA2 course as a whole, an upward shift in the distribution of marks took place in 1996, which was beyond what could have been expected by the normal fluctuations occurring from year to year (chi-square = 11,8 (5); $p<,05$). In addition, there was evidence that the standard of the academic performance of students taking the course in 1996 increased. The comments of the course lecturers indicated that 1996 was a year of very high quality of student understanding and work. This was supported by the report of the external examiner of the course, who commented very favourably on the standard of the course and of the applied research projects completed by the students.

Motivation and perceived relevance as factors influencing attendance at tutorials

Whether improvements in pass rates or in standards of particular courses can be attributed to the influence of tutorials alone is unlikely, and it is thus important to treat the positive results reported in the previous sections of this chapter with caution. There have been a number of changes in lecturing, as well as in course content between 1992 and the present. There have also been new lecturers who introduced new directions in both the RDA1 and the RDA2 courses. These changes, in addition to the introduction of the tutorial programmes and the materials used to structure tutorials, are likely to have combined in influencing the upward trend in marks across the two courses at second-year level for which student-led tutorial support has been provided.

Nevertheless, high attendance, as well as positive ratings of tutorial programmes, are important indicators of whether students find student-led tutorials relevant and useful. Comments made by students in minute chapters and in interviews concerning the student-led tutorials supporting the RDA1 and RDA2 course have been generally positive. In addition, attendance at these tutorials has been high. In contrast, the experience of second-year students with SI tutorials would appear to have been a negative one. SI tutorials were not well attended. In addition, comments made by students in minute chapters and interviews were largely negative.

There were a number of recurrent themes in these data, indicating that there were two apparent problems with the SI tutorials. The first problem lay with the style of the SI tutorials, which focused on the students' notes from lectures as a medium to understanding the concepts covered in lectures. The second problem lay with the focus of the SI tutorials, which provided support of a general nature rather than a variety of activities and materials based on analysis of students' work in a particular course area. An additional (and related) problem lay with the relationship between the SI tutors and the lecturers, who were not integrally involved in the planning and evaluation of SI tutorials.

It was clear from the themes raised in minute chapters and interviews that many students did not see the value of tutorials presented in a non-directive way by student tutors. This was linked to their experience of first-year as well as the RDA tutorials, in which the student tutors were actively involved in teaching, varying their roles between facilitation, organizing activities, explanation of difficult concepts and participant in small- or large-group work as necessary. In the first-year tutorials and in the second-year RDA tutorials, a variety of tutorial activities was introduced, within the framework of a tutorial curriculum developed jointly between lecturers and students.

The SI methodology, in contrast, assigned the student tutor a more limited role as facilitator, in a process focused on clarifying students' notes from lectures. In the SI tutorials, tutors were expected to handle student problems in a particular way, and defer student questions back to the group rather than get actively involved in explaining or reteaching concepts poorly understood in lectures. In the other student-led tutorial programmes in the department, in contrast, tutors were encouraged to use their own initiative in dealing with student problems. This might involve referring a problem back to the group, but might also involve active explanation, organization of activities, provision of supplementary readings or materials, as well as developing additional strategies in the tutors' meetings to deal with problem areas more effectively.

Our negative experience with SI was thus apparently influenced by interference from other areas of the tutorial curriculum. Where second-year students had participated in other tutorials in the department, they did not find the SI tutorials motivating or relevant. The SI tutorials lacked credibility, as they did not introduce what these students were looking for, which was direct tutoring, additional readings and materials that provided applications of concepts covered in lectures, as well as mediation of concepts in areas in which they were experiencing difficulties. Had the SI methodology been introduced in a more focused way, or in a teaching situation in which there were no other tutorials, our experience would probably have been better, and more in line with the positive results on SI reported in the literature (Lundeberg, 1990; Martin *et al.*, 1983; Maxwell, 1979, 1990, 1991).

Summary

This chapter has focused on the tutorial programmes provided by the psychology department at Wits to all first- and second-year students. In each programme, a curriculum of activities and materials has been developed linked with the content covered in lectures, but which is also open-ended in the degree of support and teaching that tutors can provide.

In each of the tutorial programmes, senior student tutors have worked cooperatively with the academic staff of the department in planning and evaluating tutorials, and in the development of the tutorial curriculum. At this time, the potential of using student-led tutorials to support mainstream teaching is broadly accepted within the psychology department. At first-year level, there is recognition of the potential of student-led tutorials as regards providing face-to-face contact with a large first-year intake, as well as in improving the retention rates of underprivileged and educationally underprepared students. At second-year level, there is recognition of the benefit of student-led tutorials in supporting courses that students have experienced as difficult.

We thus regard student-led tutorials as essential in the context of an academic department that has large student numbers and relatively few academic staff. At both first- and second-year levels, attendance at student-led tutorials has been high, and they have been positively rated by the students. In addition, the evidence at second-year level suggests that attendance at tutorials has been associated with increased academic performance.

Across the department of psychology as a whole, there are benefits from student-led tutorials in terms of relationships between undergraduate students and student tutors, as well as benefits resulting from increased face-to-face contact between academic staff and the student tutors. Students attending tutorials are encouraged to use the tutors as a resource. Tutors, for their part, encourage students to take responsibility for their own learning, but are prepared to reteach or re-explain certain sections of the course as necessary. In this respect, a broad range of teaching methodologies is used in tutorials, including group discussion, group problem-solving exercises, small group and paired student activities, individual tutoring and mediation of concepts covered in the lectures or in the prescribed textbooks for the course. In addition, student tutors are encouraged to work diagnostically, to identify students having difficulties, and to refer them to additional resources. At first-year level this takes the form of additional readings and academic development tutorials, while at second-year level this takes the form of additional readings and exercises, computer-based tuition, study groups and extra tutorials where appropriate.

Planning and evaluation of tutorials are ongoing, and based on contact between lecturers and student tutors in a weekly meeting. The tutors prepare attendance records and report on the participation of each student in their group. These reports have formed important additional evidence with borderline cases with respect to passing or failing.

At both first- and second-year levels in psychology, the results of student-led tutorials have been encouraging. At first-year level, many students attending tutorials have reported that they have helped in clarifying concepts taught in lectures and in understanding the application of concepts covered in lectures to practical examples and psychological data, as well as in preparing them for class assignments and examinations. At second-year level many students have reported that the individual attention that the tutorial system provided made a difference to their mastery of course material and provided a valuable supplement to large-group lectures. While there are some negative comments and criticisms, overall the evidence suggests that there are positive effects of attending tutorials on second-year pass rates in particular course components, and that the standard of teaching and learning has increased in those courses in which tutorials have been introduced.

At both first- and second-year levels, our conclusion is that student-led tutorials have encouraged individual participation, which has enabled students to become engaged in dialogue concerning the concepts covered in lectures. At second-year level in particular, a helpful outcome of the tutorial system has been the 'spawning' of several self-study groups. These initiatives have been started by students who have found the tutorials helpful but have felt the need for additional group-based learning to assist in their studies.

There are, however, a number of cautions attached to using students as tutors. Our experience is that without initial and ongoing training for student tutors, and a firm structure of materials and activities that student tutors can utilize as the basis for their contact with the students in their tutorial groups, a grave injustice is done to both first- and second-year students and the senior student tutors. We believe that it is inappropriate to give unstructured tutoring roles to senior student tutors with very little, if any, training, and with only minimal ongoing support. Tutoring is a very skilled enterprise. One cannot expect people to undertake it with only the barest modicum of prior training.

An initial training period is needed before student tutors move into tutorials. This needs to be supported by ongoing training which focuses on the week-to-week classroom experiences of tutors, as the basis for cooperative planning and evaluation of tutorials. We have taken some steps towards providing this type of training within a cooperative action research framework. A curriculum of structured activities and teaching materials has been developed linked to a methodology of ongoing planning, implementation, observation and reflection on tutorials. However, there are many aspects of tutor training requiring further development, and we recognize that a great deal of work is necessary in these areas.

Address for correspondence: Dr Charles Potter, Department of Psychology, University of the Witwatersrand, Johannesburg, Private Bag 3, WITS 2050, South Africa. Tel. (011) 716-111.

Chapter 10

A STUDENT-STUDENT MENTORING SCHEME FOR FRESHMAN STUDENTS

Margaret Rutherford and Mmanosi Daisy Matlou

Students entering the College of Science find it difficult to orientate themselves and so miss much of the first few weeks essential educational input. In 1996, ex-College students mentored small groups of freshmen during orientation and the first quarter of the year. The scheme was evaluated with interviews of both mentors and mentees.

Introduction

The 1994 elections in South Africa gave rise to a democratic society and the iniquitous apartheid laws no longer apply. However, no matter how willing people are, major changes take time to implement. Prior to the elections there were something like 19 different educational departments which were not only regionally but also racially segregated. One of the most important changes was the titular removal of these racially differentiated educational systems, leaving one national department with provincial offices. However, with the very large number of pupils, compulsory education for the first seven years for the first time and the rural situation of the majority of the schools, the old systems will take time to die away. This means that, in particular in secondary schools, the scene is very confused. We will look briefly at the 'old' education system and document the changes relevant to our particular situation; a detailed description of the proposed changes are documented elsewhere (South African Green Paper on Education, 1996).

South Africa's Educational System Pre- and Post-the 1994 Elections

Prior to the elections, the education of South African children was largely segregated along racial lines. There were separate education departments for white, black, Indian and coloured (mixed race) students, some of these having regional sections and all of which set their own matriculation examination papers. In addition there was an independent matriculation board which served largely the private schools. The separate departments of education existed independently, each largely ignoring the others.

The per capita allowance for education varied between the departments with the white students at the top of the allowance scale and black students at the bottom. This meant that the schools in the black system were under-resourced and in addition the teachers were, on the whole, not as highly qualified as those in the other departments.

The country now has one new education department, the students write a common set of matriculation papers and the teacher:student ratios are being adjusted across the schools. Many black students now attend former white schools but it remains true that the majority of these black students still attend schools in rural areas which are poorly resourced and staffed. The class sizes are large and the students generally resort to rote learning. (This was also mentioned by the mentors participating in the scheme reported here, who stated that the different form of learning at university led to cognitive conflict and danger of failure.)

There is still heavy attrition among black students in the educational system; the black students who reach standard 10 are the 'pick of the crop' and have already demonstrated considerable determination and talent. However, few of them have a matriculation certificate which gives them university exemption with a pass in mathematics and physical science, let alone with acceptable marks in these two subjects (Blankley, 1994). This means that the majority of black students are entering tertiary institutions to study arts subjects rather than the economically more desirable sciences and engineering. In addition, those students from schools within the previously black system who do gain entry to science or engineering have a significantly worse graduation rate than the other students.

Background to the College of Science

The University of the Witwatersrand (Wits) has for many years been involved in academic development activities for educationally disadvantaged students. While this disadvantage may be manifested in many ways, the most obvious one is a poor school with inadequate teaching facilities. In the faculty of science, the latest development is the College of Science (CoS) which took its first students in 1991. The college is fully documented elsewhere (Rutherford, 1996) but it must be emphasized that the need for such a programme is likely to exist for some time despite the rapid changes in the educational system.

Briefly then, the CoS admits students who do not qualify for automatic admission to the normal three-year programme in the faculty of science, or the four-year programme in the faculty of engineering, into a four- (or five- for engineering) year programme. These science students may be admitted with no physical science in their matriculation examinations and with a much lower mark in mathematics than that required for the three-year curriculum.

The first two years of this programme are in the CoS and then successful students join the three-year programme for their final two years (final three years for engineering). Students are admitted after a rigorous selection procedure which looks at various factors including educational disadvantage. While in its early years, the College selection procedure could use the race of the student as a measure of educational disadvantage, this is no longer so and the school attended by the student is now used in this way, together with any information provided by the applicants themselves. It is these students who were the freshman students reported on in this mentoring scheme.

The majority of students came from schools which previously fell under one of the boards catering exclusively for black students. They were therefore not accustomed to using good facilities (eg, laboratories and libraries). They were used to succeeding largely by rote learning and had not gained very high marks in the matriculation examination (the maximum points possible using the Wits calculations is 40, with 24 required for automatic admission into the science faculty and a higher number for the engineering faculty, depending on branch of study). The male students greatly outnumbered the female students and the ratio of rural to urban students was about 5:6. In addition, the majority of the students were the only representative from their school and so had no ready-made friends on campus.

The majority of these students fell into a group which, in the light of experience over the past few years, we would categorize as high-risk students. They have difficulties in adjusting to a city environment and to a very large institution (around 20,000 students). They are in general the economically poorer students and so need financial aid for both tuition and residence. In addition they have come from schools which are highly regimented and have succeeded by following instructions frequently given in poor English. Their spoken English is usually adequate but their written academic language is poor. They may spend the first few weeks of term in a fog, frantically trying to adjust to a very alien environment.

Rationale for the Mentoring Scheme

In summary, the majority of students accepted into the College of Science are:

- the first in their family to attend university;
- unfamiliar with a larger city environment;
- unfamiliar with the large university campus;
- English as a second language speakers;
- not aware of student services on campus;
- lacking information regarding university work requirements (both quantity and quality), courses available and their prerequisites and possible careers.

The university has a full week of orientation before the term starts, when clubs and societies recruit students and advice is available on course selection. The CoS has a more structured programme during this week but, despite this, many students seem lost for the first few weeks. In 1996, therefore, it was felt that more senior students who had taken the CoS route and were now in second- or third-year mainstream could usefully act as mentors for new students. The aim of the programme was to address the particular needs or problems felt to be barriers to students' adjustment to university during the first few weeks of the first term. Practical problems like failure to understand the timetable (which works on a diagonal system), not knowing how to find lecture venues, and basic needs like how to access university accommodation and financial aid were perceived as variables which could affect students' adjustment to university and subsequently their academic performance. Mentors were therefore identified as possible service providers who could assist freshmen and women with viable strategies necessary to overcome these problems.

A job description for the student mentors was drawn up and circulated to all CoS staff for comment. This was then modified and given to all staff and mentors. This document is given in Figure 10.1.

COLLEGE OF SCIENCE
Mentoring Scheme

Guidelines

1. **Main Aim**
   To give the new students an 'insider's' view of the CoS.
   Mentors meet with their group once a week, arrange with them – the tutors lecturers will help you to find a venue for your meetings.

2. **To Do: Provide information and be positive!**
   Provide information – e.g.,
   a. **They feel alien and alone** – you could give ideas about how to stay positive about academic life. Use your own coping strategies, that's why we asked you to help. We assume you have developed strategies to cope and to grow – share those with them.
   b. **Who to see about what** (e.g., Ms Matlou about emotional problems; course coordinators about problems with tutors/work; the core office about timetable problems).
   c. **When to see who about what** (e.g., progress reports, who fills these in).
   d. **Details about test/exam writing – seating at tests/exams**: how to do this, where the seating lists are published.

3. **What you should avoid:**
   This is most important, otherwise you will end up a wreck, overworked and emotionally distraught yourself. We do not want that.
   a. **You are not a counsellor** – they should not come to you with emotional, money, family problems. REFER SUCH STUDENTS IMMEDIATELY TO THE CORE OFFICE. Your task is to know who to send them to.
   b. **You are NOT a TUTOR** – you should let them give you the names of their various tutors. If they have problems with the subjects (academic problems) and ask you to 'explain the work', tell your lecturer-partner who will alert the academic staff concerned.
   c. **Try to avoid PITY-PARTIES**: Discussions where they trash the College, lecturers/tutors. Discuss but try to keep focused on solutions rather than pity.
   d. **You are not a spiritual advisor**: stay away from their religions, beliefs.

4. **What you may encounter:**
   Lots of questions about 'What the College is' (Students in JUNE 1995 did not know that they were not mainstream students). To answer questions, you may need statistical details about the CoS. We should discuss during the first meeting with lecturer-partners.
   Problems about money, emotions, family, relationships (girl-/boy-friend trouble); refer to appropriate people – do not even think about getting involved. Be sympathetic but do not get involved.

Figure 10.1 Guidelines for college mentors and tutors

Selection of Mentors

The scheme had to be voluntary since it was felt that volunteer students would be those who felt a commitment to both the CoS and the university and were not just paying lip-service for the monetary rewards. However, no mentor was to be out of pocket and those who returned to halls of residence early had their residence bills covered by the CoS or the faculties. Consequently at the end of 1995 staff in the College of Science were each asked to identify one senior student who would be willing to act as a mentor to a small group of new students. Each member of staff had one assigned mentor only. A meeting was set up at the beginning of the orientation week for both tutors and mentors to discuss the essence of the mentoring scheme. The guidelines of the job description were discussed with the group and then each pair (tutor and mentor) talked briefly together to clarify their relationship.

A day or so later in the orientation week, the incoming freshman students were divided in groups of about six persons and each group assigned to a mentor with a facilitating tutor. We attempted to group the students (mentees) according to their optional subject and also to assign a mentor who was majoring in that subject area; for example a group of new students taking the biological sciences option would have a mentor who might be majoring in genetics or botany or anatomy. This was to increase the perceived relevance of the exercise. The tutors were asked to provide support to mentors by answering queries that the mentors could not handle. Once the groups had been established the mentors took over their groups of mentees for an introductory talk. As the mentoring scheme was unstructured, each group discussed activities for the remaining days of the orientation week and then scheduled subsequent meetings. The mentors were told that the scheme was designed to respond to new students' expressed needs and so the meetings should continue until mentees felt they had no problems and the group faded away.

Evaluation

As with all new initiatives, an evaluation was felt to be essential. It was intended to provide information about the effectiveness (both time and financial) and perceived usefulness of the scheme. For this reason it was a summative process and carried out at the end of the year. It is not possible to analyse the effects of such a scheme in a quantitative manner since the factors affecting student success are many and varied and it is inappropriate to attempt to correlate a short intervention at the beginning of the year with student marks after 28 weeks of tuition. The evaluation was, therefore, necessarily a qualitative and impressionistic one. Apart from semi-structured interviews, anecdotal observations and reports from CoS staff were collected for the evaluation. Although such observations and reports are subjective, they give valuable feedback regarding the merits of the scheme.

Designing the interview questions

Three sets of similar questions were designed for the tutors, mentors, and mentees. Certain common concerns were incorporated into the designing of the interview schedules. Each facet of the scheme was probed in the interviews so that the schedules had the following main thrusts:

- Since the scheme was a face-to-face exercise, the attendance at and the frequency of the meetings was asked for.
- The scheme was designed such that it did not overload the tutors and mentors and mentees with more work; an estimate of the total time commitment was requested .
- The questions regarding the number of the mentees were asked to establish if the number was limited to what was agreed upon, ie six to eight mentees per mentor. We wanted to see if any mentor felt overloaded with queries from the mentees. This question was also designed to probe the relationships that might have been established between members of the groups.
- Since venues are heavily utilized during the university terms, we had to establish if finding venues for meetings was problematic.
- When on a new and possibly alien campus, students become curious about a variety of things. We thus asked questions about what issues were discussed at the meetings – it was also reasonable to establish if mentors were able to respond to all these queries or needed training. (They were chosen not only because of their knowledge of the university but also because of their personal experience of the CoS programme and the fact that they had themselves survived in the system.)
- Finally the perceived usefulness of the scheme was probed and new ideas on how to run the scheme were solicited. Mentors and tutors were also asked if they would participate if the scheme were to run again.

Collecting data

Groups of tutors, mentors and mentees were interviewed and the transcripts used as a primary source of data. Participants were invited to lunch time meetings (13.10 – 14.00h) as it was the only time when all parties were free. It was however difficult to persuade students to come for interviews since it was approaching the end of the year and exams were looming. As a form of incentive, a snack lunch was provided. Interviews started +/- ten to 15 minutes later than the scheduled time as mentors and mentees never arrived on time. A total of nine group interviews were carried out as shown in Table 10.1.

Table 10.1 Interview participation

Participants	*No. of groups*	*No. of participants*
Tutors/lecturers	3	14
Mentors	3	12
Mentees	3	23

The mentees' participation in interviews according to their subject group (biology, n= 8, engineering, n = 7 and earth sciences, n = 8), was a matter of convenience as the invitation to come to an interview was extended at the end of lectures, tutorials, or laboratory sessions. Of these 23, 19 met with mentors and four did not.

Procedure

The purpose of the interviews was outlined to all participants before the start. Permission to tape the sessions was sought from the participants and they were assured of the confidential nature of the proceedings. In addition to the tape recordings, brief field notes were taken. At the start of each interview session all mentors, tutors or mentees were given a copy of the relevant pre-interview questions, and were given a short time to read these and think about them. Questions were asked in the same order in each session with a few minor deviations, where additional probing or clarification was required or when the conversation naturally went in a different but relevant direction. Although the interviews were meant to end at 2 o'clock, a few extended beyond the set time as students became more talkative as time passed and they became more relaxed.

Data analysis

Verbatim transcriptions were made of the interview sessions and summaries of these constructed. The summaries were then analysed using the following items as guidelines:

- usefulness of job description
- effectiveness – time commitment and cost
- usefulness of scheme
- topics discussed
- venues used
- future participation
- requests for help/information/guidance.

While the job description was found to be useful several mentors were still unclear as to the scope of the job. They would have liked more guidance regarding the activities considered to be appropriate for their groups. Some of them felt that they would have liked to have had a training session beforehand and more preparation.

> 'I could have had more information and I could have, you know, training.'(mentor)

No one felt that the scheme was onerous in terms of their time – apart from the first meeting during orientation week when mentors and mentees usually went on a tour of the campus, the meetings rarely lasted more than 15 minutes.

> 'I wouldn't say it took much of my time.' (engineering mentor)
>
> 'The first day we met for about an hour and a half and thereafter it was just ten minutes, 15 minutes.' (first-year student)

All the participants felt that the pilot scheme had been useful. In particular, the first-year students who had not been allocated to a mentor because they had registered late felt that they had missed out.

> 'I think it is important to have a mentor especially if it's your first time around university because you don't know anybody... the mentors are helpful especially academic wise because some of us did ask what was going to be expected of us during the course of the year and they did give us some previous views.' (first-year student)
>
> 'I think it is cool to have a mentor.' (first-year student)

> 'That was very difficult (not having a mentor) because I missed all my lectures – I sat in the wrong lecture – so I came to you for help (to the College counsellor) – so it is then that I could find my way. I couldn't use the computer in the library so I lost a lot... I was unaware that other students had mentors – why should I struggle when they know how to find things?' (freshman who registered late)

The first session was spent on campus orientation in all cases. Most of the mentors included a session in the library to show new students how to access the computer system there. After this it seems as though the students were most concerned with academic matters, and, although this was outside the original brief of the mentors, they appeared to handle the questions without having to refer to tutors.

> 'Most important the outline of the course – someone who's got experience of the course... a mentor is much better (than a tutor) because she will be like a on view of the student – not like a teaching person, so you get the view of a person who studied so you get to talk to someone who is not such a big person – you feel free to talk.' (first-year student)
>
> 'I had "smaller-nyana" problems and they were able to solve them.' (first-year student)

Although the scheme was not meant to address academic issues, some mentees were grateful that their mentors gave them ideas about essay-writing skills and some course content information. Evidence of the usefulness of the mentors' help is supported by the mentees who reported that they failed the first essay which they attempted on their own and passed the next essay after receiving some guidance from the mentor.

> 'She said after writing an essay we don't submit the essay so that she can read the essay and make some comments.' (first-year student)
>
> 'After writing my first essay I failed it but the second one she helped me and I passed so I think I made progress.' (first-year student)

Due to its location in the heart of Johannesburg, Wits university was not designed to be a totally residential university. With the admission of a wider variety of students, many come from out of town; also, if they do live within travelling distance, they normally come from overcrowded homes with large families and have no study room. Such students need a place within a hall of residence. The demands for residence exceed supply. The long process of securing accommodation is compounded by the policy of accommodating students who can afford to pay residence fees first. In addition, an upfront payment of a 20 per cent deposit is required which means that students have to wait for notification of the result of their application for financial aid before being able to move into residence. In the process of waiting, students lose hope and become frustrated. In addition, the processing of financial aid applications is laborious and normally a decision cannot be made as application dossiers have outstanding information. In the past, some students deregistered, while in this group mentees reported being directed to the relevant residence office and getting an explanation about how long the process will take. Mentors used their own experience to ease the mentees' anxiety.

> 'When she came she wasn't sure that she had a financial aid package, she just came and she waited and waited and they told her that she was a financial aid package so it was like she supported us besides studies.' (first-year student)

Venues were varied and seemed to have caused few problems – most groups fixed their meetings only at the previous one. All participating mentors who were hoping to be on campus in 1997 indicated a willingness to be involved again.

The responses to a question about what should be included/excluded if the scheme were to run again were mixed. Some students said that although they felt that the campus tour was useful they did not like trailing around with a 'guide'. They could not however suggest a different way of doing this and others said that it was a 'great' way to do it! Almost all students would have liked some help on academic matters later in the year when they felt that they would have more informed questions to ask of their mentors.

> 'I think it is helpful to have a mentor although I did not use the opportunity.... Late in the year you can't cope with assignments and things, maybe if I have somebody who knows my subjects he could have helped with academic work.' (first-year student)

The mentees' groups were kept small to maximize participation and to make the group manageable for the mentor. The mentees reported that they were able to make friends within the group although they were meeting for the first time. Knowing other mentees they said was useful as they were able to learn other things from other mentees and they could also share information, material and books. A mentee reported that,

> 'The mentor is a person who can bridge the gap... for me to know other people in the group... by so doing, I know Vincent and all the people... and their friends... then I am connected even when my mentor is not there I have these guys who can be my friends and help me with the course.' (first-year student)

It will be noticed that the quotations given above are all from students. This is because the tutors who were interviewed said that they had had to spend virtually no time on the scheme and their comments were speculative. Those who did see their mentor saw them because the mentors were still being taught or supervised for a higher degree by that member of staff.

Discussion

In terms of the aims of the mentoring scheme, it appears that from the tutors', mentors' and mentees' points of view, that the mentoring scheme did assist students to adjust to university life. Campus and familiarization tours to course venues, which all mentors included in their activities, were noted as useful as most students arrived on time at venues, and seemed to know which offices offered the different services. Library orientation was noted as useful by both tutors and mentees as tutors observed that students knew which libraries were relevant to their courses and could also carry out a literature search. Both tutors and mentees reported that there was less confusion regarding the reading of the timetable, an observation which was supported by the CoS counsellor as she seemed to have had fewer students requesting assistance in reading and understanding the timetable. In previous years, the counsellor frequently repeated the same story regarding the courses offered in the CoS and the careers one could follow. With the inception of the mentoring scheme, this request was not made. This supported the mentors' reports that questions on courses were frequently asked, and that mentors dealt with such course-related queries. This was corroborated by tutors who also reported fewer queries and the mentees themselves seeming to have a fair understanding of what the CoS offers in terms of courses, careers and prerequisites to courses.

Elsewhere in this chapter it is reported that the majority of students coming to CoS come from the low socio-economic and disadvantaged communities. Such students cannot afford to finance their studies and as a result, they depend on the university's financial aid package. Mentors reported that they briefed their group about the long time involved in processing the applications and then advised them not to give up. The same applies in securing places in university residences; mentees reported being directed to the relevant offices and being able to secure a place. Evidence of this is that the counsellor dealt with fewer financial aid and accommodation queries.

In general, the tutors thought that in comparison to the previous years' groups, students who went through the mentoring scheme seemed to have adjusted more quickly and appeared relaxed and less confused. This feeling about students' adjustment and knowledge about what the university offers, was supported by tutors on an anecdotal basis during the year.

Mentors observed that mentees seemed to show less tension than they themselves had felt and were also relieved each time their queries were answered. In support of the mentors' observations, mentees reported that mentors provide some psychological fulfilment by just being available for them; hence they felt relaxed, comfortable and less frustrated.

Where to from here?

Following the evaluation of the pilot scheme in 1996, it was decided that a similar process should be carried out in 1997. However, since the time commitment required from the staff was minimal, it was decided that in general the college counsellor would act as the staff link for most of the mentors. Consequently she gave an open invitation to staff if they wished to participate but identified most of the mentors herself. These mentors will meet as a group in orientation week at the beginning of 1997 and once again be assigned a small group of new students. Modified information has been designed for the mentors in the light of the evaluation and this has been expanded to include guidelines for suggested activities. These are shown in abbreviated form in Table 10.2.

Table 10.2 Mentors' check list of activities

Part 1 During orientation week

Campus tour	*Academic matters*	*Time management*	*Insider's story*	*Student services*
Important offices – Faculty, College	Reading the timetable	Academic vs social/sporting	Personal experiences	Campus health
Venues for (a) lectures (b) tutorials (c) laboratories	Meaning of lectures, tutorials, and laboratories	Attendance – DP requirement	Coping strategies	Counselling and careers
Library orientation	Available CoS courses	Managing three courses	Survival	Accommodation office
Sporting facilities	Course expectations			Financial aid office
	Failure!			SRC

Part 2 During the academic year

General	*Academic matters*	*Referral/support*
Networking with other mentors	Put students in contact with sympathetic tutor	Remind students of available services
Occasional meeting	Share experiences	DO NOT act as a counsellor
Give students a way to find you	Be positive	

Conclusion

The mentoring scheme piloted in the College of Science in 1996 was time- and cost-efficient. It appears from all the evidence to have also been effective in easing students into university life and enabling them to concentrate on academic activities without some of the difficulties reported by previous students. The evaluation of the pilot scheme will lead to a more comprehensive evaluation (using a structured questionnaire) to be carried out in subsequent years. It has also given pointers for modifications from 1997 onwards.

Caveat

One of the difficulties with this form of evaluation is that students have a tendency to give the answers that they think the interviewer wishes to hear. This might particularly be the case here where the interviewers were the college director and the college counsellor. However, since the remarks were supported by evidence from the tutors and by anecdotal comments throughout the year, we feel that the conclusions drawn may be considered valid.

Address for correspondence: Professor Margaret Rutherford, College of Science, University of the Witwatersrand, Johannesburg, South Africa. e-mail MARGR @gecko.biol.wits.ac.za

Chapter 11

STUDENT TUTORING AT THE UNIVERSITY OF THE WITWATERSRAND: A RESPONSE TO NEW SOUTH AFRICAN EDUCATION POLICY

Carol Taylor

During the three years that have passed since South Africa's democratic government was elected to power in April 1994, much attention has been given to restructuring the country's education system. Underpinning an ideology of moving from an elite to a mass system of education has been a desire to foster modernization and democratic nation-building. A paradigm shift to student-centred learning through an outcomes-based curriculum, combining education and vocational training, has been championed by education experts to ensure the education system meets South Africa's needs as it moves towards the twenty-first century. In a context of fiscal discipline and the persistence of apartheid's legacy of educational disadvantage, student tutors are ideally placed to assist in realizing national educational goals. This chapter outlines the established network of student tutoring at the University of the Witwatersrand, drawing on two case studies to show how as a strategy it is successfully responding to the new education vision.

Introduction

In stark contrast to the age of apartheid, the new South Africa embodies principles of equity, redress and democracy. Since April 1994, when Nelson Mandela's African National Congress party came to power these values have underpinned reformist strategies in all aspects of contemporary South African society. As political transition has changed to a period of transformation their saliency is currently informing new policy in higher education.

In February 1995, a National Commission on Higher Education (NCHE) was established to advise the government on restructuring tertiary education by undertaking a situation analysis, formulating a vision and putting forward policy proposals designed to ensure the development of a well-planned, integrated, high quality system (NCHE, 1996:1). The Commission's findings have been published in two draft documents and a Green Paper which is presently being discussed in the democratic manner which has come to characterize South African public life.

Higher education is perceived by the commission as 'a key allocator of life chances and in this respect faces the imposing challenge of serving as a major instrument for the advancement of equal opportunities for members of disadvantaged groups' (NCHE, 1996:31). Its findings and recommendations are best understood to resonate with national aspirations for equality of opportunity, equitable human resource development and intellectual achievement which will ensure country-wide growth and prosperity. In NCHE's view:

> 'higher education is indispensable for realizing the socio-economic and socio-cultural potential of the country. Higher education contributes to the mobilization of resources through the production and application of knowledge, the building of human capacity and the provision of lifelong learning opportunities. In this way, it can play a significant role in improving the economic, social and cultural conditions of all South Africans.'
>
> (NCHE, 1997:42)

Implicit in NCHE's goals is a desire to rectify the legacy of an exclusivist past which prevented the potential of the majority of the country's people from being realized.

In seeking to rectify this impoverishment, NCHE endorses a unitary education system, thereby seeking to abolish the discriminatory nature of apartheid higher education. The Commission also argues for the integration of education and training in a system that will open access to all and expand on a mass scale. The notion that training with formal education is to be assumed by higher education arises out of the Commission's belief that a direct link exists between South Africa's economic growth and its need to be globally competitive, and the excellence and aptness of its tertiary education system. In this view then, higher education must produce graduates with the appropriate skills and competencies to serve the country's reconstruction and development and so facilitate the government's policy of growth, employment and redistribution (GEAR).

Much of the Commission's new direction has been well received but its attempt to link higher education directly to the economy is being contested by educationists who consider a bias towards business interests misplaced and a debate has surfaced in education forums around the soundness of the argument for universities being appropriately engaged in training as well as formal education (Chisholm and Vally, 1996; Motala, 1996). The narrow focus on students acquiring specific and clearly identifiable competencies in an outcomes based curriculum, is being challenged on the grounds that it runs counter to a traditional university education's holistic development of the individual (Greenstein, 1995; Mokgalane and Vally, 1996:9).

In considering both the Commission's vision for South African higher education and the debate generated by its proposals, the role of student-tutoring comes into focus. The relevance of student-tutors in the South African context is best understood in a milieu of challenge mitigated by constraints, of aspirations curbed by past disadvantage, and of a perceived disjuncture between training and the dissemination of theoretical knowledge as the appropriate domain of higher education.

Since transition, fiscal deficit has necessitated a reshaping of government policy from reconstruction and development (RDP) to GEAR and so it is within a context of fiscal discipline that higher education is striving to meet South Africa's needs. The National Commission on Higher Education considers the system to be comparatively well resourced but the process of massification, already begun with a 10 per cent enrolment increase annually since 1988, and representing a doubling of black students (NCHE, 1996:11) has meant that the experience of the system is one of being under-resourced, of personnel shortages faced with growing staff:student ratios and of cutbacks as funding is reallocated to meet other pressing national needs. Resources, in short, have to be found within the system if NCHE's design for higher education as a mediator of prosperity is to be realized.

Massification rightly ensures open access to higher education, but large numbers of students now entering the system bring with them the legacy of a disadvantaged apartheid education. In 1996 only 14.8 per cent of students sitting the matriculation examination received a university-entrance pass (Fast Facts, SAIRR, February 1997:1), leaving many students gaining admission on the grounds of 'possible potential to succeed' determined by specially devised university admission tests. In this regard, higher education is seeking not only to strive for excellence on a stringent budget, but accepting the imposing challenge of compensating for educational disadvantage in its efforts to provide equal opportunity to all South Africans. On both counts, student-tutors in South African higher education are well placed to provide an invaluable resource both in terms of person power and as a reservoir of intellectual knowledge and skills that can be effectively utilized in the goal of national capacity building.

Student tutors at the University of the Witwatersrand

An analysis of student tutor involvement at the University of the Witwatersrand (Wits) illustrates the possibilities of student tutors' role as a response to the policy goals of the National Commission on Higher Education. In a telephone survey I conducted in February 1997, over 1000 students (of a total university enrolment of 17,896) were discovered to be involved in student tutoring activities at Wits. Their number includes graduate students and students majoring in specific disciplines who are tutoring undergraduate students, students engaged in peer tutoring, students acting as demonstrators and students tutoring high school pupils.

Student tutors work either on a voluntary basis, in return for their student bursaries, or as a form of student employment receiving reimbursement from specially designated university funds. As student tutors, their commitment covers a range of student-driven learning initiatives such as participating in a university run schools-liaison programme whereby they go out as student tutors to local black high schools, as volunteer student tutors in a Student Tutor Education Programme (STEP), a Saturday morning campus-based programme offering tutoring in 12 school subjects and life skills to approximately 1500 secondary school pupils, assisting as student demonstrators in practical laboratory sessions in the science disciplines, providing academic support as student tutors to under-prepared students in university residence-based projects and conducting small group tutorials in degree programmes throughout the university's nine faculties.

The pattern of training offered to student tutors varies across the campus but two case studies, one from the faculty of science and one from the faculty of arts, each of which offer alternate routes of access to a university education to disadvantaged students, provide illustrative examples of student-tutor training programme design, implementation and evaluative research.

Student Tutor Training in the Faculty of Science

In recognition of the importance of small-group tutoring for effective tertiary level teaching and the special needs of educationally under-prepared students, members of staff of the Department of Chemistry at Wits have been offering student-tutor training workshops since 1991. Initially, these were of a half-day duration but as a result of research which showed that students rated tutorials as important vehicles for learning but that the level of effectiveness depended on the skills of the tutor (Meyer, 1991:1), this has been extended to a three-day training workshop since 1994. Included in these tutor training workshops are student tutors from the faculty of science, Wits College of Science, Vista University, Khanya College and Johannesburg College of Education. The programme is designed primarily for new student tutors but a special session is devoted to advanced training for experienced tutors. The workshop is based on methods that student tutors can utilize in actual tutorials. These include tutorial preparation and methodology, role play, case studies on management and attitudinal problems that student tutors might encounter in tutoring, and experiential learning in 'live tutorials' in which pairs of student tutors work with new first-year students in the College of Science, and subsequently reflect upon this experience as a part of the workshop. General skills such as interpersonal and language skills and subject-specific conceptual and study skills are also addressed during training (Rollnick *et al.*, 1996:9–12). Annual evaluative research into these workshops through questionnaires, in-depth interviews with student tutors, and workshop participants' reports show that student tutors find the support models adopted at the workshop to be extremely helpful, with workshops serving to boost student-tutor confidence and providing a valuable learning experience (ibid, 1996:15). The organizers of this particular series of workshops in the faculty of science have been concerned to provide ongoing support to student tutors during the course of the academic year, but to date due to timetable constraints and extremely heavy schedules of both staff and students it has not been possible to formalize such help and so currently staff provide assistance to student tutors on an informal and 'as needed basis'.

Student Tutoring in the Faculty of Arts

In the faculty of arts, the formal training of student tutors has been taking place since 1993. This training involves workshops offered early in the academic year by Academic Development (AD) staff on small-group teaching and management and academic reading and writing skills to which all student tutors in the faculty are invited. Thereafter, ongoing training takes the form of one-hour weekly meetings throughout the year between academic staff and student tutors in their respective departments. As in the faculty of science, this training is particularly concerned to equip student-tutors to enhance the academic development of educationally disadvantaged students who currently represent 55 per cent of arts faculty students (Wits Academic Information and Systems Unit, 1997).

The programme as it is run in the department of social anthropology is typical of arts faculty-wide student-tutor training. In this department, the AD coordinator, a lecturer and the student tutors work together in action research cycles which involve planning, implementation and reflection on tutorials. In planning sessions, the lecturer discusses aspects of tutorial content and the AD coordinator suggests methodological approaches to presenting tutorials. During review sessions, the student tutors report on their tutoring experiences and the discussion focuses on resolving difficulties and refining methodology (Taylor, 1995:70).

Since 1993, annual questionnaire evaluations and student tutor interviews and reports indicate unanimous agreement among student tutors that training in tutorial methodology is essential for successful tutoring. Student tutors express an appreciation of the supportive nature of the planning sessions and on their efficacy as discussion forums in helping overcome pedagogical and psychological difficulties encountered in tutoring academically diverse groups of first-year students (Taylor, 1995:71). In addition to these advantages the training programme has also served to facilitate a partnership in teaching and learning between academic staff and student tutors which has enhanced curriculum development in undergraduate courses in anthropology. Each review session provides an opportunity for student tutors to comment on tutorial topics and in so doing assist lecturers in enhancing the complementarity between lectures, assignments and tutorials, make reading matter more germane and refine strategies of teaching and learning generally. In this way a process of academic development has emerged which involves lecturers and student tutors working together on integrating academic skills with academic content and refining course design to accommodate the needs of educationally under-prepared students who are present in large numbers in undergraduate anthropology classes. In this way a culture of learning has evolved since the inception of this training which has academically benefited the department and the students it serves.

Relevance to NCHE's Education and Training Policy

In being characterized by skills-oriented training these endeavours to ensure effective student tutoring in the faculties of arts and science have special relevance to the National Commission on Higher Education's emphasis on education and training. NCHE endorses the following 'generic competencies' as essential skills in which undergraduates should become proficient (as summarizedby Motala in *EPU Quarterly*, September 1996:11).

(1) Reflective Understanding of the Learning Process
(2) Conceptual Thinking
(3) Critical Evaluation
(4) Problem Solving
(5) Decision Making
(6) Planning and Organizing of Activities
(7) Data Collection
(8) Application of Ideas and Techniques
(9) Cooperative Team Work
(10) Practising Democratic Principles.

Rollinck *et al.*'s findings in an opening session survey conducted among a total of 106 participants at the 1994 and 1995 science faculty training workshops reveal the existence of a high correspondence between what the Commission deems to be desirable 'generic competencies' that students should acquire as part of their tertiary education and what prospective student tutors perceive to be their needs for competent tutoring (1996:8–9) (see Table 11.1).

NCHE's skills or competencies can be categorized as analytical, organizational and communicative. The skills for each category depicted in the top set of boxes in Table 11.1 represent those designated by NCHE, while specific skills that student tutors perceived to be necessary for competent tutoring and requested as a part of their workshop training are in the bottom set of boxes. A clear correspondence is evident in each category.

In terms of analytical skills, student tutors are concerned to understand group dynamics, to be competent in assessing cognition, to be adept at integrating skills and content and to be successful pedagogically. They are conscious of the need for good organizational skills for effective tutoring and obviously aware of the importance of sensitive communication skills in the interests of fostering objectivity and independent thinking in the students they tutor.

In the case study of the department of social anthropology student-tutor training programme, participant-observation research since 1993 shows that

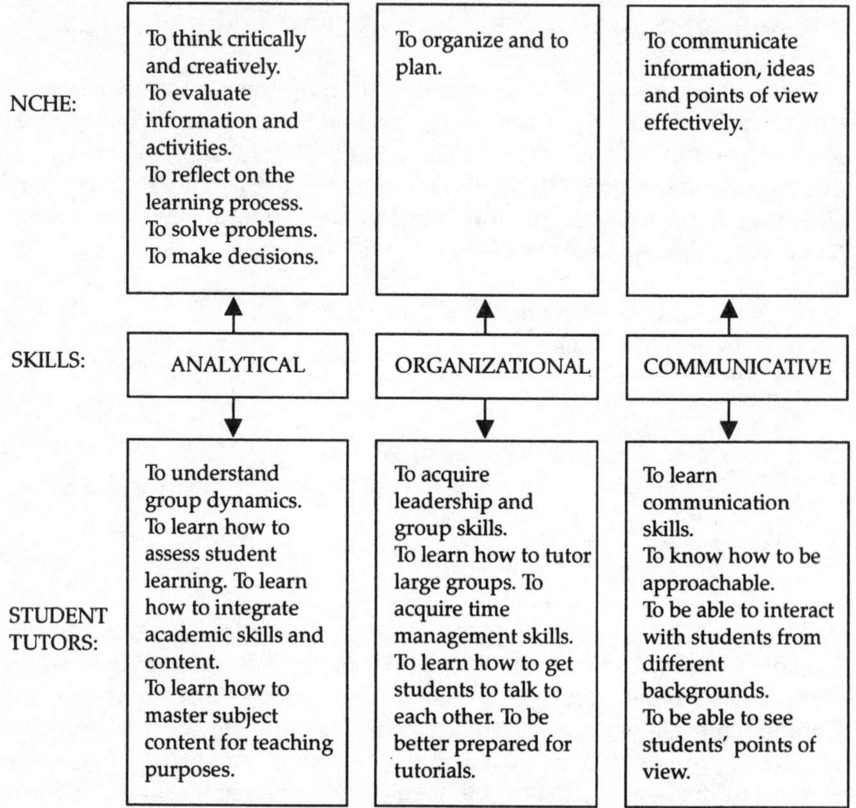

Figure 11.1 Skills endorsed by NCHE and requested by student-tutors

being involved in the process of organizational and analytical skills practice in helping design, implement and review tutorials provides student tutors with an opportunity to acquire and perfect the type of skills which NCHE deems to be a necessary part of current undergraduate educational training (Taylor, 1995:70–71). Evaluative research based on year-end reports and open-ended interviews conducted annually since 1993 with a total number of 16 student tutors, has revealed them to be consciously striving to develop communication skills that will ensure effective learning. The parallels between NCHE's skills and competencies and those acquired by student tutors participating in this training programme are depicted in Table 11.2.

In Table 11.2, NCHE's generic skills are again itemized in the top set of boxes, with skills acquired by student tutors being represented in the corre-

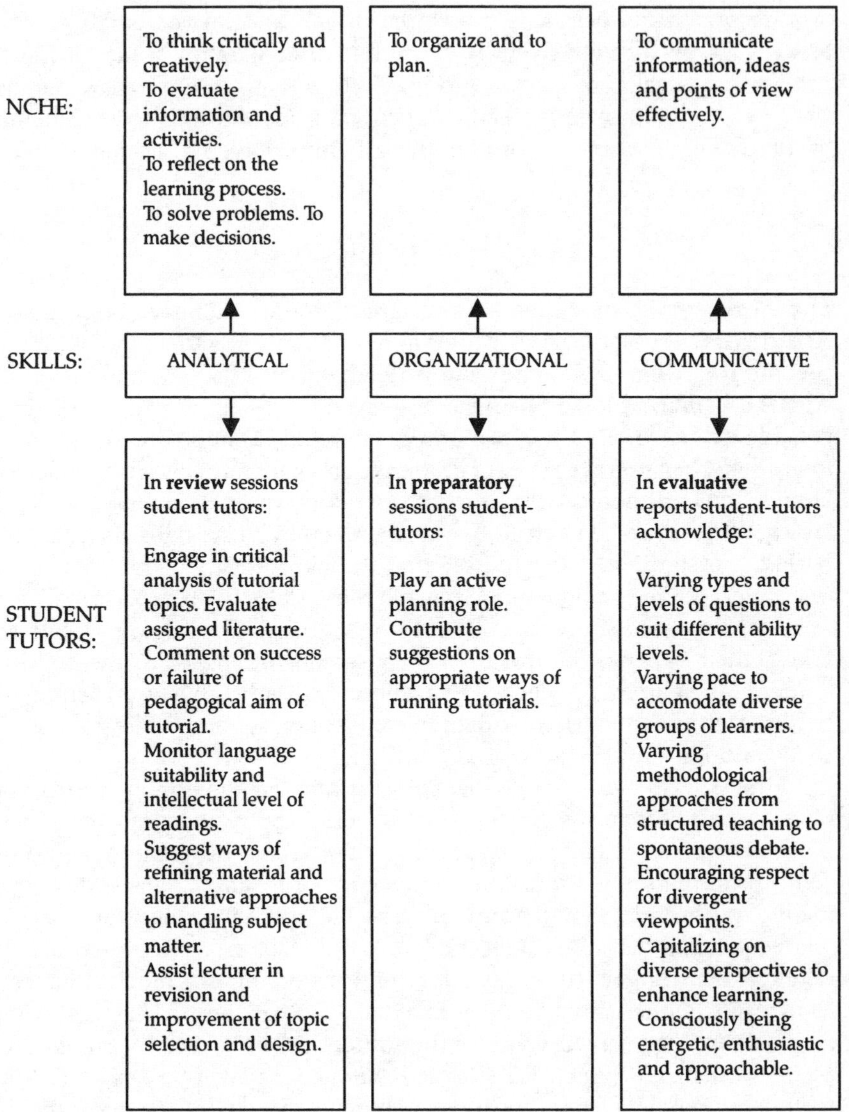

Figure 11.2 Skills endorsed by NCHE and utilized by student tutors

sponding set of boxes underneath. In the organizational and analytical skills categories, student-tutor participation in an action research cycle of planning, conducting and reviewing tutorials affords them an opportunity to acquire organizational skills in tutorial design and implementation, and analytical skills through critically examining tutorial topics, academic literature, pedagogical approaches, and intellectual levels of tutorials. Ongoing practice in communicative skills appropriate to tutoring heterogeneous groups of students are apparent in the communicative skills category.

Conclusion

These case studies of student-tutor training in the faculties of Science and Arts at Wits suggest that such programmes not only articulate well with but predate the National Commission of Higher Education's (1996) vision of education and training. In being skills-driven programmes of learning they provide evidence of an integration of competencies and content, an optimally beneficial interweaving of academic and general skills with academic knowledge and theory with practice. As tutors, students themselves have anticipated and voiced a need to acquire precisely those skills endorsed by NCHE. It is significant also to note that student tutors have reported their realization of the essential need to teach these skills, in an explicit manner, to under-prepared students in their tutorial groups (Taylor, 1995:75). In so doing, their experience concurs with research findings into the specific academic development needs of educationally disadvantaged students currently entering the South African higher education system. (Adler *et al.*, 1997; Dison and Pinto, 1995; Potter *et al.*, 1994).

In the skills debate, then, educationists opposing the notion of incorporating training into university education would appear to be adopting a too narrowly instrumentalist view of skills training. As this chapter suggests, contrary to the impression that a university education's holistic development of the individual will be impaired by incorporating skills training into degree programmes, the intellectual and professional development of students participating in student-tutor training programmes is much enhanced as a result of their involvement in what Goodlad terms 'study service' (1995a:4). And the way forward for the academic development of under-prepared students, in which Wits student tutors are playing a key role, is to further refine skills training and teaching methods and to continue to develop through research more finely tuned evaluative assessment of student's acquisition of these skills.

In the South African context, the involvement of student tutors is not only demonstrably beneficial to student tutors and the students they assist, but student tutoring can additionally be viewed as an appropriate response to two other important needs of South African higher education – finding resources within the system given fiscal constraints, and the system's need to enhance its human resource development in order to produce 'professionals with globally equivalent skills to strengthen the country's enterprises, services and infrastructure' (Green Paper on Higher Education Transformation, 1996:7). Student tutors are an invaluable resource as tutor educators at Wits; in fact, given their numbers it is clear that the system would be much impoverished without them. As participants in a teaching and learning enterprise, they have drawn attention to the need for developing the skills of under-prepared students in higher education and engage in this process themselves, and while helping others they gain in intellectual development and receive training in and perfect skills that are of particular importance both to their own career goals and South Africa's pressing developmental needs.

Address for correspondence: Dr Carol Taylor, University of the Witwatersrand, Department of Social Anthropology, Private Bag 3, Wits 2050, Johannesburg, South Africa. Tel. (011) 716-1111. Fax (011) 716-2766. e-mail 031Carol@muse.arts.wits.ac.za

Chapter 12

'I UNDERSTAND MORE THAN I UNDERSTOOD': EXPLORING THE POSSIBILITIES OF USING STUDENTS AS TUTORS IN SOUTH AFRICAN TOWNSHIP SCHOOLS

Line Sørensen and Ian Gregory

Student tutoring in schools in South Africa has neither been widely accepted nor developed. This chapter considers the findings of a grass-roots study on the feasibility and potential of using student tutors in South African township schools, as a contribution to the reconstruction and development of the nation's education system.

Explanation of Terms

The expressions 'black' and 'white' are used purely as terms of identification of the systems under which the racial segregation of apartheid took place, the legacy of which still affects contemporary South African society. The terms are not used as a form of categorization of the people.

The term 'township school' is used to identify the schools in the so-called township areas of South Africa. The townships, often characterized by harsh living conditions, were designated living areas for large groups of the 'non-white' population during the apartheid era. Today South Africans may legally live where they choose, but due to economic constraints the townships are still a reality.

Introduction

Background to the study

The concept of student tutoring in schools in South Africa has neither been widely accepted nor, as far as the authors are aware, has it been developed. There have even been claims that student tutoring in schools would not be possible in South Africa today, although the need for more investigative work in this area has been identified by Rutherford and Hofmeyr (1995: 233–47).

In order for student tutoring to succeed an existing model cannot simply be transplanted into the South African environment. A new model must be designed which takes account of the developing nature of the country and conforms to the South African education system. This chapter details a study which focused specifically on the possibilities of introducing student tutoring in schools in this new environment.

The study was undertaken by invitation of the Academic Development Programme (ADP) of Rhodes University, Grahamstown, South Africa, and hosted by the iKhonco ('Chain') project. Ikhonco is an ADP initiative in which township school pupils receive tutoring help on the university campus outside school hours. Ikhonco acted as a basis for this study which explored using tutors in school during school hours and focused on maths and science.

Study objectives

In order to assess the possibilities of using students as tutors in schools the following objectives were defined:

- To characterize the South African context in which tutoring is placed.
- To identify needs in secondary education with a view to assessing the benefits of using students as tutors in township schools.
- To assess whether the environment allows for tutoring intervention.
- To identify the critical issues involved with using students as tutors in township schools.

Investigation and methodology

Student tutoring in schools is a new concept in the South African context and is surrounded by a natural scepticism. A pilot project could therefore not be implemented before groundwork into the feasibility of the concept had been undertaken. In this study an approach was adopted in which the authors themselves combined active tutoring in schools with practical research 'on-the-job'.

Tutoring

Phase I: getting started

The authors visited five township secondary schools during a period of three months in 1996. The first school was visited for two weeks, the others for one successive week each. Science and mathematics teachers were offered assistance in their classes. For those teachers who accepted assistance, the authors assumed the role of tutors in the classroom and worked closely with the teachers. The authors did not prescribe a way of working, but allowed the most appropriate tutoring methods to evolve. By taking on a dual role as both tutors and educational researchers it was possible to gain direct experience of the tutoring situation, to observe the tutoring process and to gather background information on the education system.

Phase II: growth

The initial tutoring yielded such positive feedback from the schools that it was decided to include two tutors from Rhodes University in the study. One of the schools from Phase I was visited twice a week for four weeks. The authors and the two new student tutors attended school together, thus reinforcing the tutoring that had been offered so far, and allowing observation of the new situation.

Evaluation

The tutoring activities in Phase I were evaluated by means of questionnaires filled in by the pupils whereas feedback from teachers was oral. The aim of the evaluation was for pupils and teachers to reflect on the tutoring experience, but was also used as a means of feedback for the tutors themselves. The evaluation form used was a modified version of the standard form found in the BP Tutoring Resource Pack (Hughes, 1991).

Scale of the study

Table 12.1 indicates the scale of the study in terms of the teachers, classes, pupils and lessons involved.

Table 12.1 The scale of the study

Number of *teachers* involved	15
Number of *classes* involved	39
Number of *pupils* involved	1017
Number of *lessons* attended	99

All class levels in secondary education were included in the study.

The Situation – Tutoring in a South African Context

The national education system

The new South Africa is a young and rapidly changing nation. Apartheid, however, left behind some particularly damaging legacies. There is a need to construct an education system based more on equality, and the ability to produce more practically skilled and employable workers. The development of human resources through appropriate education and training is a key part of the Reconstruction and Development Programme (RDP), a national effort to build those areas of the society where the need is the greatest (Garson, 1996).

Reform of school education is therefore a high priority on the government agenda. During apartheid the content, purpose and funding of education for different population groups was different. The schooling system is now beginning to change and a route to equality is being found. Integration between the previous 'white' and 'non-white' schools has been slow, however; most people are more concerned with dilapidated schools, unqualified teachers and overcrowded classrooms.

A further cause for concern is the culture of protest that, although diminishing, is still evident in schools whose pupils and staff used to be highly politicized and wary of interaction with other institutions. After the 1994 elections schools began to open up, enabling more direct interaction to develop between schools and other institutions, such as historically 'white' universities.

The higher education system is also undergoing dramatic change. The National Commission on Higher Education has proposed a radical shake-up by introducing 'massification' of higher education, moving away from the traditionally elitist and skewed base. The scale of the imbalance in representation of different population groups is borne out by figures indicating that 60 per cent of the white student-age population are in higher education, compared to only 10 per cent of the black student-age population (Reddy, 1996).

Rhodes University, like other tertiary institutions, is facing pressures due to increasing student numbers, reduced resources and demands for transformation. The university is located in Grahamstown in the Eastern Cape, the poorest of South Africa's provinces with an official literacy rate in the province of 59 per cent, and a severe unemployment situation.

The need to ensure that students entering higher education from disadvantaged backgrounds are better prepared, and that more of them enter science and technology related studies, means that tertiary institutions are taking a more active interest in the welfare and development of pupils in the schooling system as well as of their own students.

Township School Characteristics

The five township schools included in this study can be characterized by a number of factors, of which the most important are described here.

The schools have a varying standard of facilities; most lack adequate equipment for science teaching and some also lack the essential resources required to run a school. Overcrowding is therefore commonplace, with class sizes of up to 60 pupils not being unusual.

Pupils enter secondary school at Standard (Std) 6 level at the age of 11, proceeding up to the end of school matriculation exams in Std 10. However, the age distribution among pupils in one class is often wide, with up to ten years separating the youngest and oldest.

The majority of pupils come from a disadvantaged background. Their families can in many cases not afford to pay school fees, buy school uniforms, provide their children with appropriate winter clothing or a staple diet. This often has a direct impact on school attendance and academic achievement.

Pupils can choose to take the lower grade or higher grade matriculation exams. The syllabus content for these grades is different, but pupils of both levels, and therefore of vastly different abilities, are grouped together in one class. Teachers often find it impossible to cater for the learning needs of all the pupils.

Teaching is traditionally based on 'chalk and talk', all classroom work being done by the teacher writing on the blackboard and talking. Tutoring in the classroom would therefore require a significant change in method. To achieve this change is perceived as difficult in the current environment, and is one of the reasons why concerns have been expressed about the ability of tutoring to function in South African schools.

This situation is compounded by estimates from the Rhodes University Education Department which suggest that 60 to 70 per cent of 'science' teachers in the Eastern Cape are under-qualified (Boltt, 1996). Many of them have qualified in other areas of teaching and have been drafted into science to cover shortages.

Pupils' motivation with science is low. One reason for this is the lack of hands-on experience of the subject due to equipment and staff shortages. A second reason is that science and maths syllabi are generally based on the 'western' model which often does not coincide with the day-to-day experience or cultural background of the pupils.

Corporal punishment was banned from schools in 1995. This has led to a perceived decrease in standards of discipline within many schools as no replacement system of discipline has been implemented or recommended. The problem has manifested itself for instance in school uniform not being worn and homework not being done.

Disruption in the schools was a regular occurrence during the apartheid era. The situation in 1996 had improved, but in the three-month period of this study there were still around five days of disruption. Disruption often occurs without warning, and can involve either pupil non-attendance or teachers spending the day on tasks such as union meetings or disciplinary hearings.

Tutoring in Township Schools: Critical Issues

This section summarizes the issues that are considered critical to the possible development of student tutoring in schools in the Grahamstown situation.

Acceptance of tutoring

A main hindrance to beginning tutoring is the possible initial resistance of teachers, due to the perception of the student tutor as a threat to the teacher's competency and authority. In this study, teacher resistance was found only to be an initial problem. Once tutors had been in the classroom for a few hours, the teachers began to adapt lesson patterns and teaching methods by finding ways of involving tutors in the lesson, not only accepting the tutor's presence but finding ways of utilizing the resource. This further meant that 'tutor accommodating' teaching methods were not a prerequisite for the introduction of tutoring, but rather tutoring could be instrumental itself in bringing about change.

Teacher involvement

Tutoring will only be successful with those teachers who volunteer to accommodate tutors in their classes. Those teachers who were assigned tutors by their superiors in the school were invariably unwilling to incorporate tutors into their classroom activities. For tutoring to work efficiently it was also helpful for teachers to be directly responsible for organizing the tutoring in which they are involved..Teachers then developed a personal ownership of and commitment to the tutoring.

Teacher training

The teachers involved in this study had not worked with tutors in the classroom before and were initially uncertain about how to utilize them. Some teachers mistook the tutor for a 'general purpose' helper, used to routinely mark homework or to apply discipline. This highlighted the need for basic teacher training in order to acquaint the teachers with the tutoring concept and the way tutors should be used.

Tutee target group

Std 7 to Std 9 pupils were identified as those who will benefit most from tutoring. Std 7 pupils must choose their matriculation subjects and tutor involvement can therefore guide and motivate pupils to choose appropriate subjects. Tutoring can further support the academic foundation for matriculation in Std 8 and Std 9.

Std 6 and Std 10 were found to be less suitable for tutoring. Std 6 pupils are new to secondary education and the classes are exceptionally large. This situation would benefit greatly from tutoring, but it may be too challenging for a new programme to provide the number of tutors required for the class to benefit. Tutoring at Std 10 (matriculation level) was needed, but did not always function well due to the nearness of major examinations. Work tended to focus on syllabus content, rather than on exercises and classwork.

Language and communication

Language was found to be as important as academic content in tutoring. The language of instruction in school is English which many pupils find difficult to cope with, since their mother tongue is Xhosa and they may have only had limited exposure to English outside of school. The pupils' command of English may therefore depend to a large extent on the teachers' ability and commitment to speaking English in class. Student tutors who are able to speak English can help address language problems that may inhibit learning and assist the development of the pupils' language skills. Although recognized as important, issues concerning the use and support of other languages in school, such as Xhosa, are not considered here. In this study, differing first languages of the tutor and tutee did not create a barrier to communication.

Logistics

School timetables are based on a cyclic plan consisting of more than five days, which means that lessons taking place on any one weekday will be different from week to week. The number of days in a cycle often varies from school to school. Timetable coordination proved to be one of the major obstacles in making student tutoring function on a regular basis. As university students became involved in Phase II, it was initially difficult to integrate university and school activities due to the lack of coherence between the cyclic plan of the school and the fixed weekly timetables of the university.

It was found that close cooperation between teacher and tutor could help overcome this obstacle. Teacher and tutor made a general agreement on weekday time slots in which the tutor was available and in which the teacher had lessons in the relevant subject, albeit with different classes. Every week the teacher and tutor would agree which of the time slots were appropriate. In this way, the tutor was assigned to a particular teacher rather than a class.

Similarly, the issue of transport became pressing when student tutors were involved who had to fit in the tutoring between lectures. The only method of public transport to reach the area is the 'Community Taxi', which in the short term proved to be a satisfactory mode of transport for the tutors, but in the long run a permanent solution must be found.

The tutoring in this study was evaluated by pupils and teachers. The evaluation was designed to allow them to reflect on the tutoring experience.

Pupils' Evaluation

A total of 216 responses from maths and science pupils were received, ranging from Std 7 to Std 10. The questionnaire consisted of two sections, the first containing multiple-choice questions yielding quantitative results, the second containing open, qualitative questions.

Quantitative

Table 12.2 gives responses to the first section of the questionnaire. The questionnaire was designed to be as consistent as possible with the approach used by other well-established tutoring projects. The Pimlico Connection has successfully implemented this form of evaluation since 1979.

Table 12.2 Opinions of the pupils about the tutoring they received (216 responses)

Pupil responses to evaluation forms. With tutoring, lessons were:			
more interesting	91%	less 1%	the same 8%
more enjoyable	92%	less 3%	the same 5%
I learned more than usual	87%	less 0%	the same 13%

The results indicate a high percentage of positive response to the tutoring experience. The results are affected by a number of factors:

- tutoring and the individual attention it provides in class was a change to the normal rote-learning environment which occurs in most schools
- the authors were from overseas and therefore had 'interest value' for the pupils beyond the purely academic
- the tutoring at each school was concentrated over a one- or two-week period only. There was not enough time for the 'novelty value' to wear off
- a general reluctance to express criticism.

It is predicted that the figures for an established project would be less than these results. Even with a downward shift the responses are still likely to indicate the value and potential of tutoring in the schools. This can be shown by comparing the above results with those from two well-established projects in the UK, given in Table 12.3.

The comparison between results from the various projects indicates a difference of between 40 and 70 per cent in positive response. Although surprising, it must remembered that the tutoring projects used as a comparison have applied student tutors in different environments.

Table 12.3 Opinions of the pupils in the STIMULUS project, Cambridge University, and the Pimlico Connection project, University of London (Goodlad and Hirst, 1990:90; PC, 1995)

Pupil responses to evaluation forms. With tutoring, lessons were:	*STIMULUS*	*Pimlico Connection*
more interesting	30%	54%
more enjoyable	29%	55%
I learned more than usual	24%	54%

Qualitative

All the responses to open questions were categorized according to the topics shown in Table 12.4.

Table 12.4 Frequency of recorded responses for different topics

Topic	*Frequency recorded in responses*
Help, explanation and understanding	86 %
Tutor attitude and behaviour	25 %
Tutor as knowledge resource	15 %
Learning culture	11 %
Relationships	9 %

Help, explanation and understanding

Help was identified as being given in the form of individual attention, at a pace appropriate to the pupil's ability. Pupils expressed feelings such as '[the tutor] helps me when I make mistakes and we are working together'. The tutor was seen as someone who can help the pupil understand, someone who is easy to understand and someone who has the time to give explanation.

Tutor attitude and behaviour

The tutors' attitude and approachability was often linked to the way help was given. One pupil put it this way: 'they are accessible and they don't accelerate'. The pupils also emphasized the attitude and behaviour of the tutor through expressing what they felt tutors should not do – a tutor who did not arrive on time in class, for instance, was 'bad'. Tutors who arrived on time served as an example to the pupils themselves to be on time for class.

Tutor as knowledge resource

The pupils recognized the tutor as someone who was knowledgeable, or who was a source of information, providing input in the form of access to university books or information on tertiary study and careers: 'they even ask us about our careers and give us information about it'.

Learning culture

Having a tutor in the classroom made pupils reflect on the process of learning. One pupil observed his own higher level of activity and involvement in the classroom due to the presence of tutors, and tied this to learning more: '[I am] feeling active when they are in the class because I learn much more'.

Similarly, a perception of learning methods was brought up: 'When we have tutors we see the different way of learning'. This contrasts with negative comments, '[I don't like it] when the tutors want us to change the style of our teachers and take their style'. The tutor using different approaches to the teacher challenges the knowledge and methods the pupil has already learned and might therefore be perceived as a threat, perhaps also to the teacher's authority. In general, this is an indication of how pupils might react to fresh approaches brought by the tutors.

Relationships

The perception of the tutor as a peer, a friend, or even family, was expressed this way by one pupil: 'They are trying [to help] by all means as [if they were] our brothers or sisters or parents'.

Two pupils touched on the problem that the tutee might feel inferior to the tutor. One pupil expressed this as a problem of the tutee having 'less experience', whereas another pupil pointed out that the tutor helps the tutee but the tutee never helps the tutor. This pupil was concerned about revealing problems to the tutor, without being able to balance the relationship by helping the tutor in return: 'They do not come with their problems. They just help us with our problems'.

This might relate to the African values of *'Ubuntu'* where helping each other is a natural part of human interaction. The Xhosa saying *'Izandla ziyahlambana'* ('the hands wash each other') illustrates the cultural necessity of helping each other.

Teacher Evaluation

Fourteen teachers participated in the study. Their feedback can be summarized as follows:

- tutors are able to pay special attention to individuals when the teacher is dealing with large groups
- tutors give pupils a chance to participate in class
- tutors make the pupils work harder
- tutors are interested in improving the learning of the pupils
- the tutors come for a short period of time; when pupils get to know them they are gone
- tutors must not spend too much time with one pupil; they must divide their time such that they reach more children within a period.

Teachers did not refer to the acceptability and practicality of having tutors in the classroom, but appeared to have rapidly accepted the tutors and proceeded to look at how to utilize the tutor resource even better. One teacher said: 'The periods of their visit should be increased. They should not work just with higher classes, but, as a proper foundation, also with lower classes.'

Discussion

What are the needs in township schools which tutoring can address?

Tutoring intervention is not for its own sake but can address specific needs. The needs in the township schools that tutoring can address and the associated benefits were defined as follows:

- a reduction in class sizes by effectively increasing the teacher:pupil ratio;

- assistance with the pupil's learning through individual attention;
- motivation of the pupils' interest in maths and science, encouragement of homework and attendance in class;
- development of the pupil's language and communication skills;
- academic support for teachers;
- assistance with the development of pupil-centred learning in the classroom;
- development of pupils' consciousness of their own ability to learn;
- support of prospective university students;
- career guidance to aid matriculation subject selection.

There are specific areas where the involvement of students as tutors *in* schools can help address needs *outside* the school environment:

- providing a bridge from school to university, both academically and culturally;
- supporting prospective university students and 'massification' of education;
- students improving transferable and marketable skills;
- students wishing to help others achieve and give something back to the community.

Is the environment in township schools suitable for tutoring?

Concerns have been expressed about the suitability of the environment in township schools to tutoring activities, the main concern being the threat a university student might pose to a teacher's authority and competency. This study encountered the result that the teachers involved often developed new group and class work methods in which the tutor was utilized as an additional rather than substitute resource, hence 'removing' the tutor as a threat. The development of new methods in the classroom also counteracts the concern that traditional 'chalk and talk' teaching methods could not be changed to allow for tutoring activities.

To summarize, the following factors were identified as contributing to the environment in the township schools being suitable for tutoring:

- enough teachers will voluntarily accept tutors for tutoring to be beneficial in school;
- teachers are flexible in adapting teaching methods that can accommodate tutoring;
- school disruption is at a level that will not interfere greatly with tutoring;

- differing first languages between tutor and pupil is not problematic;
- the logistical problems of organizing tutoring can be overcome (timetable coordination and transport).

What makes the South African tutoring situation unique?

The value of *Ubuntu* (loosely translated as 'humanity' or 'solidarity') plays a powerful role in the tutoring relationship in South Africa, as it does between all human interactions in the Xhosa and many other African cultures.

First, in the freer learning atmosphere that is created with tutoring, pupils will naturally form into groups in preference to working individually. The group dynamic ensures that everyone is pulled along by the group and that no individual is left behind. For example, if the tutor works with a group and one member 'sees the light', he or she will be happy to help the rest of the group catch up. Thus a healthy 'tutoring-within-tutoring' activity naturally develops.

Secondly, the pupils often see the tutors as providing a one-way flow of 'help' from the tutor to themselves. Within the concept of *Ubuntu*, it is important that the interaction is mutually beneficial. With tutoring this is hard to achieve in practice, but if the tutor is visibly happy to be with the pupils and explains why he or she wants to tutor, the pupil will feel more at ease.

Thirdly, the development of 'scientific thinking' at school is difficult. One reason may be that the culture is built and procreated through story-telling and the handing down of information through generations, without challenging those who are more senior. Science, however, requires a more exploratory approach to learning. Tutors who come from the same background as the pupils may help embed an understanding for scientific thinking in the pupils without crossing cultural values.

Conclusion

The concept of student tutoring in schools in South Africa has neither been widely accepted nor, as far as the authors are aware, has it been developed. The aim of this study was to assess the possibilities of using students as tutors in schools by combining tutoring in the schools with parallel research and evaluation.

Tutoring intervention was shown to help address specific needs in township schools. Tutoring contributed to the development of school resources through, for instance, the effective reduction in class sizes, the academic support of teachers and the development of pupil-centred learning. By giving individual attention, tutoring increased pupils' academic motivation, and encouraged class attendance and homework.

The environment in the schools, with underqualified teachers and an emphasis on 'chalk and talk' teaching, would not at first glance be seen as suitable for tutoring intervention. It was found, however, that the introduction of tutoring can itself initiate the change to a pupil-centred learning atmosphere in which tutors can be utilized.

The study concludes that the success of a future South African tutoring in schools programme is likely to hinge on the awareness and handling of a number of critical issues such as teacher involvement, teacher training and logistics. The fact that tutoring functioned in practice, that it fulfilled specific needs in the schools and that feedback from pupils and teachers was positive, argues a strong case for the further development of student tutoring in the South African environment.

In the words of one pupil from Ntsika Secondary School who experienced tutoring, 'I understand more than I understood'.

Address for correspondence: Ian Gregory, c/o 31 Beech Court, Ponteland, Northumberland NE20 9NE.

PART F: NEW DIRECTIONS

Chapter 13

INSTITUTING AND DEVELOPING STUDENT MENTORING AND TUTORING IN NAMIBIA: CONSTITUENCIES, NEEDS, PROSPECTS

Fritz Becker and Barnabas Otaala

This chapter presents the Namibian case for resolving the inherited asymmetry in basic and tertiary education. Selected approaches needed to redress and improve the distorted learning/teaching potential of individual students and teachers are investigated.

Overcoming Asymmetries in Education?

In considering the wide academic interest in crucial issues demanding action from all constituencies involved in and committed to resolving asymmetric access to education both in Namibia's different regions and their societies, it seems that the examination of the genesis of Namibia's educational and cultural development in the pre-independence era lost its impetus during the first six years of independence. This is no surprise. The study on *Namibia: Perspectives for national reconstruction and development*, for example, which was conducted by the United Nations Institute for Namibia (UNIN, 1986) in Lusaka, presents an exhaustive but concise account of the main asymmetries in education stemming from past colonial domination and apartheid education. In addition to other key sectors of national development, this study outlines the educational philosophy and scope of action to be taken in order to introduce structural changes in the educational system on Namibia's independence (UNIN, 1986:505–49).

> 'A hundred years of colonial domination of Namibia characterised by calculated racial segregation, ethnic fragmentation, economic exploitation and cultural subjugation, has left a social order which needs revolutionary transformation. The speed and extent of any such social transformation depends on the setting, timing, content and method of the national education system and on the programmes on cultural emancipation.'
>
> (UNIN, 1986:505)

The determination to overcome the 'neglect of the limited educational facilities for Namibians in most parts of the territory' (UNIN, 1986:509) in an independent state, and to eradicate 'the internal inefficiency in the education system' (UNIN, 1986:514) imposed by the apartheid regime, transformed education into a showpiece of change, receiving high political priority and great financial support, human capital and international consultancy. Sources such as the following all exemplify the vigorous effort to keep promises made on independence and to monitor failure for amendment or record success to be sustained:

- the report of a presidential commission on *Higher Education in Namibia* (Turner, 1991) which considers potential structures, tasks, challenges and routes of future development in higher education;
- the University of Namibia (UNAM): *First Five Year Development Plan 1995–1999* which reflects the commitment of all university constituencies, accepting the development path not dictated by esoteric ivory tower attitudes, services or courses, but prescribed by peoples' needs in lifelong education and in trans-mural research;
- the strategic publication *Toward Education for All: A development brief for education, culture and training* (1993) which 'translates the Namibian philosophy on education into concrete and implementable government policies';
- the public annual education statistics, translated, for instance, into the reader-friendly brochure called *A Profile of Education in Namibia* (1996).

In the past six years primary, secondary and tertiary educational systems saw fundamental changes embedded in the overall educational reform launched in 1990. It is common knowledge that, while being implemented, any reform of such magnitude and complexity, filled with areas of social policy-making, attracts discussion and debate among the various constituency groups, subsequently triggering action for modification, reflection and appropriate adjustment within the politico-economic and socio-cultural processes of development in Namibia (Becker,1993:169–76). In times of such reforms (which touch the roots of social fabrics by redefining the access to educational systems in a more equal on-merit-only affirmative action approach), it sometimes appears to be difficult to master aspirations and expectations, to calm impatience or make up leeway and time when experimenting with 'winds of change'. It is also difficult to convince all involved in the reform of education that their work is not tantamount to Sisyphean labour. In order to prepare oneself for potential disappointment regarding reforms changing the pattern and structure of higher education, the *Report on Higher Education*, for example, cautioned its readers when stating:

> 'The greatest problem which higher education will face in the short term is to find an adequate supply of qualified entrants. The matriculation system has proved itself entirely inadequate as a means of providing university entrance while it will take some years before the IGCSE (International General Certificate of Secondary Education; FB/BO) and the new school curricula will have had time to affect the supply of higher education entrants.'
>
> (*Report on Higher Education*, 1991:viii)

As to tertiary education, this statement anticipates one of the many key roles the national university is expected to play. The policy document *Toward Education for All* is indeed quite specific in its assessment:

> 'One of the University's principal responsibilities will be to participate in improving our education system as a whole. Directly, the University will be central to the expansion of our pool of well prepared secondary school teachers. Both directly and indirectly its education faculty will help refine the philosophy, shape the curriculum, and develop the materials of our education institutions, both residential and non-residential. And its research programmes will help us see how we are doing and how we can do better.'
>
> (*Toward Education for All*, 1993:111)

Both education for all and lifelong learning are exposed in the development brief *Toward Education for All* (1993:1–16). The firm promotion of these ideas within the context of the Namibian situation reflects the fact that providing the material and non-material infrastructure in addition to human capital for formal education constitutes only one element in the endeavour to lead the multifaceted and (perhaps) ambitious Namibian education programme en route to success. In fact, it is common knowledge that political, economic, and social factors as experienced in a teaching/learning environment are also instrumental in achieving educational success. It goes without saying that the philosophy of education for all (and its complementary concept of lifelong learning) represent an holistic approach to improving the formal and non-formal body of knowledge required to master more easily the skills of survival in the physical and non-physical reproduction process of any human being's lifecycle. Apart from the ever-important examination results, it has become equally necessary to always act knowledgeably and avoid fatal perils such as HIV infection or substance abuse. In this regard, *Toward Education for All* suggests that 'a culture of lifelong learning will help our society react effectively to the challenges we will surely face. One example is AIDS. Ignorant, we become its victims. Or we can learn to manage and eventually master this affliction' (1993:14).

Annual education statistics disclose structural and regional disparities in the achievements of learners. This is not only owing to the vast and unevenly populated landscapes of arid Namibia. In part, this situation results from factors and variables such as insufficient basic infrastructure of schools, under-qualified teachers, restricted resources, and attitudes toward learning and teaching environments.

In Namibia, the performance of lecturers and students alike is evaluated at tertiary level throughout the academic year. This exercise leads to all concerned being in a position to specify their needs for an improved output in the future. In this system of tertiary education the weak performance records of students often emerge from poorly supported formal and informal learning/teaching environments which include family. As the university community accepted the challenge of fulfilling the high expectations conferred on all constituency groups at UNAM, it became necessary to merge the existing student-centred philosophy of pastoral care to which the majority of university staff subscribed, with the holistic approach to lifelong learning under the umbrella of the development brief: education for all.

In essence, this conclusion means that the university needs to establish a sustainable tutoring and mentoring scheme as a means to provide 'solutions to specific problems – rather than adopt them just for the sake of it' (Goodlad,1995a:3). At UNAM such schemes should start small as experience suggests, but would reach out ultimately to the secondary and primary level of education far from the capital region.

Constituencies in Basic/higher Education: A Profile

In starting to integrate tutoring and mentoring into the systems of basic and higher education in Namibia it might be worth remembering that this experiment also aims at discovering unexplored educational teaching and learning opportunities as well as dormant organizational possibilities.

As the national university bears the responsibility for the preparation of the future generation of well-educated secondary school teachers, it would be ultimately desirable if an iterative approach to evaluating all tutoring and mentoring activities could result in responding to student demands. These demands may refer to individual situations occurring along the route of learning. They also may be interpreted as an amalgam of ideas, needs, frustrations and enjoyment which could find their way into syllabi and curricula after careful analysis.

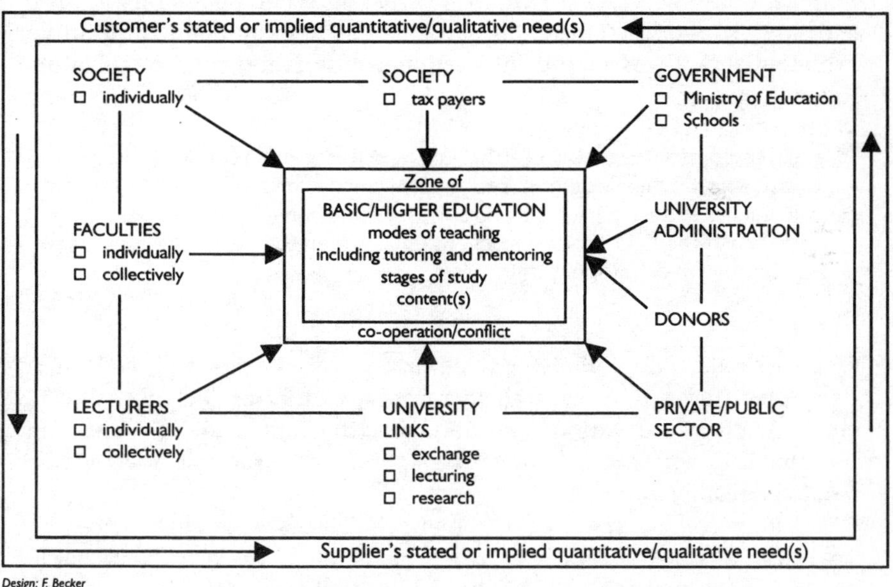

Figure 13.1 Constituency groups in basic/higher education

Figure 13.1 assembles constituency groups in basic/higher education with reference to Namibia. The outer frame of this overview reflects the assumptions that basic and higher education meet the needs of customers. The larger rectangle lists a number of groups and institutions which usually have a deliberate or an inadvertent influence on education through their institutional roles and functions. The most crucial objective in this drawing is, however, the zone of cooperation or conflict, surrounding the smaller rectangle in the central part of the figure. This zone attempts to visualize organizational culture, fostered through communication, pooling of resources and ideas, or through networking private–public partnership(s) alike.

The objective of achieving and, later, sustaining high quality standards within this specific area of cooperation is to provide the means of (re-)production which, *inter alia*, would strive to ensure high standards in learning/teaching and research, assisted by total quality management.

Needs: A Statement of General and Targeted Challenges

In questioning whether psychology is responsive to development problems in third world countries, Kagitcibasi has recently pointed out in her Presidential Address of the International Association for Cross-Cultural Psychology:

> 'If psychologists can make a "niche" for themselves in high priority research toward societal development; if they can provide some solutions to human problems encountered in the process of social change and thus assert the relevance of the field for development efforts, then the status of psychology will improve in developing countries.'
>
> (Katgitcibasi, 1992:3)

One can similarly claim that if educationists were more practical and focused more on using action research to respond to the myriad of challenges encountered in our various educational settings, then the relevance and usefulness of formal education in responding to societal development would be readily apparent.

What are some of these development challenges, and what suggestions can be put forward to address at least some of them? The rest of this chapter answers these questions. We briefly outline challenges related to academic progress, to the threat posed by HIV/AIDS, and to the threat posed to health by substance abuse. We then proceed to indicate ways in which the concept of student mentoring and tutoring can be applied to alleviate some of these threats.

Challenges in the academic progress of students

One of the most basic tools used to determine the quality of education has been and continues to be performance in public examinations. Namibia has experienced changes in the public examination system at senior secondary level. Prior to independence the Cape matriculation system was used as a tool to determine progression from secondary education into universities and other tertiary institutions, as well as to the world of work. As part of the education reform process in 1993, the then Ministry of Education and Culture formally adopted the International General Certificate of Secondary Education (IGCSE) and the Higher International General Certificate of Secondary Education (HIGCSE) as the type of examination to replace the Senior Cape Matriculation Examination. These examinations were implemented for the first time on a nation-wide scale in 1994–5.

The results of the November 1995 examinations were published in January 1996. These results were not terribly good; in fact many pronounced them disastrous. The effect has been that many students have been admitted to university and other tertiary institutions with serious deficits which necessitate additional tuition and tutoring of students.

The threat posed by HIV/AIDS

Namibia, like the rest of Africa, is facing an HIV/AIDS pandemic. Work elsewhere, such as in Uganda, has shown that knowledge of HIV/AIDS and their causes has recently increased among the general populace and youth in particular, but their attitudes and practices have not changed.

Factors that impede HIV/AIDS prevention control efforts, particularly in developing or most populous countries, include ignorance about the nature and modes of the spread of HIV infection, denial by many individuals and societies that AIDS is relevant to them, complacency despite the pandemic's magnitude, and the traditional reluctance to discuss sexual matters.

The threat posed by substance abuse

There is evidence that the use of tobacco, alcohol and drugs is on the increase in Namibia, particularly among the young. According to the latest figures from the Namibian Drug Enforcement Bureau (DEB) 19–26-year-old young adults had been extensively targeted for the introduction of hard drugs in the past year (Strijdom, 1992). However, alcohol was again the number one drug of abuse amongst the out-of-school youth. It should also be pointed out that there is a close link between substance abuse and the spread of AIDS

(Strijdom, 1992). Namibian school children experiment with tobacco and alcohol from the age of 9. This carries on up to the age of 12. At 13 years, a rapid increase in the numbers of children involved in substance abuse has been found among both sexes.

Mass education of Namibian youth through the public school system is not taking place, for reasons that include the following:

- teachers have not been trained to assist learners in solving the problem of substance abuse;
- schools do not have the resource materials to assist teachers – literature, posters, videos;
- most schools and school committees do not see such education as a priority, and they are not enlightened about the need for such education.

Prospects: A Delimitation of Foci of Implementation

To address some of the challenges posed in the preceding section related to academic work, and to health hazards posed by the spread of HIV/AIDS (and other diseases), we propose through mentoring and tutoring some practical, cost-effective solutions involving the University of Namibia, other tertiary institutions, and secondary and primary schools.

Academic assistance centre for students on campus

It is proposed to institute at the University of Namibia and the Polytechnic of Namibia an academic assistance centre in order to pay attention to students who come from disadvantaged groups or who feel they need additional help. In an academic assistance centre, services could include the following.

Peer tutoring

Students may request a tutor for any of their courses (predominantly in the science faculty where we experience a high failure rate). The centre would maintain a list of student tutors who have successfully completed courses in various disciplines. These students would then assist those who need help at times mutually agreeable to both parties. Student mentors and tutors will be able to contribute to each of the following activities.

Mathematics room

Teaching mathematics is an intractable problem in many places. Making a 'Maths room' available would be an attempt to solve this problem in Namibia. The room would offer tutoring for maths courses from college algebra to calculus. It would be a drop-in service open for students at specified times, as availability of tutoring staff dictates.

English language and study skills support

Courses offered would include taking notes, reading, writing and speaking. Also to be provided would be individual advice and group workshops on study skills. We already have a compulsory course for all first-year students offered by the language centre, but we are sure there are other individuals/groups who require specialized attention.

Services for students with disabilities

There is a need to coordinate services for students with disabilities. To date UNAM may not have experienced many cases requiring special help, but from requests such as that presented to senate last year for a student to have a longer time period to write their examination because of some physical disability, it seems there will be an increasing need for us to be sensitive to the needs of students with disabilities and to respond to them appropriately. The Department of Educational Psychology and Special Education could be asked to suggest some guidelines.

Student employment

To make some of the above-named suggestions possible it might be necessary to arrange to hire students in a variety of roles (although there are issues to be negotiated concerning deploying paid and unpaid tutors in similar activities as tutors for courses already successfully completed by them eg, as note-takers for other students or as computer lab assistants). The stipend paid to them would be minimal compared to the important tasks they would be performing. Moreover, in acting as tutors for fellow students they gain in more ways than one, including the experience that comes from successfully explaining a concept to another learner. To implement these various possibilities, financial assistance would be required and there are many possibilities of sponsorship from industries that benefit from graduate recruitment.

Academic assistance for students in secondary schools

In addition to the type of assistance described above for students in tertiary institutions such as the University of Namibia and the Polytechnic of Namibia, there is assistance that could be provided by university students, particularly student teachers to secondary schools.

In many disadvantaged rural, peri-urban and urban secondary schools it is not unusual to have a staff:student ratio of 1:50. Under these kinds of conditions effective teaching and learning is not easy. This situation could be alleviated through a student tutoring system. It is proposed to deploy University of Namibia and Polytechnic of Namibia students (at mutually convenient times) to assist secondary school teachers as student tutors, initially in the capital city of Windhoek, and eventually in the more remote rural secondary schools.

HIV/AIDS and drug addiction prevention through peer tutoring

As already indicated, there is an alarming rate of the spread of HIV/AIDS in Namibia as well as an increasing amount of drug addiction particularly among the youth in secondary schools as well as in tertiary institutions. If HIV/AIDS and drug addiction prevention and sex education programmes are to prove effective, teachers must receive professional training in how to teach these subjects. The best way to train teachers initially in this area is through pre-service professional training.

In the meantime, however, the use of peer tutoring could be an effective remedy to address these health hazards. It is proposed to mount a Schools HIV/AIDS and Population Education Programme (SHAPE). Its goal would be HIV/AIDS and sexually transmitted disease (STD) education in schools in Namibia to control and prevent their spread and the related problem of drug addiction among schoolchildren.

To realize this goal it is proposed to launch the University of Namibia and Polytechnic of Namibia Student Welfare Society with the following short- and long-term objectives.

Short-term objectives

Among the many short-term objectives the following three are highlighted:

- To train peer educators (students) and teachers about HIV/AIDS, and drug addiction.
- To equip them with the necessary knowledge, skills and information on the nature and spread of HIV/AIDS and other STDs, as well as on drug addiction. Students would be in a strategic position to create awareness among their peers at the university and the polytechnic and in secondary schools, about the danger of these health hazards.
- To provide them with the necessary skills for advocacy and to form anti-AIDS clubs in secondary schools and at institutions of higher learning.

Long-term objectives

The main long-term objectives would include the following:

- To raise a general awareness so as to be able to create and mould a virus-free generation that includes youngsters of the age group 5–15 years.
- To undertake activities encompassed in the above-named objectives, the student society referred to will need some funding for the training of peer educators (students) and teachers, the payment of teachers, as well as for advocacy.

Peer tutoring in health-related problems in primary schools using Child-to-Child approaches

The idea of Child-to-Child was started in 1979 during the International Year of the Child, and it has since spread to over 70 countries worldwide. The Child-to-Child programmes are designed for children who are often caretakers of younger siblings, future parents, communicators of information to their parents and other caretakers and community members and, as such, capable of improving conditions affecting health and development.

Child-to-Child is an approach that helps children to help others, and in health education this strategy is being used in different ways all over the world. In this section, we emphasize the two main ways in which the approach is used: in schools and within the communities around the schools; and in youth groups where children join together to spread health ideas to communities.

Child-to-Child approaches can also be used in other subject areas such as agriculture and environmental studies, but here we concentrate on health. Three important goals of the Child-to-Child approach include:

- linking health and education together within communities and so improving the life of both children and adults;
- involving children as well as adults in actively improving health in communities;
- encouraging children to take action individually and as a group so that they can benefit both themselves and others without giving themselves extra burdens.

The methodology is active and fun for children in that the concept 'Child-to-Child' emphasizes:

- meaningful, active learning, using a variety of approaches and methods;
- activities which are interesting and fun for children to do.

How the Child-to-Child approach helps children

This approach helps children through targeting four major areas as identified below.

Knowledge and skills

It develops knowledge and understanding of important health issues in communities. It promotes a wider understanding of health as something more than absence of disease and thus an awareness of:

- links between a healthy person and a healthy environment;
- links between physical health and the health of the 'whole person' (mind, body, spirit).

It develops active skills to help children prevent disease and help those who are sick. It develops thinking skills of:

- identifying problems and solving them;
- communicating ideas to others;
- examining actions and results: What have we done? Was it useful? How could we do it better?

This knowledge and these skills increase children's capacity to improve their own lives.

Attitudes

Child-to-Child also aims to develop desirable attitudes in children both through what children learn and how they learn it. It develops:

- their self-confidence, because they are planning and taking action;
- their sense of responsibility, because they are being trusted to do things that are important both for themselves and for others;
- their sense of cooperation, because they are working together.

Changes in behaviour and practice in children

Child-to-Child also aims to achieve changes in behaviour and practice in both younger and older children, eg:

- improved health habits resulting in better personal and community hygiene (eg, children wash their hands more often and fill in mosquito breeding places);
- more care and attention to the health of others (eg, children care for the safety of younger children);
- better use of available resources to improve health care (eg, children provide oral rehydration using rice water).

Effects on families, schools and communities

In addition to helping children, the Child-to-Child approach also helps families, communities and schools through:

- helping to make closer links between education and health workers, at community level (and at higher levels, too);
- helping to bring changes in health knowledge and practice, through the knowledge that children can spread and the example they can provide (with the help of their teachers, youth leaders and health workers);
- helping to provide a model of an active methodology in health linked to doing and helping in the community so that these approaches may be used in other subject areas;
- increasing the respect that a community gives to its children (as it sees how they can take responsibility to improve health).

In Namibia, Child-to-Child was formally introduced towards the end of the first year of independence (Mostert and Zimba, 1990), at a major workshop held in Windhoek, with participants coming from health, education, non-governmental organizations (NGOs), and communities. More recently a series of workshops was held in both northern and southern Namibia (Otaala, 1994a, b). During the workshops teachers and health workers are provided with selected health messages that they can pass on to older children who in turn can pass them on to their younger brothers and sisters, other children, their parents, and the communities from which they come. Selected Child-to-Child activity sheets such as *Playing with Younger Children*; *Preventing Accidents*; *Road Safety* and *Immunisation* have been translated from English into Oshindonga for use by primary-school teachers and children in Owambo land, one of the most populous parts in Namibia.

Currently there is a proposed pilot project to examine the working of the Child-to-Child approach in colleges of education and selected nearby satellite schools. As a result of operating and monitoring this project over a period of time it would be possible to assess better the potential of Child-to-Child as an approach in health education, the potential of colleges of education in promoting such an approach, and the value of health education as a model for promoting more active, learner-centred, relevant and community-related learning in other areas of the curriculum, and within the school as a whole (Otaala, 1995). To enable the project to be initiated there is need for seed funding.

Evaluation of Child-to-Child Programmes

As Pridmore (1996:7) points out, 'although the flexibility and adaptability of the Child-to-Child approach has enabled it to be used in a wide range of contexts, there has been little systematic attempt to analyse what can be accomplished by the approach'. However, as reported in Lansdown's (1995) review of Child-to-Child literature, some recently conducted national evaluations strengthen considerably the existing evaluation data.

Evans's study (1993) sponsored by the Aga Khan Foundation is the most comprehensive evaluation of Child-to-Child programmes to date. Conducted in India, the programmes reviewed took place in seven different settings between 1986 and 1990, and both qualitative and quantitative data were collected. The evaluation concluded that 'Child-to-Child was an effective way to bring health messages to children, particularly in schools, and that it was sustainable because it was continuing in all settings evaluated after evaluation funding had ceased' (Pridmore, 1996:8).

In Botswana the 'Little Teacher' programme was set up by the Child-to-Child Foundation, aimed at enabling older children to help prepare younger ones (pre-school) for school entry and to take health messages home to their parents. The overall conclusion of the evaluators was, that 'There is ample evidence that this programme has had a substantial impact on the Botswana community. ... The programme enjoyed substantial objectives achievability and has had a non-trivial impact on the Botswana school community' (Babagura *et al.*, 1993:47).

Concluding Remarks

There are many challenges that face African developing countries, including Namibia. They range from constraints on the educational system to deliver high-level manpower previously lacking due to colonial legacies, from combating crime such as drug addiction to the fight against HIV/AIDS. We have tried to indicate a modest start which could be made deploying students as tutors and mentors to tackle in a most cost-effective way the varied challenges.

This start is entirely consistent with the wish of the Vice Chancellor of the University of Namibia, Professor Peter H Katjavivi, who at the 1997 commencement day of the university addressed the students as follows:

> 'As the privileged few of our society, you owe the underprivileged masses, out there, a great deal. My dream for 1997 is to see you, our students, going out to our local schools, going out to our society in general, going out to our youth, sensitising them about social evils, such as drug substance abuse, juvenile crime, HIV/AIDS, to mention but a few. I see you, during your holidays, going out to our rural masses, and helping to make the illiterate literate, and sharing your knowledge with them.'
>
> (Katjavivi, 1997:2)

We are aware of the fact that the foregoing deliberations have taken a descriptive stance. It appears to us that, in the context of Namibia, the concept of tutoring and mentoring as usually perceived may require some further investigation to provide for an encompassing element which would be embedded in socialization as children grow up and develop, and youth matures.

Address for correspondence: Dr Fritz Becker, University of Namibia, Private Bag 13301, 340 Mandume Ndemufayo Avenue, Pioneerspark, Windhoek, Namibia. e-mail foebecker@unam.na

Chapter 14

CASTING THE NET: PEER ASSISTED LEARNING ON THE INTERNET

L A Beardon

Peer assisted learning moves into a distance learning mode, extends beyond the present geographical limitations, and contributes to the personal and cognitive development of ever more pupils and peer teachers. Children's questions are answered personally by university students. Aims, methods, funding, quality control, teacher involvement, home and school links, video-conferencing, mirror sites, and research and evaluation are all discussed.

Introduction: Planning for the New Information Age

As we near the end of the millennium, there is in prospect an era when information technology, and in particular the Internet, will open up the possibilities of peer assisted learning (PAL) to many more children, including those in remote places as well as those close to centres of higher education. The peer teacher and learner can either meet in 'real time', see and talk to each other using video links and write on the same 'whiteboard', or they can e-mail each other which avoids scheduling complications and enables each one to contribute to the exchange at a time when they find it convenient to do so.

Present-day technology makes this possible; the technology is being refined and improved, costs are coming down and the numbers of schools and homes that have Internet connections are increasing exponentially. Digital television could bring down the cost dramatically because a network computer does not need much memory and users do not have to invest in expensive hardware and software that soon becomes obsolete. Cable companies are backing experiments with digital television and network computers that enable the subscriber to have access to a vast 'library' of educational and recreational CDs, to all the latest software and to a comprehensive range of reference and information sources, and to use this system from their own living room at home or from school. In one such experiment pupils at home can access video film taken on geography field trips and answer questions on it for their homework, teachers can use snips to make up worksheets for the next day's lessons, and both can be printed out next day in school. In the future, more possibilities for electronic PAL will open up, if these experiments lead to more schools and homes having access to network links with better video contact.

If the information-rich community is to share information around the world it is likely to be electronically. It can no longer be argued that computers, and the avenues that they open along the information highways, only affect the minority, the already over-privileged. It is far cheaper to access libraries and information sources, and to print out the pages you are really interested in, than it is to travel to the source or to order the book by post.

A recent estimate given in the February 1997 newsletter of the Mathematical Association claims that 80 per cent of secondary schools in the UK now have Internet access. Although access for a whole class is still relatively rare, schools are developing their own internal networks and can also download suitable sites for use off-line. Telephone and cable companies, and political parties, are competing to offer attractive deals to schools. We can only speculate what the combination of commercial and political interests, as well as those of the educational community, will promote. Wherever these developments lead, it is clear that links over the Internet have already become part of our culture; they will increasingly creep in to affect more and more of what we do, changing many of our habits and altering ways of doing things that have been established for generations.

PAL will be no exception. Not only can people access the world's libraries from wherever they live, work or go to school, but they are also able to have their questions answered, sometimes by experts, often by other people like themselves who share a common interest. The culture of the Internet is one of a free exchange of ideas, not as yet sabotaged by commercialism and the profit motive. E-mail news and special interest groups have grown up through which people can discuss their, often highly specialized, interests and learn from each other; this is PAL in action. You float a question out on 'the ether' and back come answers from unexpected places around the globe. Setting up news groups for school students is one way of promoting

PAL, and giving it the extra dimension of possible new friendships with people far away.

An alternative to sending university students out into schools to help children learn is for university students to staff an 'Ask an Expert' answering service, fielding questions on their own area of specialized study. With effective quality control, monitoring and back up, such services could have most of the advantages of visits to schools without the disadvantages that spring from incompatibility between certain classroom cultures and the presence of student tutors. The use of the term 'expert' here would need to be justified by the presence 'in the wings' of real experts to help out with questions that the university students cannot confidently answer themselves. One form of PAL will not replace the other: both can have a strong ingredient of interpersonal contact, and both could claim to raise the aspirations of young people through 'the role model' effect. The author is engaged in a new electronic PAL experiment, to run alongside a ten-year-old conventional one, and this chapter describes the early days of the development.

STIMULUS and NRICH

The Cambridge STIMULUS PAL project enables university students to help as volunteer classroom assistants in local schools. Though very successful within its scope, STIMULUS and similar projects in many parts of the world, have geographical limitations and have been hitherto limited to face-to-face contact. The National Royal Institution Cambridge University Mathematics Enrichment Project, hereafter referred to as NRICH, begins a new phase, extending PAL into an entirely new mode of distance learning. Pupils at school or at home will be able to have their mathematical questions answered by e-mail. Video-conferencing will be set up, limited at first, but in time this may bring a new meaning to 'face to face' in relation to PAL. The peer teacher and learner smiling in recognition of each other, or over the pleasure of climbing some intellectual hill together, may be in different towns, or in different countries.

Building on the experience of the Cambridge STIMULUS project, the benefits of NRICH will be extended to a much larger group of children. Links with mathematics enrichment work in Australia and Hong Kong and PAL projects worldwide are contributing to this development. Many of the lessons learned will be applicable to other projects, to other subjects apart from mathematics, and to school and university students working within cultural and educational environments very different from those in the UK.

The philosophy and background, and the 'RI' in NRICH, can be traced from 1826 when Faraday gave the first popular science lectures for children at the Royal Institution in London; it is linked to the inspiration of the Christmas Holiday Lectures first on radio and now on television, and also to the Royal Institution Mathematics Masterclasses, held in the impressive nineteenth-century splendour of Albemarle Street, and also in the 'Out of London Groups'. The Royal Institution has developed a national network of Mathematics Masterclasses (RIMM) and each year a new group of over 2500 teenagers attend. The author, with a band of fellow volunteers, has run RIMMs for many years in Cambridge, but has always felt that they were sadly limited, providing for relatively few children, from a limited area, for a limited time. What about a national system (hence the N) to be served from Cambridge, to provide extracurricular and enrichment opportunities for all children? Children can access NRICH from home or from school, and it is intended to give teachers help in extending their ablest pupils and in running maths clubs. School students need not say 'Goodbye' after the last RIMM but rather 'We'll keep in touch on the net'. NRICH will provide a mathematical stimulus of a different nature from the RIMMs and from national competitions; it will be available to many more young people who cannot presently benefit from the existing provisions, and it will extend throughout their school years from age 5 to 18.

As well as an electronic 'Ask a Mathematician' answering service staffed by university student volunteers, the NRICH Online Maths Club will provide continuous and sustained support to help young people maximize their potential. They will be able to participate as individuals or as a member of a school mathematics club. Some children are isolated because they do not know other people of their own age with similar mathematical talents and interests, and such children will benefit from the contacts they make over the Internet. The project will offer opportunities to pupils who are not sufficiently challenged by the mathematics in their school and it will also provide inservice training for teachers and all the resources they need to run maths clubs in their schools.

The emphasis is on communicating, sharing, explaining and enjoying mathematics, with a regular supply of new material on the Internet and interaction with school and university students beyond their schools. Excitement will be heightened by the interactive nature of the contact and exploring the educational possibilities offered by the Internet. There will be a fortnightly Internet magazine; articles on a variety of mathematical topics; challenging puzzles and problems with solutions submitted by the children themselves; the opportunity for pupils to publish their own brain-teasers and jokes; news groups for pupils to exchange ideas and one for teachers and parents; video-conferencing so that professional mathematicians can interact with pupils in their schools and schools can link up across the country; and an archive of resources and materials on the Internet.

This is the ideal time to be developing the use of the Internet to bring to school students and to their teachers up-to-date mathematical materials, to extend their awareness and understanding beyond the confines of school syllabuses and to heighten their appreciation of the nature of mathematics, their awareness of the range of applications and their understanding of the significance of some of the new developments. There is a need for high quality educational material on the Internet specially designed for use by schools.

Setting up the project

The idea for NRICH is a synthesis with nothing very original. Problem-solving workshops, as observed in 1994 in Australia, run by Terry Gagen and colleagues from the University of Sydney, seemed a good alternative to RIMMs, particularly for rural areas. The use of the Internet was obvious: we could include more children by providing mathematical activities for an ever-growing net-workshop and we could reach mathematically talented and hitherto isolated youngsters. The Internet also provides a means of extending PAL to many more children. In August 1995 letters were written to professors of mathematics, to learned societies and to the Royal Institution with a draft proposal, and the serious business of fund-raising started in the Autumn of 1995 with backing from the Royal Institution.

By July 1996 approximately 60 per cent of the funding had been raised to run the project from September 1996 until December 1999. In 1996/7 a one-year feasibility study with 34 Norfolk secondary and middle schools is being run by the Inspection Advice and Training Services of Norfolk County Council. In January 1997 the NRICH Centre in Cambridge opened in preparation for extending the services to all the schools throughout the UK starting in September 1997.

In August 1996 it was agreed that a mirror site would be established in Hong Kong and joint evaluation and research will be carried out. Children will work on the same problems and exchange ideas through NRICHtalk, the online discussion group for school students. NRICH will provide the PAL service for school students in the UK; other centres may enjoy a link with NRICH, and set up their own answering services. Technical developments and knowledge will be freely shared.

Among the aims of NRICH is the extension of PAL into a distance learning mode and so to contribute to the personal and cognitive development of both the pupils and the university student peer teachers. To achieve this NRICH will provide an electronic answering service whereby young people will be able to ask mathematical questions that will be answered personally by students from the University of Cambridge. Quality control will be exercised through rigorous selection and training of volunteers, and through checking samples of question-and-answer exchanges.

A management group of four was set up with the director to run the NRICH centre, a representative from the Royal Institution, another colleague from Cambridge who is in charge of research and evaluation, and one of the inspectors from Norfolk Local Education Authority to run the Norfolk pilot. An advisory board has been appointed to represent the sponsors, to receive half-yearly reports from the management group, to monitor the work of the project, and to commission an independent evaluation in the third year. The advisory board includes professors from other universities and a school teacher from another area.

The web site to serve the Norfolk pilot schools opened in November 1996 providing problems and links including NRICHtalk, an electronic discussion group for pupils and NRICH support, a similar group for parents and teachers. The electronic answering service started in May 1997 for Norfolk schools and in September 1997 for school students throughout the UK. The success of the project will depend not only on the quality of material offered but also on the design of the World Wide Web pages, on the efficiency of the computer system, on avoidance of delays due to overloading or breakdowns, prevention of the intrusion of undesirable material onto the system, effective safeguards and monitoring of the answering service and the accessibility to users.

The staff of the project at the NRICH centre includes the director, a teacher, two graduate student assistants and the computer officer, all part-time. The teacher assists the director in liaising with schools, teachers and pupils, editing the newsletter, monitoring the answering service, training student volunteers and teachers and promoting the project. Two graduate students work for six hours a week, assisting in all the work of the project including the preparation of newsletters and checking solutions, and they spend some time as peer teachers on the answering service. The university students, who act as peer teachers and answer questions from school children using e-mail, are trained and registered with the project, and they work for three hours a week in a voluntary capacity.

The e-mail question-and-answer exchanges are stored, and the time each student volunteer spends on line is logged. Quality control is exercised by the selection and training of the volunteers, and by checking samples of the question-and-answer exchanges recorded. All these exchanges are stored by topic and an archive will be built up including 'most frequently asked questions'. If the demand warrants it then selected university students will be paid to do additional hours. In the third year of the project specially selected and trained university students from other universities may be invited to volunteer to act as peer teachers for the project.

Research, development and evaluation

The research and development is now focusing on a system for children to exchange ideas and discuss solutions to mathematical problems over the Internet with the equipment available to them. Setting up the answering service will also require innovative design. All aspects of the work of the project will be evaluated, half-yearly reports will include reviews of the work of the project, an analysis of the evaluations and questionnaires, revised strategic plans and targets, accounts, and annual budgets. An independent evaluation will be conducted. There will be research studies to assess the effectiveness of the strategies used by the project in raising children's understanding of mathematics beyond the confines of the National Curriculum and other examination syllabuses. The project will provide data, and there is considerable scope, for further research to be undertaken. The team will welcome research associates.

PAL on the Internet

There are good reasons for all school and university students involved to be registered so that the project team can check that the users are who they say they are. Anyone trying to use the 'Ask a Mathematician' answering service online who has not already registered will be told the registration procedure, advised to send their question with their registration application, and told that it will be dealt with promptly while their registration is being processed. School groups will be encouraged to make a joint registration so that, where a group of school students have a question they have worked on together, there will be a single spokesperson for the group asking the question.

Several messages to and fro may occur between the school student and the university student and, when the question has finally been answered, the university student will sign off. At this point one of the project team will classify the completed question-and-answer series, by topic and age group, and it will be stored, with no editing, in the research archive. Some of these question-and-answer exchanges will be edited and published online.

Although some technical difficulties over the use of different systems disappear in the use of e-mail, considerable difficulties remain when the exchange involves mathematics with formulae and diagrams. The project is developing advice for users on e-mail attachments and scientific word-processing that is simple enough for use in schools.

A sample of the question-and-answer sequences will be monitored both for accuracy of the answer and the quality of the explanation. A quality assessment will be given for the peer tutoring based on two four-point scales. For the university student, the assessment will be one of the following: 'good explanation'; 'average explanation'; 'poor explanation'; or 'impossible to assess'. For the school student the assessment will be: 'seems to understand well by end of exchange'; 'partial understanding'; 'poor understanding'; or 'impossible to assess'. In order to maintain validity and reliability, these assessments will be moderated.

Data will be kept so that the project team can readily check how much time each university student spends, the average time spent each week, the date and length of each session, the number of completed exchanges, and any quality grades given. Similar records will be available for each school.

The system is being designed so that the project team is alerted if any exchange is unduly long, if the total time for any university student is more than four hours in one week or less than one hour, if an individual school student asks more than five separate questions in a week or if any question has remained in the entry phase queue for longer than a week. Normally questions should be answered within five days.

Recruitment will target all mathematics undergraduates and graduate students, and particularly members of maths societies, using both the direct approach to the students themselves (mailshots) and through directors of studies. Volunteers will be recruited at the end of the summer term for the following academic year starting in the autumn, much as STIMULUS volunteers have been recruited for the last ten years. All mathematics undergraduates have e-mail accounts and receive notices about their courses via e-mail. Volunteers will be able to log on to the 'Ask a Mathematician' service from any computer on the university network, and will also be able to come into the project centre for advice or to work there. Two graduate students will work for the project and will take a turn at answering the questions when there is a need. Some of the volunteers are PhD students who are around in the university during the university vacations; they will be called on to staff the service at that time as there will be less help from undergraduates. Volunteers will be able to staff the service from remote locations and some will do so during university vacations. If there are too many questions coming in for the number of volunteers, plus the two paid graduate students, then to keep pace with them, as a short-term measure, the best of the volunteers who want to do this will be paid for a few extra hours over and above the three hours per week that they do for free. Eventually there may be recruitment of individual students from other universities and there has been some consultation about this.

Regular initial training sessions will be held and selection of volunteers for the service will be based on successful completion of the initial training and on academic achievement. Informal inservice training and social events will enable university students to discuss their experiences and to offer suggestions. Networks will be established so that university students can assist each other, when they need to do so, to find answers for questions. There will be a need from time to time for university students to ask for help in answering a question, and there will be university teachers to whom they can turn for help when necessary. If the question is more general (like for example, 'How do I study for my advanced level on my own?') then the university student will refer the question to the project team.

The Use of the Internet by School Pupils

One recent UK paper (Corbett, 1997) describes a case study of a secondary comprehensive school which set up an installation with 18 networked workstations and a UNIX server, providing whole-class 24-hour access to the Internet. It describes how the Internet has been used as a powerful teaching and learning tool, including the exchange of information between fellow students around the world via web pages or e-mail, and asking experts direct questions by e-mail.

A low-cost model for educational networking of the 83,000 public US schools based on linking local computer bulletin boards at the school level (Hughes, 1993) maintains that the biggest cost of this model is not the hardware, software or network costs, but the learning demanded of teachers, administrators and the public. In the four years since this paper was published, there has been a big change in public awareness. While it still remains true that teachers may not use the Internet to best effect in their teaching for some time to come, PAL on the Internet, such as that offered by NRICH, is accessible to many pupils even without help from their teachers.

Mailing lists for school students such as NRICHtalk facilitate PAL, much of which is initiated by pupils themselves. An account of the KIDSPHERE mailing list, how the service is used by students and teachers around the world, and the value to the subscribers, is given in Carlitz (1995).

Comparison of PAL in the Classroom and PAL on the Internet

The title of this chapter is 'Casting the net: peer assisted learning on the Internet' and this title has been chosen to point to one of the essential differences from PAL in the classroom. When the 'traditional' PAL placement is organized the coordinator, teachers and volunteers know exactly which group of pupils are to be the subjects of the PAL. In the case of PAL on the Internet, the school students themselves have a choice in the matter. How this will affect the learning will be an important area for research and evaluation but it is conjectured that it will make a critical difference. This is not to suggest that either system is to be preferred to the other, or that one will supplant the other. Education at its best encourages students to want to learn and, when NRICH casts its net, a measure of the success of the project will be how much interest it sparks off and how many school students are caught up in a wave of enthusiasm and send in questions to be answered.

Another very significant difference is that the culture of the classroom will have a much smaller effect on peer teaching and learning than in the 'traditional' schemes. Studies of PAL in the classroom have shown that although many teachers can, and do, use PAL as an effective educational strategy, this is a much undervalued resource. A focus on classroom management skills and teaching strategies shows that only a minority of teachers have high levels of skill in working effectively with university student volunteers, using them to mediate between themselves and some of their pupils in order to achieve their teaching objectives (Beardon, 1996). In this paper Beardon explores the 'triangle of relationships' between the class teacher, peer teacher and learners and the strengths of the systems which lead to the most effective peer tutoring. The actual implementation is less effective in secondary schools than it is in primary, and overall it is shown that class teachers do not consistently make the best use of student tutors as a resource. For example, a study carried out by Beardon, involving 141 volunteers over three years from 1994 to 1997 in 25 schools, showed that, according to the volunteers, 24 per cent of teachers told them the learning objectives for the lessons, 39 per cent of teachers took the help of the volunteers into account when planning their lessons, 44 per cent of teachers made good use of the subject knowledge and skills offered by the volunteers, 55 per cent of teachers made the best possible use of the help of the volunteers, and in 61 per cent of the classes the teachers introduced the volunteers making it clear to the pupils that they were students from the university. These percentages, albeit recording the necessarily subjective judgements of the student volunteers, speak for themselves.

In electronic peer tutoring the triangle of relationships which must underpin PAL in the classroom is reduced to a two-way pattern. It has the advantage that there is an extra element of choice involved for both participants. As already mentioned, the school student first decides that he or she wants to ask a question. In the model which uses e-mail (rather than real-time video links) the university student can browse through the questions and choose the ones that he or she feels best equipped to answer. This in itself should lead to a better quality of explanation. Moreover the university student has time for reflection, and even for consulting others, before answering the question, which is not a regular feature of PAL in the classroom.

The personal contact and human relationship dimension will be different in the two contexts, and comparisons of this effect will also make interesting research studies. It is conjectured that the informal 'chatty' nature of the e-mail culture will go a long way to establishing a friendly relationship between peer teacher and learner, that school students will always know that the peer teacher is a university mathematics student, that supplementary questions relating to such aspects will be more frequent than in the classroom, and that there will be a comparable 'role-model' effect. School students will be able to find out first hand about studying mathematics at university and, for school students who do not live near a university, there will be a much bigger impact. In the case of the real-time video links the personal contact will feel closer and interaction will be more spontaneous and more like PAL in the classroom.

Conclusion

This chapter has described PAL on the Internet in relation to a project that has more claim to potential than proven achievement. However, a careful study has been made of the best ways to develop and retain the advantages of an existing PAL scheme, extending it to use the electronic medium, and conjectures have been offered, all in the expectation that cooperation and the sharing of ideas will assist others in setting up and evaluating similar schemes.

Address for correspondence: Mrs L A Beardon, University of Cambridge, Department of Education, 17 Trumpington Street, Cambridge CB2 1QA. Tel. 01223 336282. Fax 01223 332894. e-mail LAB11@cam.ac.uk

Chapter 15

MENTORING GIFTED PUPILS

Joan Freeman

Mentoring provides a specialized form of educational help for gifted pupils whose special educational needs cannot be met in school. This may be when the pupils need a broader and more advanced approach than the school can provide, in the identification of unrealized gifted potential, in realizing creativity in high-achieving school learners, helping those of high potential who are underachieving, those who have been accelerated in their education, and the encouragement of the lifelong continuation of gifts. Students in tertiary education are particularly suitable for this, particularly from the emotional point of view. Organizing mentoring calls for care in matching, timing, emotional concerns, communication and evaluation.

Introduction

Mentoring provides a focused form of enriched education for gifted pupils whose learning needs cannot always be met within the normal school system. The gifted are defined here as those who either demonstrate exceptionally high-level performance, whether across a range of endeavours or in a limited field, and those whose potential for this has not yet been seen. This has to be judged in comparison with others of similar age, experience and opportunities. Aptitudes may range across different areas, such as intellectual, artistic, creative and physical abilities, or be limited to one or two (Freeman, 1997a).

Distinguishing high-level potential – as distinct from production – is particularly difficult because of the wide variety and changing nature of human abilities as they develop. Gifted children, who are 'merely' working at above average level are easily missed. To fulfil high-level potential to a level of excellence in any area, a child needs the means to develop, which not only includes the material to work with, but a focused and challenging education for which mentoring can be essential.

The arguments about precise definitions and the identification of such children have been active for over half a century, and will doubtless continue. Consequently, there are perhaps 100 definitions of 'giftedness' around, almost all of which refer to children's precocity, either in psychological constructs, such as intelligence and creativity, but more usually as high marks in school subjects (Hany, 1993). In formal school education, for example, social or business talents are rarely considered, and physical and artistic prowess is frequently seen as an inborn talent which merely has to be honed into excellence by practice.

IQ tests can neither distinguish the processes of learning and thinking nor predict creativity (Cropley, 1995), and because they only measure a narrow band of intellectual behaviour they cannot predict other aspects of life, such as what career a person is likely to follow or how individuals will cope in social situations. In fact, drive and energy have often been found to be relatively more predictive of life success in high-IQ children (eg, Albert, 1992; Holahan and Sears, 1995; Schaie, 1996; Subotnik *et al.*, 1993).

To some extent, the way a very able child is identified depends on what is being looked for: whether it is academic excellence for education, innovation for business, or solving paper-and-pencil puzzles for an IQ club. However, it is educationally more productive (and more scientific) in searching for high-level potential to look at the dynamic interaction between individuals and their opportunities for learning; to recognize achievement within the context of what each has available to learn with. If gifted pupils are only to receive their educational help from school this will restrict the quality and variety of what they can achieve. The student mentor can helped to broaden the pupils' viewpoint, not only in the subject selected for expansion of learning, but in areas that the school may not have considered.

Research shows that the highly able are not a homogeneous group, whether in terms of learning style, creativity, speed of development or social behaviour. Student mentors working with gifted children would be particularly valuable in enabling individual pupils to see ahead, and to provide the encouragement and sense of identity that teachers and parents cannot.

Although mentoring has been known in business, the arts, and in vocational education for many years, it is not usual in the school context. The mentoring of gifted pupils is a particularly appropriate activity for older students in tertiary education, many of whom are likely to have been gifted pupils themselves and so can understand the special problems that may arise. In addition, because they are not distant in age and experience they are able to set up a bond of sharing exploration within the subject area in a learning partnership that is beneficial to both.

The Special Value of Student Mentoring of the Gifted

Gifted pupils may need more than school can provide

Schools are institutions run for the benefit of the majority and it is sometimes difficult for them to provide the individual attention that a member of a minority such as the gifted may require. Over and over again, research shows that the child's own interests are an excellent and often neglected indicator of future adult attainment (eg, Hany, 1996); yet teachers are so heavily occupied that they are not always able to discover those interests nor to provide the time and energy to help individuals to develop them.

In a survey of the research on prediction, Trost (1993) calculated that less than half of 'what makes excellence' can be accounted for by measurements and observations in childhood. Although intelligence and other cognitive factors appeared to be the most reliable indicators, given a high-level of aptitude the key to future success lies in keenness and dedication. Rich educational circumstances must be present to promote the intrinsic motivation that is vital for outstanding progress in the school years; it goes with curiosity and love of learning which Renzulli (1995) calls 'task commitment'. Student mentors can become closer than can teachers to individual pupils, and so guide them to develop what they are keen to work at, separately from the school curriculum. Studies of mentoring in high school programmes for the gifted emphasize the importance of presenting gifted pupils with a variety of 'hands-on' experiences (Zorman, 1995).

An example of such work takes place at the Technological Centre for the Galilee, dedicated to the study of ecology, that uses mentoring to achieve extremely high pupil achievement. The scientists work with the local comprehensive school, from which teenage boys and girls have been invited over the past 18 years to work on their own projects. They are not selected in any way. The centre has the specific aim of developing scientific thinking, using projects such as the effects of magnesium on plants, cultivating wild mushrooms or the effects of hormones on fish reproduction. The youngsters design and do original work to which there are neither answers nor (often) methods, such as aspects of Ph, then continue to work with the data at school. The teenager has to prepare and write a proposal, which is discussed with the mentor (usually a PhD student) before he or she can begin, either alone or in a group. Each one has to be able to work on a computer, eventually to summarize and provide a dissertation. The organizer says that by the time the children leave at 18, some are better than MScs.

Mentoring can help identify creative potential which is not school-style

Some psychologists, such as Eysenck (1995) find that a high IQ score is at the root of all creative genius, but others that creative success cannot be separated from social forces, such as encouragement and motivation. Kaufman and Peters (1992), in their follow-up of American Presidential Scholars, found that the only creative way in which those individuals used their vast memory banks was as props for their self-esteem! However, they also found that 58 per cent of them reported that it was mentors who gave them the support to reach that pinnacle.

Creative thinking involves emotion and personality, including enough confidence and courage to consider new approaches to problems, rather than hiding in the security of familiar and accepted ways of thinking. The conflict for the high school achiever is between the need for emotional control for academic excellence and that of a more free and open-minded approach needed for creative endeavour. Youngsters who were extremely successful academically were found to be creatively inhibited because of the narrow focus and pressure of their school education (Freeman, 1991, 1995). In her 14-year comparison study of gifted and non-gifted children, Freeman found that the former were sometimes inhibited in their creativity by the heavy load of academic work they were obliged to do to reach university. Some of the gifted young people felt this omission strongly, most noticeably the boys and the scientists, who were often the most deprived in that way.

Indeed, Sternberg and Lubart (1995) found that the high-IQ student often has considerable problems in producing original insightful ideas. More than 200 teenagers in the Yale summer programme were divided via Sternberg's Triarchic Theory of Intelligence into 'high analytics', 'high creatives' and 'high practicals' on the criterion of their scores in a given ability being outstandingly better than those for other abilities. These groups were compared with a balanced-gifted group (equally high in all three areas) and a balanced-above-average control group. All the young people took a very challenging college-level psychology course, at the close of which they were assessed for basic (traditional) recall, analysis, creative use and practical use. The high analytics – those who had often been identified as gifted by IQ – did worst of all on the creativity tests. The authors concluded that these pupils had rarely been asked to make a creative effort, but had conformed to expectations of being good scholars by using memory to gain high marks. In agreement, investigations into American prize-winners in both arts and sciences showed that a very high intelligence was not always necessary for outstanding results – sheer memory was much more useful (Walberg, 1995).

The problem for teachers is to enable intellectually gifted pupils, who have the ability to achieve top grades in examinations, to keep a playful, creative approach to their work and general outlook. An environment in which the exceptionally able child can prosper all round must be balanced, implying enough time with other people to make good social relationships and develop interests outside study areas. Mentors can make all the difference.

The gifted who are underachieving can be helped through mentoring

Gifted pupils may not succeed at school for two main reasons – emotional problems or inadequate provision of learning materials – as indeed is the case with any child. But in addition, they may find a mismatch of thinking styles between instruction and learning style. West (1991) examined the lives of ten famous visual thinkers, including Einstein, Edison and Churchill, all of whom had underachieved at school. He presented research which indicated that the visually talented can encounter particular learning problems in a normal classroom where teaching is linear, one fact following another in a specified order.

Although teacher judgement of giftedness is not reliable, naturally their judgements will affect their expectations and treatment of pupils, such as in the organization of learning groups and selection for examinations, which will in turn affect the way the pupils react to education. Teachers' personal attitudes towards the very able vary greatly; some feel resentment while others overestimate their all-round abilities (Chyriwsky and Kennard, 1997; Ojanen and Freeman, 1994). Although teachers have been found to judge the highly able consistently, in that they will pick the same kind of children (Hany, 1993), the relationship of those judgements to objective measures varies considerably. Bennet *et al.* (1984:215), found that 40 per cent of potential high achievers had been underestimated by their teachers. In Southport, Tempest (1974) found that out of 72 6-year-olds identified by their teachers as gifted, only 24 had IQs of 127 or above and seven had IQs of under 110 – but two children with reading ages six years in advance were not nominated as gifted.

Teachers are not always helped by checklists of the supposed characteristics of the gifted, which are widely varied. Some of the items can be confusing, many being socio-cultural rather then specific to aptitude. A child asking a lot of questions, for example, can either be seen as gifted or as attention-seeking, or perhaps lives in a home where questioning is encouraged rather than one where children are encouraged to work things out for themselves. It would be important for mentors to work with underachieving potentially able pupils to help them overcome their problems, not only in a counselling manner but in terms of subject matter and expanding outlooks.

Mentors assigned to possibly bright pupils who may be underachieving eg, the culturally disadvantaged, those with incorrect gender expectations (Freeman, 1996), or emotional problems at home, are better placed than teachers to give the personal attention and inspiration needed to lift a pupil's self-concept and in broadening horizons and possibilities allow the untapped high-level potential to flourish.

The gifted who are accelerated can be helped through mentoring

Moving pupils up by a year or more beyond their age group is something which only happens to high-achieving pupils, and it can bring emotional problems. In a review of American research on emotional development of the accelerated gifted, Cornell *et al.* (1991:91) concluded that 'few authors have examined socio-emotional adjustment with adequate psychological measures', and few have looked at the long-term effects. No data have emerged from any study to indicate which students will fare well in early college entrance programmes. There are many different types of acceleration, of which mentoring, working with an expert in the field, can be one form.

The major problem with grade-skipping, the most common procedure, is that the child 'hurried' on in that way may be not be either physically or emotionally mature enough to fit in socially with the rest of the class. Intellectually, certain subject areas (such as language) require the appropriate life experiences that come with age, and without these the necessary conceptual development may be lacking. Physically, a 4-year-old is not as adept as a 5-year-old, for instance, and particularly for grade-skipped boys, their apparently late physical development encourages the 'little professor' image as being hopeless at everything which is not school-learning (or music). The role of the mentor with accelerated pupils is to offer a companion/guide who is working on the same lines and who understands the emotional and intellectual problems of learning at a level beyond age-peers.

To encourage the life-long continuation of gifts

Evidence from follow-up studies shows that high marks in school do not provide a reliable indicator of adult careers – teachers and academics excepted (Holahan and Sears, 1995; Subotnik *et al.*, 1993)! The gifted child does not necessarily become the gifted adult. Giftedness is a continuous developmental phenomenon that can rise – and fall – over time: 'late bloomers' do exist and can be missed if identification is not continuous (Gottfried *et al.*, 1994).

Overall, schools appear to have relatively less effect on the fulfilment of gifted potential than that of average ability children, possibly because they do not, on the whole, focus on the development of their special gifts. In addition, because precocity is the usual identifying feature of young gifted children it is probably the reason for its later apparent loss, often called 'burn out', which is usually due to the others catching up. It is as though a boy is two years in advance for height at 12 and becomes known as very tall, but because most others have a later growth spurt he ends up just a little taller than the average man. The Goertzels' (1978) study of 317 eminent people found that two-thirds of them were not in any way precocious, and Gardner's (1993) study of seven world-changers found that even by the age of 20 only Picasso's future world status was apparent.

Mentors can provide the stability and continuity that pupils may need to continue functioning at an exceptionally high level. This foundation is essential if the outcomes of early precocity are to be continued in a life-span perspective. But without clarity in such aims, attempts at mentoring may not always be successful.

Specific Mentoring Concerns with Gifted Pupils

Most student mentoring of schoolchildren is aimed at raising standards, often in high-risk and underachieving populations. Mentoring pupils who are already functioning at a higher level of learning is different.

To begin with, the mentor should be aware that the gifted pupil can comprehend the subject area in a greater depth and breadth, and at a faster pace, than most others of the same age. Because of their exceptional advancement a gifted child could benefit from mentoring at a younger age than others (Zorman, 1995). There are sometimes false assumptions about these pupils, for example that a gifted child is equally able all-round, which can be confusing because of the sometimes unbalanced or 'dysynchronous' learning of many such children (Terassier, 1985).

A highly motivated youngster who is keen to pursue a chosen path of learning may need help in deciding whether to broaden their interests or focus on one area for long-term excellence. The mentor also has to know that gifted children at different stages will show passionate interest in certain areas that may not last (Winner, 1996), so that time to be spent on the child's current passion may have to be negotiated! Several American universities (eg, Columbia, William and Mary College) have developed student mentoring programmes for gifted pupils that often attempt to broaden pupil outlooks by integrating the classroom and the community, many culminating in a product, such as a public exhibition of work. Evaluation via self-reports (eg, Beck, 1989) found that participants rated such programmes more highly for the promotion of life-skills than subject work.

Most student mentoring of the gifted pupil takes place in the United States. This means that most information about mentoring is based on American educational systems and standards, which may not be entirely appropriate for other countries. For example, how teachers perceive the gifted and consequently the proportions they identify has been seen to vary considerably between different cultures. German teachers have been found to estimate 3.5 per cent of children as gifted, Americans 6.4 per cent and Indonesians 17.4 per cent (Dahme, 1996). Even within the USA, percentages of the child population identified as gifted vary between 5 and 10 per cent across the states (OERI, 1993). What is more, in the USA, whole-class mixed-ability teaching is normal, and in fact in most states ability or interest grouping is actually prohibited. This is countered to some extent by special programmes; even by '1990, 38 states served more than 2 million gifted students', and since then 'the number of programmes for gifted and talented youngsters has grown substantially' (OERI, 1993:iii). In an overview of gifted American pupils' attitudes to school, Winner (1996) is clear that they are often dismissive of what is available to them, and in order to progress to excellence they must find mentors and teachers outside, especially in art and music.

In such circumstances mentoring can provide a lifeline for children whose needs cannot be met in the ordinary school. Many who won the Westinghouse Talent Search had done their work out of school in a hospital or university library (Subotnik, 1988). Usually a university teacher or laboratory supervisor acted as a mentor. Many children who go to the large summer camps for the gifted report that the mentors they found there were their most valuable resource (Durden and Tangherlini, 1993).

In a review of mentoring for the gifted, Zorman (1995) points out that in almost all cases where individuals reached the heights of creative achievement they received intellectual and spiritual support from another individual who served as a mentor. This is true even at the highest levels: Zuckerman (1983) found that about half the Nobel laureates she studied had had another laureate as a mentor. Charles Darwin had just such a special relationship of shared intellectual passion with his tutor at Cambridge. The results of a 22-year follow-up of 220 mentored and non-mentored young adults by Torrance (1984) indicated that the mentored subjects had reached significantly higher levels of education. Werner (1989) too found in a similar study of 698 children in Hawaii that the ones who achieved at an exceptional level, even those at high risk, had had the support of a mentor. In retrospective studies, both Torrance and Pizzini (1985) have shown that at times when the gifted individual met barriers on the road to achievement it was their mentors who gave them the encouragement to keep going.

Choosing the Student Mentor

The most difficult challenge in all mentoring is finding the right match between the people involved. Mentoring the gifted calls for special understanding of how it is to be gifted, and the ability to help these special children. One can use Goodlad's (1997) analogy of map-reading as an example of how to learn: how would a mentor deal with a future cartographer who can already use a map with enthusiasm and expertise far in advance of age-peers?

For the gifted pupil, more than one mentor may be needed to attend to different aspects of a subject area. There is also the need for the mentor to be aware of any embryonic jealousy, competitiveness and frustration with regard to a gifted protégé. This is particularly important for student mentors because of the short age difference between them and the pupils, and their possible lack of experience outside education. Successful student mentors for mathematically gifted pupils (Stanley *et al.*, 1990) were themselves found to be extremely talented and had experienced mentoring.

Gifted children can act as peer-mentors, for example, in a creative writing project or the learning of computer languages. It provides them with the opportunity to take responsibility, to assess their own cognitive as well as interpersonal skills. The same rules would hold for them – the peer-mentor must be able to present a valid, honest critique at the end of what has been done together, both as a teacher specialist and as a friend. However, there is a danger in peer-mentoring that advanced learners may be exploited, as Freeman (1991) found. Instead of spending time on their own learning they are obliged to help others who are less able or advanced. It must be clear that the peer-mentor really wants to play that role and does not feel coerced and resentful.

Ideally, the student's teaching style and the pupil's learning style should be compatible: some mentors might use a gentle, encouraging style, while others might hold highly idiosyncratic views about the teaching process influenced by their own not too distant experiences in school.

Mentoring and counselling to improve self-esteem have been found to be effective in promoting a more realistic acceptance by gifted girls of their abilities (Arnold and Subotnik, 1994), notably in helping them to integrate family and careers (Beck, 1989). Beck also found that boys often look for other males as mentors, and girls for a female model who can help them take risks and work independently. However, it is more difficult for gifted girls to find a mentor, as women experts are less easily found, especially in the sciences. Boys generally prefer a mentor who is a skilled expert, hard working and able to motivate and prod them, whereas girls generally prefer one who encourages and praises, acts as a friend, instils confidence and inspires them. Interestingly, the female Presidential Scholars who had received mentoring were similar in their salaries to the males, whereas those without mentoring had lower salaries than the males.

Of the American Presidential Scholars, 66 per cent said that their most valuable mentoring came from teachers, at either high school or graduate level, although teacher-mentors could sometimes set unreasonably high standards (Kaufman *et al.*, 1986). For the gifted who may have much less need of classroom teaching, mentoring calls for some teacher accommodation, so that pupils can leave their classes occasionally to work with their mentors. Mentoring, though, can also be done before school, during the lunch-break, or (more usually) after school. A teacher might continue the work of the mentor for keen pupils after school, or a specialist teacher could extend the mentoring role to a small-group project, such as the production of a play.

Specific Educational Aspects of Mentoring the Gifted Pupil

- *Modelling*. Student mentor offers the protégé the mentor's personality and level of skill or knowledge with which to identify.
- *Keeping tradition*. Mentors not only encourage the development of a knowledge base, but also pass on the processes of acquiring it, including curiosity, and cultural thinking about the area. This is what many high achievers have great need of as the foundations for their future work.
- *Offering direction*. A good mentor will help the gifted pupil to develop his or her own plans for the future and ways of achieving them. For the multi-talented this can be a considerable problem.
- *Suggesting a new language*. The gifted pupils are offered new ways to think about reality: their frame of reference may expand to take on

extra meanings, as they learn to look at familiar problems in new ways.

- *Providing a mirror.* The mentoring relationship should expand pupil awareness of the self through honest feedback, allowing them to analyse their thinking and their own development. This is something the high achiever may not have time to do in the scramble for high marks.

Emotional Aspects of Mentoring the Gifted

The mentor must be willing to share, listen, care, encourage, and accept the protégé's mistakes – especially important for some of the many pressured-to-be-perfect gifted pupils – and act as a role model. There are special problems of other people's attitudes towards them which the gifted encounter in being different (Deslisle, 1992; Freeman, 1991, 1997b).

Some student mentors (who are themselves learning the job of student) may find it difficult to relinquish their domain over a keen and highly able protégé who has stretched the limit of their ability to intellectually nurture and assist. This problem has even been found with mentors of little children (Shore, 1995). But when the relationship has reached a point of diminishing returns it must end or it will stagnate. Often, though, the gifted and their mentors keep up long-term informal contact (Zorman, 1995).

The gifted protégé's potential development is very dependent on self-esteem, which can be put at risk when requests for advice are met in a sneering or hostile way. But it is also threatened if advice from the mentor is constant and unsolicited, possibly to meet their own psychological needs. Mentors should realize that any rejection of their ideas by bright youngsters with ideas of their own should not be taken personally.

Gifted pupils can be keen and demanding, risking overusing the mentor's time and good will. However, the mentor should always be positive and supportive, and continually reinforce the confidential nature of the relationship. Even for the keenest protégé's the contract should include time spent in other areas of life. The mentor can offer to support other matters concerned with administration, such as making arrangements for visits, but responsibilities that belong to the evaluator or others should not be taken over.

Ways of Starting up Student Mentoring for Gifted Pupils

- Start small, with a few pilot projects.
- Build a resource file of possible mentors through local institutes of

tertiary education. In finding good mentors, it is important to describe what is expected to everyone involved, and to acknowledge the existence of other support, such as extra classes that the pupil may be attending.

- The integrity of the mentor in this position of trust is vital: it may well be necessary for schools to obtain references before a mentor starts, while the activities must be monitored by some other responsible adult, preferably in the school.
- Allow enough time for administrating, finding, thanking, travelling, discussing, evaluating, and so on; this is likely to be much more than expected.
- Arrange it so that the organizer can communicate to all interested persons. Keep copies of all written and verbal communications. Important notices should be posted to all concerned.
- A volunteer, probably the teacher whose idea it was to start the scheme, should explain to staff, parents, and students what mentoring is and why it is particularly beneficial to bright pupils.
- It is important to be flexible in developing a mentoring scheme so that other staff members will become convinced of its value for pupils who they may feel are already advantaged.

Overview

The essence of mentoring gifted pupils is to help them realize their considerable potential, not only at school but for the rest of their lives. Here are three clear aims for mentors of gifted pupils:

1. Think independently to promote higher-level thinking and problem-solving.
2. Develop profound worthwhile interests.
3. Develop originality, initiative and self-direction.

The assistance of older student mentors would be of great practical help and, with preparation, welcomed by most schools. The care with which a student mentoring scheme for the gifted (and potentially gifted) is set up for any school or education authority is not only likely to affect the future lives of the pupil participants, but because of their outstanding potential it may well affect all our lives in their future productions.

Mentoring gifted pupils

Address for correspondence: Professor Joan Freeman, School of Lifelong Learning and Education, Middlesex University, Trent Park, Bramley Road, London N14 4YZ. e-mail J.Freeman@mdx.ac.uk

PART G: MAKING IT HAPPEN: PRACTICAL GUIDES TO ACTION

Chapter 16

A FOUR-STAGE MENTORING MODEL THAT WORKS

Joseph Pascarelli

A four-stage mentoring schema, part of a national action research initiative, has been used in designing and installing a variety of youth mentoring programmes in several states, higher education institutions, as well as local school communities. Four stages of mentoring – initiation, cultivation, transformation and separation – describe the development and growth of protégé from a state of dependence and low self-confidence to one of autonomy and self-reliance. Specific skills and competencies of mentors are identified along with descriptions of effective behaviours that mentors use to empower youth.

In the United States, we are becoming increasingly aware of the extraordinary cravings of today's youth for caring, belonging, connectedness and meaning and, as a result, are reinventing mentoring – a renaissance of one of the oldest natural-support relationships dating back to the Greeks. Sociocultural changes that include diminishing family roles, lack of positive social networks, the transfer of family caretaking responsibilities to already overburdened schools, and lack of community resources for youth all point more and more to the need for providing youth with more significant others in their lives to guide, support, coach and, in some cases, simply to mentally and physically attend. These needs are universal and do not confine themselves to any one geographical region or one specific demographic or economic population. Youth need older youth and adults in their lives to support and nurture healthy development and to provide the connection that links one generation to the next.

New models are emerging on state-wide, regional and school/community levels inviting older students, community members, professionals, representatives from the business sectors, and others to become mentors – to spend approximately an hour or so each week for a year or a year and a half interacting with a young person around various themes: career interests, tutoring needs, hobbies, and simply relating and caring. Regardless of the particular theme that brings together the mentor and protégé, we are learning that these powerful relationships have significant impact in helping youth find a place in the world, a purpose for being, and a belief in self.

A Research Agenda

The initiative was launched as an action research project that began with formal inquiry (field studies) into the nature of mentoring programmes that existed in New York City and 14 other cities and their surrounding metropolitan areas throughout the state of New York. Locally recognized, successful mentoring programmes were identified and a randomly selected group of programme coordinators, mentors and protégés were interviewed. Among the programmes identified were those that served special populations of both mentors and protégés (ie, Hispanics, young women, potential early school leavers, homeless youth, youth with disabilities, etc). From these interviews, common characteristics of the programmes, the mentors and protégés, and their interactions and relationships were identified and plotted. A two-tiered process was used. Initially, the researchers identified characteristics common to all programmes and then selected a cluster for in-depth analysis (case studies).

At the same time, a formal and extensive literature search was conducted that resulted in a knowledge synthesis product entitled, 'Mentoring: a journey not a destination' (Lorentz and Pascarelli, 1988). The study was multi-disciplinary and addressed the fields of education, psychology and anthropology, including the special areas of adult learning and systems development.

Findings from both the field studies of mentoring practices and the knowledge synthesis served as the foundation for conceptualizing the four-stage mentoring schema presented in this chapter and for developing a training design prototype implemented in New York State. The schema and training prototype were adopted by the state-level policy advisory board of the New York State Mentoring Programme, comprised of a collection of professionals from education (early childhood through higher education), youth-oriented social service agencies, as well as from the business, government and religious sectors.

Replication, including adaptations of the training and implementation model, have occurred in the Virgin Islands (The Governor's Youth Mentoring Programme), the state of Oregon (The Oregon National Guard Mentoring Programme), and in schools and educational communities in other regions of the country. These regions represented a range of demographic settings (eg, urban, suburban and rural), as well as diverse and special focus groups.

Various assessment methodologies have been used to measure both process outcomes (the delivery of the mentoring programmes) and impact (social and academic development of the protégés). Specific to this chapter, information has been gathered on barriers and enhancements to student growth and include pre- and post-surveys and feedback forms completed by protégés and mentors, school-based data (ie, attendance, grades, etc), teacher assessment information (ie, homework completion, classroom attentiveness, etc), and interviews and case studies conducted with both protégés and mentors.

All programmes have stemmed from the collaboration of schools, colleges and universities and sectors of the broader communities. In most instances, they were mentoring systems whose elements included: conducting a formal action research study focusing on local contexts; designing and developing a mentor training system; establishing policies and infrastructures; acquiring human and materials resources; creating collaborative arrangements; identifying and matching mentors and protégés; coordinating interactions; providing assistance and training; and assessing impact.

Central to all of this, however, have been three core questions that guided the overall initiative. They were:

1. Since the mentoring relationships moved from protégé dependency to autonomy and greater self-reliance, could this process be described in discrete and developmental stages?
2. If so, were there certain skills, competencies and behaviours that were used by successful mentors at various stages that could contribute to the knowledge base on effective mentoring?
3. Further, if these could be identified, did they have potential to frame a training programme for mentors that would increase the likelihood of quality mentoring relationships and also be used to describe the mentoring process to others involved in all other aspects of installing these programmes?

Some Key Learnings

Returning, then, to the knowledge synthesis mentioned earlier and the main focus of this chapter, initial research findings suggested that significant growth could be traced throughout a mentoring relationship and this growth could be observed and measured by an increased ability to solve problems, to make responsible decisions, to consider values, choices and consequences before taking action, and to stand up for beliefs. Increased self-confidence and ego strength lead to a healthy sense of being. The protégé, having experienced a solid mentoring relationship, is more likely to act on beliefs, assess actions, and project into other situations as a result of the support provided by a mentor.

In all of this, a mentor functions as a guide and supporter, establishing trust and demonstrating empathic understanding while, at the same time, introducing new and often contradictory ideas and helping the protégé develop a positive sense of the future (Levinson *et al.*, 1978). The mentor builds on the skills, competencies and talents of the protégé rather than attempting to be a problem-solver with a solution in search of a problem, a fix-it person, or a formal teacher. The mentor engages in restrained guidance, gentle but firm nudging, and reflective feedback while focusing on the protégé's activities in plotting, reflecting and acting in responsible and self-directed ways (Daloz, 1986).

Mentoring is a natural process grounded in the belief of human potential. Temporal in nature, it is based on trust, mutual attraction, enjoyment in talking together, attentive appreciation of each other's ideas and thinking, mutual respect for the autonomy of both the mentor and protégé, and is sustained by excitement and affirmation of both parties (Haensly, 1989).

Often a proactive role, a mentor supports a protégé not just through intensive listening but also by testing the protégé in different environments and different activities whether the basis of the mentoring relationship is career interest, hobbies, tutoring, or simple caring and friendship. The mentor intends to provide the protégé with the skills necessary for self-discovery. A sound mentoring relationship helps the protégé learn to build networks in areas of interest or concern and this skill is used to develop lifelong connections with people and environments.

The challenge of a mentor is to help the protégé turn experiences into knowledge that can, in turn, be used for growth and action. This is an iterative process which is anchored in explicit demonstrations of effective two-way communication, respect for the autonomy of the individuals, and mutual trust. The mentor's primary responsibility is to empower the protégé to gain a fuller sense of plotting a life map and the capability for autonomous, responsible action. This map must value those parts of the self calling for connectedness and relationship; it must indicate landmarks, point out dangers, suggest possible routes and destinations, but leave the walking to the individual (the responsibility of the self to construct the map) (Levinson *et al.*, 1978).

Mentors, research findings revealed, grow and obtain a sense of fulfilment, a renewed sense of purpose and a deeper insight into the self. To give to another – to care, support and nurture the growth of another – is indeed self-growth. Mentors trust and believe in human potential and are able to translate these values into actions by becoming mentors. Many assume the role so they can give back to society – to provide others with the kind of support they themselves received at certain life stages. Others want to help protégés acquire solid values having to do with learning, working, and having a purpose in life. Erikson (1950) labels this as a condition of generativity – the realization of the continuity of life and the flow of generations. Still others simply (but profoundly) wish to 'be there' to encourage and empower. There is a creed that describes their message to protégés:

> I am here for you.
> I believe in you.
> I will not let you fail.
> You have the power.
>
> (Pascarelli, 1991)

The inspiration for this creed emerged as a result of identifying and adapting the four-stage conceptual schema that is described in the next section of this chapter. The schema eventually became the basis for designing and implementing mentor training systems, including training and development events in the states and several school/communities, higher education environs, and school/business sectors identified earlier in this chapter – continually being refined and adapted to each of the multiple contexts in which mentoring initiatives were installed.

The Developmental Stages of Mentoring

It is important in presenting the schema to recognize that, although it is described in discrete, normative stages, and as a linear system, the mentoring relationships themselves are indeed dynamic, episodic and non-linear. It is intended to provide an understanding of a complex phenomenon and not a prescribed, closed developmental path.

The contributions of Kram (1980) and Phillips-Jones (1982) have been most useful in framing the four-stage schema that describes the journey of the protégé growing from a state of dependence that constrains and inhibits potential, through a set of experiences that develop certain skills, attitudes and/or habits, and finally to a state of responsibility, autonomy and independence. The conceptual model identifies four developmental stages: initiation, cultivation, transformation, and separation (see Figure 16.1).

Initiation

The *initiation* stage of a mentoring relationship consists of a set of experiences during which mentor and protégé are discovering mutual attractions – including each other, enjoying talking together – attentive appreciation of each other's ideas and thinking, and learning about each other's interests. This is the 'checking-out' stage: the protégé sensing experience, knowledge and authenticity; the mentor, a chance to influence, a willingness to connect, and the potential of fulfilment. The specialness of the relationship emerges with the protégé realizing that he or she has been chosen by the mentor while the mentor recognizes the unique opportunity to connect and be valued by helping the protégé make meaning of his or her experiences (Klopf and Harrison, 1982).

Mentors during this early stage need to focus on certain skills and competencies. Among the key ones are respect, warmth, genuineness, being 'for' the protégé, and entering the protégé's frame of reference. Respect is demonstrated by actively attending and listening, being open to learning, regarding the protégé as unique, and being inviting and acknowledging as contrasted with evaluating, discounting, placating, or projecting boredom.

The communication of warmth is primarily non-verbal – smiling, close proximity, eye contact, natural and pleasant tone of voice, positive head nods, and body movement (eg, leaning in, facial expression congruent with content of conversation). Aloofness, 'canned warmth', or inappropriately intimate warmth will be read by the protégé as artificial, patronizing, or insincere.

A mentor must be natural or genuine – behaving in spontaneous, open and non-defensive ways. There is a need to be able to express thoughts and feelings without creating filters between mentor and the protégé, never trying to control or manipulate. The mentor needs to drop external roles and enter into a kind of rolelessness.

Being 'for' the protégé in a non-sentimental but caring way will not only increase communication but will also demonstrate to the protégé that the mentor is ready, centred and valuing the interaction. A mentor ensures that

INITIATION	CULTIVATION	TRANSFORMATION	SEPARATION
	MENTOR'S CREED		
I am here for you	I believe in you	I will not let you fail	You have the power
	SELECTED SKILLS AND COMPETENCIES		
◆ Respect ◆ Warmth ◆ Genuineness ◆ Being 'for' the protégé ◆ Entering the protégé's frame of reference	◆ Facilitative responses ◆ Empathy ◆ Advice-giving ◆ Self-disclosure	◆ Providing feedback ◆ Exploring the immediacy of the relationship ◆ Goal-setting ◆ Critiquing	◆ Embracing ◆ Integrating ◆ Empowering

Figure 16.1 Stages of the mentoring relationship

few distractions or interruptions occur during meetings, that no signs of apathy or wanting to leave occur, and that he or she places their body to make themselves present to the protégé. Physical attending – using eye contact and fixed focus, facing the protégé free of blockages (eg, tables, desks), and maintaining a natural tone and well-paced voice – are all effective.

The beginning of empathic understanding occurs during this early stage as the mentor tries to move from seeing the world from one perspective to shifting to the lens of the protégé. This does not occur easily but rather unfolds as the protégé's world, perspective and ideas are explored. The mentor must be clear on not stereotyping or ascribing attributes to the protégé based on generalizations made about a peer group. The uniqueness of the protégé's context and frame of reference must be underscored. In this case, entering the protégé's frame of reference marks the first growth experience for the mentor in gathering information and seeking to understand the protégé's attitudes and positions. This can best be accomplished if both mentor and protégé have a common experience and are able to share reactions with each other.

Initial bonding occurs fairly quickly during this stage, usually after the first few meetings. Of course, there are cases in which the matching does not work – interactions are guarded, the protégé is reluctant and perhaps resentful, or the mentor becomes frustrated. In such cases, the relationship should be terminated; it is not worth pursuing. Mentoring relationships must remain voluntary; both the mentor and protégé must navigate the prospective relationship. Mentors cannot be concerned with their own egos and protégés must be honest, open and non-exploitative. The relationship must be comfortable and grounded in connectedness.

Cultivation

The *cultivation* stage is marked by opportunities for the mentor to encourage, affirm and accept the views of the protégé. The mentor intentionally builds on the strengths of protégés – skills, competencies, talents and interests – and, very sparingly, shares his or her own. The protégé recognizes being viewed and valued in a new light with another human with whom there is no history – being accepted by who the individual is rather than what the individual has done. In a more free environment of trust and respect, the protégé can share dilemmas, probe for understanding, and request reactions and feedback. The mentor is stimulated and feels validated and valued.

The selected key competencies in this model are facilitative responses, empathy, advice-giving and self-disclosure. Mentors, at this stage, must recognize that they are not problem-solvers, teachers, or surrogate parents. Their role is to illuminate issues, lead the protégé through critical analyses of situations, and help the protégé look at options, consequences and solutions. They encourage protégés in curiosity and creativity to view the world from multiple perspectives, and to learn, in short, that there is usually 'more than one right answer'. This is accomplished through the use of the mentor's facilitative responses. The mentor actively listens and communicates back the content and tone of the protégé's messages with accuracy and equal intensity. At the same time, the mentor synthesizes the communication and makes mental notes of important items or hunches for future use. The test here is to avoid judging, imposing, confronting and most of all dominating.

Part of facilitative response behaviours is the demonstration of empathy. This is not only being able to understand the protégé's experiences, but also to be able to 'tune in' to emotions associated with the experiences. The protégé needs to know that the mentor understands beyond the level of the immediate response, that underlying feelings are identified on the affective level of the mentor. The protégé in these instances often validates the mentor, thereby permitting the mentor to move beyond the immediacy of the situation.

Advice-giving needs to be addressed cautiously. The temptation to give direct answers and solutions, to volunteer opinions too quickly, to share experiences too early is high, and must be curbed. Too-early responses will either shut down the interaction or provide the protégé with the 'mentor's solution' and foster dependency. Advice-giving, therefore, must first be appropriate, concrete and confirming. This is a mutual learning experience and often includes both mentor and protégé working collaboratively as partners, but for the mentor always with a preoccupation of keeping the protégé at the centre of decision-making and growth.

The focus of all mentoring interactions must remain on the protégé. Mentors seldom engage in 'I' statements or use their experiences as 'lessons' for the protégé. This will deflect from the value of the protégé's experience and hinder the growth journey. Of course, when relevant to the protégé's interests and concerns, or if used to reveal the mentor's uniqueness, self-disclosure may be helpful in sustaining the interaction. Effective mentors do not meet their protégés with masks; they are easy to get to know.

Transformation

The *transformation* stage is marked with taking risks and translating intentions, beliefs and feelings into action. The protégé begins to take responsibilities for actions, to test assumptions, and to reflect with the mentor on actions taken. The protégé moves toward increased autonomy and self-confidence and begins to increase ego-strength and belief in self. Key competencies include providing feedback, exploring the immediacy of the relationship, goal-setting and critiquing.

Providing feedback enhances growth and firms up the relationship if given appropriately – timely, concretely, and non-judgmentally. The mentor must earn the right to give it. The protégé, on the other hand, must be ready to receive it; this occurs only when the protégé believes that the mentor is deeply concerned about well-being and growth – after multiple interactions and experiences. Under these circumstances, feedback can also be confrontational, especially if it is intended to help the protégé to face the reality of a situation.

The relationship between mentor and protégé needs to be assessed often, especially at this stage in light of the fact that the mentor will be providing feedback and critiquing proposed actions to be taken by the protégé. Exploring the immediacy of the relationship involves the assessment of the strengths and nature of the relationship, the identification of barriers and obstacles, if they exist, and the sharing of feelings of satisfaction, frustration and/or ambivalence about the relationship. This, of course, is both sensitive and risky since either party may not be prepared to hear about perceived deficiencies or strains in the relationship. Nevertheless, the point here is to share perceptions and attitudes in the present, work toward resolving issues, and move on.

Planning a positive future begins with goal-setting. Some behaviours that the mentor can exhibit in supporting the protégé include showing enthusiasm for interests, skills and talents, providing positive reinforcement for accomplishments and risks taken, and encouraging exploration of possible futures. The mentor can help a protégé reflect on values, examine choices of actions, and develop some future scenarios of what it would be like to act on these values. Protégés, especially those who have experienced failure and have a low level of self-esteem, have difficulty in seeing themselves in a positive, long-range future and do not value planning one. A mentor motivates the protégé to place focused energy on the impossible dream – the protégé's dream.

The mentor, at this stage, assists the protégé in testing assumptions, challenging thinking, and examining the relationship among intentions, values, goals and ensuing actions. Critiquing, as contrasted with providing feedback, tends to include more subjectivity and draws more on the experiences and values of the mentor. This is risky and dependent on the extent to which they have built a firm relationship based on mutual trust, caring and cooperation. Mentors now are able to share opinions and biases without the risk of shutting down the thinking of the protégé or over-influencing the protégé, thereby limiting his or her growth in personal decision-making and empowerment. Mentors, however, must continue to take great care when critiquing not to over-personalize, judge, or create feelings of inadequacy or defensiveness. If the mentor engages in critiquing during the early stages of the relationship, the relationship is not one of mutuality but one of domination, telling and dependency. Critiquing is appropriate only at these later stages of the relationship.

Separation

The final stage of the schema, actually a beginning path for the protégé, is *separation*. It represents the culmination of the mentoring arrangement – a time for the protégé to move beyond the relational parameters of the nurturing arrangement and act on learnings. It marks the beginning of empowerment – taking risks, inventing and trying out new approaches, striking out on one's own, and beginning to act on one's vision of a positive future.

This is the stage at which the mentor begins to work out of his or her role. Another way to think about this is to view the mentor as moving away from the role of guide or coach and closer to that of a peer. Often greater levels of openness occur accompanied by increased levelling with each other, even productive confrontation and more mature interactions. Often the separation does not occur without strain. The protégé may become overly sensitive to the mentor's suggestions, testy about sharing decisions, or over-reactive to sensitive issues as he or she uses new abilities. Mentors, on the other hand, may find themselves viewing the protégé as touchy, non-receptive and even ungrateful. Though not apparent, the protégé is likely to take on the admired qualities of the mentor more fully, but in doing so, can experience rejection as part of separation (Levinson *et al.*, 1978).

This is the most critical stage of the schema – a time for reflecting, acknowledging, making learnings explicit, and projecting. Three important skills and competencies identified are: embracing, integrating and empowering.

Embracing

The mentor, during this stage, is not just acknowledging and affirming, but is embracing the protégé as a unique individual with growth potential. This is more than warmth and acceptance: it is closer to the non-sentimental and unconditional positive regard of Rogers (1961), the 'Yes' of Buber (1958). It is no longer necessary for the mentor to be overtly aware of the verbal and non-verbal skills and competencies identified in earlier stages. The mentor is natural, positive and focused on installing confidence and independence in the protégé.

Integrating

It is essential for the mentor to facilitate the 'taking stock' of the relationship and the mutual journey, to identify patterns and integrate the experience. This is more than a review; it is rather a matter of identifying those key incidents or stories that illustrate significant learnings, new skills and growth in self-confidence. It is taking responsibility for one's actions and linking all of them into patterns and themes. The value of experimentation, learning from failure and relying on intuition is stressed; the growth from dependency to autonomy is made explicit. Protégés also need to be reminded that gains have been made by the mentor – that the relationship was not uni-directional. Mentors need to share their sense of renewal, satisfaction and pride.

Empowering

Empowering the protégé, of course, has been the overall goal of the mentor. Throughout the journey, the mentor has been assisting the protégé to articulate a sense of meaning and purpose, to explore personal standards by which to judge oneself, to recognize that it is possible to have control and power over what matters. The protégé acknowledges personal strengths, holds a belief that there is always something new to learn, views most problems as challenges, and expresses a positive sense of purpose and vision. The mentor uses a repertoire of facilitation skills to draw this out from the protégé and to make the growth explicit.

Making Meaning of the Schema

On a basic level and as the foundation of training, the schema provides new and experienced mentors with an understanding of the four stages of mentoring. Included in this are those key skills and competencies of which they need to be aware, be somewhat skilled, and mindful as they immerse in the intensity of a mentoring relationship. For coordinators of mentoring initiatives, the schema can help to identify the stages of development of various mentoring arrangements and to use this information in planning peer mentor dialogue sessions and designing resource and training materials.

From a leadership perspective it can generate some key questions that contribute to sustaining programmes: What needs to be done to sustain interest and excitement for the protégé during the initiation stage? What needs to be done to test compatibility of the mentor and protégé during this stage? What can be done to increase the momentum so that the interactions move beyond the initiation stage to the cultivation stage? How can a relationship avoid getting stuck in one stage and move on to the next? To what extent are both parties feeling satisfied and/or energized? What are the indicators of the relationship that suggest a particular stage of development? How can the protégé be weaned from the attachment to the mentor during the final stages? What is the meaning of the experience for both the mentor and protégé? For the coordinator or manager of the programme? To what extent has mutual learning and growth occurred?

These questions guide the spirit of inquiry, the testing of assumptions, the search for connections that drive our action research journey – the quest to generate new knowledge and shared meaning about mentoring. Within this is the hope for today's youth and the legacy from one generation to the next.

Address for correspondence: Joseph T Pascarelli, EdD, School of Education, University of Portland, 17741 NW Connett Meadow Court, Portland, Oregon 97229. Tel. 503 690 0260. Fax 503 690 8661. e-mail pascarel@uofport.edu

Chapter 17

MAKING A STUDENT TUTORING SCHEME WORK

Sinclair Goodlad

The research and case studies reported in the preceding chapters contain many useful suggestions for making a tutoring scheme work. To help readers 'pull it all together', Appendix A offers a checklist of those matters to which attention must be directed if a scheme is to work. The suggestions made are the fruits of scanning the research literature, practical experimentation, and more particularly listening to numerous accounts of the gritty details of tutoring schemes that somehow seem to slip through the cracks of formal research procedures. The object, therefore, of this short, concluding chapter is to emphasize a few key issues. (Those requiring more detail are referred to *Peer Tutoring* by Goodlad and Hirst, 1989.)

Define Aims

As the number of schemes grows, and as different schemes arise in a single institution (as in the University of the Witwatersrand – Chapters 9, 10 and 11), it becomes more important than ever for the precise aims of each scheme to be written down. A 'statement of intent' can not only focus the minds of all concerned but can prevent 'turf' issues arising with people feeling that areas of their jurisdiction are being interfered with or ignored.

Structure the Content

For the organizer of a tutoring scheme, a major decision concerns the degree of control to exercise over the content of the tuition/teaching. The two extreme conditions are (a) when tutors are given complete responsibility for choosing materials, and (b) when tutors operate with programmed texts and/or CAL (computer-assisted learning) in which steps for the tutee are laid down very precisely.

It has long been known that striking benefits to tutees can come from the administration by tutors of programmed materials (see, for example, Ellson, 1986; Ellson and Harris, 1970; Ellson *et al.*, 1965, 1968, 1969; Harrison, 1969, 1971a, 1971b, 1972a, 1972b). Not only does careful structuring ensure that learners are given material in appropriate sequence, but it has also been found that tutors still find the human interaction with their tutees rewarding. Tutors' originality and creativity can be built around the content whose structure is the prime responsibility of the trained teacher. Tutors, in short, do not reinvent the wheel; rather, they use other people's wheels to travel further and faster.

Emphasis on structuring the content may seem like a counsel of perfection to organizers who may be responsible for placing numerous tutors; but they can at least urge the receiving teachers to use the tutors to best effect by focusing the tutoring on clearly-defined tasks for the pupils/tutees.

Define Roles and Logistics

When tutoring schemes have failed, it has often been because 'things got in a muddle' and people who should have been told something were not. Yet another reason for writing things down! From the list under this heading in Appendix A, the roles of coordinators and receiving teachers are crucial. Tutoring is a complex, collaborative activity: it is vital that initial thought be given to the division of responsibilities so that everyone feels comfortable with the scheme.

Get Secure Finance

We are probably now nearing the end of a 'golden age' when corporate sponsors have given sustained and generous support to student tutoring schemes – though it is to be hoped that this generosity will continue! Russell Elsegood and colleagues, in Chapter 8, give sound advice on how to nourish good relationships with sponsors.

As young people come to rely more on the support of fellow students or visiting tutors from neighbouring universities and colleges, it behoves organizers to seek ways of institutionalizing tutoring. Sometimes this has been through a university's schools liaison office, with the necessary and important task of attracting young people into further and higher education. More fruitfully, tutoring can be woven into the basic procedures of further and higher education institutions by becoming part of the accredited study of the student tutors. This way, the activity becomes a legitimate charge upon the university or college's core funding. Chapters 1, 5 and 6 offer suggestions about how this may be done, and much of the case-study research reported in other chapters emphasizes the important personal and professional transferable skills that students can acquire by being tutors and organizers of tutoring.

Train the Tutors/Mentors

Not surprisingly, it has been known for many years that untrained tutors are less effective than trained ones (see, for example, Conrad, 1975; Niedermeyer, 1970). Evidence about this continues to be produced (see, for example, Fuchs *et al.*, 1994; Shore, 1995). The particulars of training will, of course, depend upon what the tutors are going to do; but the items listed under this heading in Appendix A constitute the irreducible minimum of matters that need to be addressed.

Support the Tutors/Mentors

Good structure in the content of what is to be tutored can prevent student tutors from feeling bewildered and lost; accreditation of their work within the framework of their own degree studies can ensure opportunities for them to talk through, and think through, their work with experts. However, recognition of their work (whether or not they are being assessed) is fundamental. This is a key task of an organizer. Certificates, photographs, parties all help to oil the wheels – and teachers find it very rewarding to talk with tutors about their common task. One of the single most difficult aspects of inter-institutional tutoring (with, say, students from a university visiting a school) is to find time for teachers and tutors to meet; but persistence is necessary not just for recognizing the tutors but also to ensure that the scheme is delivering what is intended.

Evaluate the Scheme

If we are to develop student tutoring not just as an interesting appendage to formal education but as one of its basic procedures, we must accumulate abundant evidence of how it works and what it can deliver. Classical psychometric studies may be neither appropriate nor possible; but detailed case studies (often in the form of annual reports on schemes for purposes of accountability) can be an indispensable source of ideas to inspire other people. Reports can also offer tutors something tangible to take away at the end of their period of service; and reports can be very effective fund-raising tools.

The contributors to this book, and those who have generously supported us, hope that the contents will inspire others to join what is now becoming an educational revolution – albeit with tools forged many years ago! Just as a motto in tutoring is 'Each one teach one', so let us act on a similar one – 'Each one reach one'! If you have found this book interesting, tell someone else! Word-of-mouth is by far the most effective way of spreading good ideas.

Appendix A

SETTING UP A TUTORING SCHEME: A CHECKLIST OF KEY ISSUES

Define Aims

- What problem(s) are you trying to solve?
- Is the activity a substitute for, or a complement to, something else?
- Objectives for tutors/mentors?
- Objectives for tutees/mentees?

Structure the Content

- Base on the skills-needs of tutees/mentees.
- Use a systematic sequence of planned tasks.
- Specify procedures clearly to develop independence in tutees/mentees.

Define Roles and Logistics

- Time and duration of sessions.
- Space – including anticipating noise problems.
- Meetings – frequency, purpose.
- Selection of tutors/mentors.
- Selection/matching of tutees/mentees.
- Role of sending teacher.
- Role of receiving teacher.
- Role of coordinator.
- Documentation/materials.

Get Secure Finance

- Source.
- Amount.
- Continuity.

Train the Tutors/Mentors

- How to start.
- Content of the syllabus.
- How to praise.
- How to avoid doing the work for tutees/mentees.
- How to cope with trouble.
- How to vary the content of sessions.
- How to end individual sessions.
- Record-keeping.
- How to end the tutoring/mentoring arrangement.

Support the Tutors/Mentors

- Give them good written materials.
- Build into their curriculum.
- Devise appropriate assessment/reward.

Evaluate the Scheme

- Keep records of who did what.
- Use rating scales for specific items.
- Collect reflective anecdotes.
- Measure what is measurable.

  but
- Don't hassle people.

Appendix B

BRIEF REPORTS ON A SELECTION OF MENTORING AND TUTORING SCHEMES

1. **Title of scheme:** UNF Link: A Service Learning Mentoring Programme
2. **Overall purpose of scheme** To motivate middle school students to pursue academic goals. Build student self-concept. To provide service learning opportunity for university students.
3. **Tutors/mentors (description and number)** 13 per semester.
4. **Aims for tutors/mentors** To develop group facilitation skills. To learn about urban environments. To develop a meaningful relationship with younger person.
5. **Tutees/mentees (description and number)** 39 per semester
6. **Aims for tutees/mentees** To expand life space, increase aspirations. To enhance self-concept. To motivate lifelong learning.
7. **Subject/substance of work** Mentors engage mentees in learning activities as vehicle for development of relationship.
8. **Year in which scheme started** 1994.
9. **Duration of each cycle** 1 semester for mentor; 2 semesters for mentees.
10. **Type and length of training of tutors/mentors** Mentors have 20 hours' training and weekly meetings for progress reports and reflection.
11. **Outcome measures** Focus groups; journal entries; reflective term papers.
12. **Source and nature of finance** Department of Psychology; Honors Program.

13. **Report(s) available** Yes.
14. **Person to contact** Dr Afesa Adams.
15. **Address** Department of Psychology, 4567 St Johns Bluff Road, Jacksonville, FL 32225, USA.
    Telephone 904 646 2807 **Fax** 904 928 3814 **e-mail** aadams@gw.unf.edu

1. **Title of scheme:** National Literacy Corps
2. **Overall purpose of scheme** To improve literacy levels of high school and primary school children while increasing motivation toward academic studies.
3. **Tutors/mentors (description and number)** 800 high school students.
4. **Aims for tutors/mentors**
   1. Improved reading and writing skills.
   2. Increased motivation toward studies.
   3. Improved critical thinking skills.
   4. Ethic of service.
5. **Tutees/mentees (description and number)** 2500 students grades K–5.
6. **Aims for tutees/mentees** Improved reading and writing skills; improved self-confidence.
7. **Subject/substance of work** Literacy.
8. **Year in which scheme started** 1995.
9. **Duration of each cycle** 1 year.
10. **Type and length of training of tutors/mentors** Teacher training – 20 hours. Tutor training –15 hours.
11. **Outcome measures** Survey; normed reading tests.
12. **Source and nature of finance** Federal and corporate grants.
13. **Report(s) available** September 1997.
14. **Person to contact** Carol W Albritton, Director.
15. **Address** PCT & S, Henry Avenue and School House Lane, Philadelphia, PA 19144, USA.
    Telephone 215 951 0343 **Fax** 215 951 0345

1. **Title of scheme:** Reading PALS
2. **Overall purpose of scheme** To raise achievement in literacy through 1:1 support with tutor and develop knowledge and expertise of tutor.
3. **Tutors/mentors (description and number)** Students, pupils, parents, volunteers; 100+.
4. **Aims for tutors/mentors** To be able to support a beginning reader. To have some understanding of the process of reading and activities to develop literacy skills. To be able to choose appropriate books.
5. **Tutees/mentees (description and number)** Pupils in secondary schools – usually Y7. Developing in pupils in primary schools.
6. **Aims for tutees/mentees** To develop self-esteem and raise achievement in literacy.
7. **Subject/substance of work** Literacy.
8. **Year in which scheme started** 1994.
9. **Duration of each cycle** 10 weeks to 1 year.
10. **Type and length of training of tutors/mentors** 10 weeks at 2 hours per week plus a minimum of 1 hour working with the tutee. A total of 60 hours is needed for credit.
11. **Outcome measures** Improved reading scores in standardised tests.
12. **Source and nature of finance** SRB and Local Education Authority – Manchester City Council.
13. **Report(s) available** Yes.
14. **Person to contact** Andrea Bernstein/Sue McCaldon.
15. **Address** Manchester Literacy Centre, MANCAT, Mostou Campus, Ashley Lane, Manchester M9 4WU.
    Telephone 0161 205 1227 **Fax** 0161 205 1228
    e-mail sue@mccaldon.demon.co.uk

1. **Title of scheme:** Arizona Postponing Sexual Involvement
2. **Overall purpose of scheme** Secondary students teach younger children (age 9–13 years) the Postponing Sexual Involvement (PSI) curriculum over 6 weeks. Emphasis is on decision making, responsibility and peer refusal skills for the prevention of teen pregnancy.
3. **Tutors/mentors (description and number)** In 4 Arizona communities over 200 tutors/mentors work with 2500 younger children.
4. **Aims for tutors/mentors** Gain skills and experience in leadership, communication and social influence.
5. **Tutees/mentees (description and number)** 2500 age 9–13 years.
6. **Aims for tutees/mentees** Gain skills to postpone early sexual activity.
7. **Subject/substance of work** PSI curriculum.
8. **Year in which scheme started** 1995.
9. **Duration of each cycle** 6 weeks.
10. **Type and length of training of tutors/mentors** 30 hours of training in curriculum and skill building.
11. **Outcome measures** Pre/post tests.
12. **Source and nature of finance** US Dept of Health and Human Services and local school districts.
13. **Report(s) available** Evaluation report.
14. **Person to contact** Dr Sherry Betts.
15. **Address** FCR 208, University of Arizona, PO Box 210033, Tucson, AZ 85721-0033, USA.
    Telephone 520 621 3399 **Fax** 520 621 9445 **e-mail** sbetts@ag.arizona.edu

1. **Title of scheme:** Academic Development – Faculty of Arts
2. **Overall purpose of scheme** Support all first-year students within specific subject disciplines: psychology, languages, immunology, etc enrolling for BA degrees and who are from an educationally deprived background. All tutors and tutees must be enrolled students at the university.
3. **Tutors/mentors (description and number)** 54 for the faculty in total.
4. **Aims for tutors/mentors** Assist with academic skills, social skills, general support ie, finding way on campus, etc.
5. **Tutees/mentees (description and number)** First year students (numbers vary within each discipline from 1 tutor : 25 tutees to 1:50).
6. **Aims for tutees/mentees** Successfully pass their first year courses.
7. **Subject/substance of work** Students choose their own subjects to make up 10 credits being BA course.
8. **Year in which scheme started** 1994.
9. **Duration of each cycle** 1 academic year (Jan–Oct).
10. **Type and length of training of tutors/mentors** 2 full days training on groupwork, study skills, etc. Monthly tutor forum – discuss success/failure. Weekly discussions with subject lecturers.
11. **Outcome measures** 2 x semester reports/students' overall pass-rates.
12. **Source and nature of finance** University funding.
13. **Report(s) available** Yes.
14. **Person to contact** Dr Ann-Louise de Boer.
15. **Address** Manager, Centre for Academic Development Programmes, Faculty of Arts, University of Pretoria, South Africa.
    Telephone (012) 420 2635 **Fax** (012) 420 2404
    e-mail deBoer@libarts.up.ac.za

1. **Title of scheme:** Youth Opportunities Unlimited Mentoring Programme
2. **Overall purpose of scheme** Aim to encourage at-risk high school students from the inner city to stay in school and achieve to their potential. YOU acts as consultants in establishing mentoring programmes eg, to the University of the West Indies.
3. **Tutors/mentors (description and number)** 120 volunteer adults (university students and business people/professionals).
4. **Aims for tutors/mentors** Opportunity for community service. Mentor training. 1:1 relationship with young person giving career guidance and academic and emotional support.
5. **Tutees/mentees (description and number)** 140 11–17-year-olds from inner city referred by Guidance Counsellors.
6. **Aims for tutees/mentees** Complete high school and go on to higher education and/or employment or skills training. Gain work experience, career guidance and emotional support.
7. **Subject/substance of work** 1:1 relationship. Training and recruitment of mentors.
8. **Year in which scheme started** 1991.
9. **Duration of each cycle** Ongoing.
10. **Type and length of training of tutors/mentors** Orientation training. Ongoing mentor training (workshop/seminars) once every 6 weeks.
11. **Outcome measures** Number of students achieving higher education/employment. Feedback from participants. Decrease in drop-out rates.
12. **Source and nature of finance** Income generating activities. Private sector donations. Some from donor agencies, eg, USAID.
13. **Report(s) available** No.
14. **Person to contact** Kylie Brown or Betty Bowen.
15. **Address** 74 Arnold Road, Kingston 5, Jamaica, West Indies.
    Telephone (876) 968 6784 **Fax** (876) 968 0979
    e-mail jspence@toj.rom

1. **Title of scheme:** Alumni Fund Student Tutoring Scheme
2. **Overall purpose of scheme** To encourage young people to see HE as a realistic option. To enhance the learning situation and help young people to fulfil their potential.
3. **Tutors/mentors (description and number)** Approx 100 students from engineering science. Business and arts and social sciences faculties.
4. **Aims for tutors/mentors** To encourage young people; act as role models; communicate their knowledge; contribute to the community; to increase self-confidence.
5. **Tutees/mentees (description and number)** Pupils in primary and secondary schools and in FE College. Approx 1500.
6. **Aims for tutees/mentees** To understand their subject better through extra one-to-one attention; to increase their self-esteem.
7. **Subject/substance of work** Usually working in subject classes related to degree; some in learning support; technology and general work in primary schools.
8. **Year in which scheme started** 1992.
9. **Duration of each cycle** Approx 12 weeks, 2 hours per week.
10. **Type and length of training of tutors/mentors** Half-hour general presentation; 2 hour training session; 15 minute interview (mainly discussing matching/placement).
11. **Outcome measures** Evaluation forms distributed to tutors, teachers and pupils.
12. **Source and nature of finance** University's Alumni Fund (£1500 per year). Possible travelling expenses in Glasgow from Glasgow Education Department.
13. **Report(s) available** Yes.
14. **Person to contact** Imelda Devlin.
15. **Address** Schools & Colleges Liaison Office, University of Strathclyde, Graham Hills Building, 50 George Street, Glasgow G1 1QE.
    Telephone 0141 548 4248 **Fax** 0141 552 7362
    e-mail I.Dev@mis.strath.ac.uk

1. **Title of scheme:** The Mentoring Programme
2. **Overall purpose of scheme** To encourage older, more advantaged youths to see value in assisting (either through tutoring/counselling/mentoring) the disadvantaged, academically weaker younger children.
3. **Tutors/mentors (description and number)** 25 mentors, 11–12th year of education, preparing for A-levels.
4. **Aims for tutors/mentors** To guide and counsel, tutor; character formation; leadership and teamwork; role modelling.
5. **Tutees/mentees (description and number)** 25–30 protégés.
6. **Aims for tutees/mentees** To aspire to do better, tap their potential. To realize their strengths and build their self-esteem and worth/confidence. To prepare them for the real work by providing that link.
7. **Subject/substance of work** Academic: helping out in schoolwork; learning basic skills like communication, teamwork, public speaking. Non-academic: 'fun' activities: telematch/origami/outdoor games.
8. **Year in which scheme started** 1995.
9. **Duration of each cycle** 1 year 2 months.
10. **Type and length of training of tutors/mentors** 2–3 weeks, Counselling Workshop, Teamwork Programme. Actually fairly limited range of workshops for youths – a problem we are trying to address.
11. **Outcome measures** Journal writing (reflection by individuals). Post-mortems of each period. Post-session meetings.
12. **Source and nature of finance** BP Singapore.
13. **Report(s) available** None yet, except occasionally in BP editorials.
14. **Person to contact** Ms Ranjit Dhaliwal.
15. **Address** St Andrew's Junior College, 2 Malan Road, Singapore 210661. **Telephone** 272 5301 ext. 24 **Fax** 272 3586 **e-mail** nji@moe.edu.sg

1. **Title of scheme:** I Have A Dream Foundation – Colorado
2. **Overall purpose of scheme** Drop-out prevention and academic assistance programme which supports students completing high school and promotes post-secondary school attendance by students of colour.
3. **Tutors/mentors (description and number)** Approx 150 volunteers in both roles.
4. **Aims for tutors/mentors** Promote academic remediation and achievement of grade levels in reading and maths.
5. **Tutees/mentees (description and number)** Over 300.
6. **Aims for tutees/mentees** To have a positive learning experience with an adult role model.
7. **Subject/substance of work** English, readings, maths, some science.
8. **Year in which scheme started** 1988.
9. **Duration of each cycle** 10 years (grade 4 through initial college year).
10. **Type and length of training of tutors/mentors** 2–5 days over first month. Insufficient, based on learnings from this conference.
11. **Outcome measures** Students more successful from grade to grade. Students improve significantly on standardized tests.
12. **Source and nature of finance** 85 per cent private resources; 15 per cent government.
13. **Report(s) available** No.
14. **Person to contact** Keely Felice, Executive Director.
15. **Address** 1566 Peace Street, Denver, Colorado, USA 80220. **Telephone** 303 861 5005 **Fax** 303 861 5008 **e-mail** mkfelice@aol.com

1. **Title of scheme:** Cross Cultural Peer Pairing
2. **Overall purpose of scheme** To assist in the academic acculturation of international students. To promote cross cultural communication/ understanding.
3. **Tutors/mentors (description and number)** Approx 450 per annum.
4. **Aims for tutors/mentors** To explore cross-cultural issues with their partner. To together plan/prepare a report for assessment.
5. **Tutees/mentees (description and number)** See 6 below.
6. **Aims for tutees/mentees** NA. In this programme they are both equal – they 'mentor' each other. All are tutors/mentors.
7. **Subject/substance of work** Cross-cultural issues; academic acculturation issues.
8. **Year in which scheme started** 1995.
9. **Duration of each cycle** 1 semester.
10. **Type and length of training of tutors/mentors** Students who volunteer are enrolled in a subject (human communication) and receive ongoing training within classes. Subject runs for one semester.
11. **Outcome measures** Formal evaluation by students. Standard of reports prepared.
12. **Source and nature of finance** Office of International Programs (University body).
13. **Report(s) available** NA.
14. **Person to contact** Anna Harley.
15. **Address** Department of Industry, Professional and Adult Education, RMIT University, PO Box 71, Bundoora, Victoria, Australia. **Telephone** 03 9468 2813 **e-mail** a.harley@rmit.edu.au

1. **Title of scheme:** The Pimlico Connection
2. **Overall purpose of scheme** Principal objectives are: To assist in making science, mathematics and design and technology more enjoyable and accessible for the school pupils who act as tutees. To offer students of Imperial College realistic practice in communicating concepts and ideas, and to do something to take the strain off teachers in schools near to the college.
3. **Tutors/mentors (description and number)** Higher education students as tutors in local primary and secondary schools. 1996/97 = 132 registered, of which 86 in nine secondary and 46 in five primary. Of the 86 tutors in secondary schools 52 science, 27 maths, 4 CDT and 3 in French.
4. **Aims for tutors/mentors** To improve their communication skills, including communication of ideas and concepts; interpersonal skills; self-confidence; patience; awareness of people from different social backgrounds. Of obvious benefit to tutors who are interested in teaching as a career.
5. **Tutees/mentees (description and number)** Primary and secondary school pupils in all age groups from Nursery to Year 13.
   Classes are normally described as being of mixed ability. Number of pupils involved is not known but is extensive, based on the involvement of 14 schools.
6. **Aims for tutees/mentees** To benefit from another adult's presence in helping with queries. Those with language problems, relatively slow or fast learners and those with a tendency to disrupt are able to receive extra assistance to aid progress. To give an extra dimension to their groupwork taking place in a practical or project situation. To benefit from constructive oral communication with the tutor in order to encourage discussion of ideas. To increase aspirations by finding out about Imperial College and the opportunities that exist beyond school (mainly upper primary and secondary).
7. **Subject/substance of work** Tutoring focuses on the following subject areas: mathematics; science; design and technology; French (piloted at one school during 1996/97).
8. **Year in which scheme started** 1975.
9. **Duration of each cycle** Last week in October to February half-term holiday (approx 14 weeks).

10. **Type and length of training of tutors/mentors** All newcomers are required to attend a two-hour 'familiarization/training' session presented by the programme coordinator and the Pimlico Connection Student Society Committee. Aims: to inform prospective student tutors of the scope of the scheme; to familiarize those interested as to the role of a tutor within the classroom; to allow an informed choice as to whether to participate. Objectives: to emphasize the commitment involved and the subject areas involved; to impress upon those interested the need to view the act and purpose of tutoring from an adult/teacher's perspective; to summarize the key components/ guidelines of the tutor-teacher-pupil partnership; to cover the issue of support which tutors should expect from the programme; to suggest the kind of situations students are likely to find themselves in.

11. **Outcome measures** All tutors are requested to complete an evaluation questionnaire. All schools are given the opportunity to offer feedback to the programme coordinator. Discussion of key issues takes place between the programme coordinator and The Pimlico Connection Society Committee (regularly) and The Pimlico Connection Discussion Group (twice a year) which comprises tutors, teachers and past coordinators.

12. **Source and nature of finance** Running costs funded by Imperial College and Old Centralians Trust. Annual Report funded by BP.

13. **Report(s) available** Annual Report produced by Programme Coordinator.

14. **Person to contact** Mr Adrian Hawksworth.

15. **Address** Schools Liaison Office, Room 321 Sherfield Building, Imperial College of Science, Technology and Medicine, Exhibition Road, London SW7 2AZ.
Telephone (+44) 0171 594 8044 **Fax** 0171 594 8002
e-mail a.hawksworth@ic.ac.uk pimlico@ic.ac.uk

1. **Title of scheme:** Student Tutor Service at Cape Technikon
2. **Overall purpose of scheme** To raise awareness of the potential of peer tutoring. To establish a central tutor office functioning as a coordination centre. To involve senior students in administrative leadership. To pilot a range of student tutoring projects.
3. **Tutors/mentors (description and number)** 93 senior student tutors.
4. **Aims for tutors/mentors** To facilitate understanding of academic subjects. To assist with social development. To support under-prepared students.
5. **Tutees/mentees (description and number)** First-year students.
6. **Aims for tutees/mentees** Voluntary attendance; inspire an enthusiasm for learning; academic success.
7. **Subject/substance of work** Maths; engineering; history of design; information systems and computer technology; literacy; English.
8. **Year in which scheme started** 1997.
9. **Duration of each cycle** (Not given).
10. **Type and length of training of tutors/mentors** Generic skills: trust building; explaining; listening; questioning; group work; 6–10 hours.
11. **Outcome measures** Attendance; pass rate; benefits to tutors, tutees and lecturers.
12. **Source and nature of finance** Institutional budget; academic vice-rector's budget.
13. **Report(s) available** Yes.
14. **Person to contact** Cheryl Hewson, Student Tutor Coordinator.
15. **Address** Academic Development, Cape Technikon, PO Box 652, Cape Town 8000, South Africa.
    Telephone (021) 460 3335 **Fax** (021) 45 2034
    e-mail chewson@hyper.ctech.ac.za

1. **Title of scheme:** BP Student Tutoring in Scotland
2. **Overall purpose of scheme** Raise aspiration and motivation of school pupils to continue their education/training beyond school.
3. **Tutors/mentors (description and number)** Approx 1500 students from universities and FE colleges throughout Scotland.
4. **Aims for tutors/mentors** Enhanced transferable skills: confidence, communication, etc. To act as role models for tutees.
5. **Tutees/mentees (description and number)** Approx 10,000 pupils in primary and secondary schools in Scotland.
6. **Aims for tutees/mentees** Make lessons more enjoyable, interesting. Raise their aspirations/motivation to participate in FHE.
7. **Subject/substance of work** Various. The student tutors work with pupils in the classroom either on a one-to-one basis or with small groups. The support is always under the direction and supervision of teachers and takes place across the curriculum.
8. **Year in which scheme started** 1991.
9. **Duration of each cycle** Annual, normally October to April.
10. **Type and length of training of tutors/mentors** 2 hours interactive training using BP resources.
11. **Outcome measures** Evaluation questionnaires available for students, teachers and pupils.
12. **Source and nature of finance** Financed from varying sources, usually local government, HE/FE, EBP.
13. **Report(s) available** Yes.
14. **Person to contact** Joe Hogan, BP Student Tutoring Fellow (Scotland).
15. **Address** Merksworth HS, Gockston Road, Paisley PA3 2NG.
    Telephone 0141 887 5141 **Fax** 0141 848 7814

1. **Title of scheme:** Peer Tutoring
2. **Overall purpose of scheme** Peer tutoring as part of independent study.
3. **Tutors/mentors (description and number)** 6–12 2nd year engineering students.
4. **Aims for tutors/mentors** Organization; transferable skills; initiative.
5. **Tutees/mentees (description and number)** Local schools – various classes of 5–8, 8–12, and 12–16 year-old pupils.
6. **Aims for tutees/mentees** Enhance and expand lesson materials.
7. **Subject/substance of work** Various – CDT; computing, etc, including project work eg, weather stations, satellite images, computer packages.
8. **Year in which scheme started** 1989.
9. **Duration of each cycle** 1 year.
10. **Type and length of training of tutors/mentors** Half-day at school and introductory training at university.
11. **Outcome measures** Questionnaires; diaries; report; feedback from school.
12. **Source and nature of finance** HEFCE, because the tutoring is part of a credit-rated module 'Independent Study'.
13. **Report(s) available** No. The students' self-assessments are returned to them.
14. **Person to contact** Dr Bill Hooper.
15. **Address** University of Exeter, School of Engineering, North Park Road, Exeter, EX4 4QF.
    Telephone 01392 263 661 **Fax** 01392 217 965
    e-mail r.m.hooper@exeter.ac.uk

1. **Title of scheme:** Mentor/Monitor project University of Amsterdam
2. **Overall purpose of scheme** Supporting pre-university students in their orientation on future studies and profession by providing experiences of university students in their studies and student life. Special attention for students from non-traditional/non-academic backgrounds.
3. **Tutors/mentors (description and number)** 150.
4. **Aims for tutors/mentors** To convey the correct information to the pupils, the student mentor must form a clear picture of his or her own education. By doing this, the student mentor may gain a better understanding of his or her own choices (self-reflection); communication skills; earn some money (fl.500 a year).
5. **Tutees/mentees (description and number)** Approx 300 16–17-year-olds.
6. **Aims for tutees/mentees** Better views on university life, better preparation for university studies (emotional, skills, content of subjects, etc).
7. **Subject/substance of work** Visiting schools and university and vice versa; educational orientation programme.
8. **Year in which scheme started** 1996.
9. **Duration of each cycle** September – June.
10. **Type and length of training of tutors/mentors** 1 day training in communication skills.
11. **Outcome measures** By monitoring all students. Results: less drop-out; better study results.
12. **Source and nature of finance** Half from university, half from Ministry of Education.
13. **Report(s) available** Yes, Newsletter.
14. **Person to contact** Willeke Jeeninga or Frank van Kampen.
15. **Address** Universiteit van Amsterdam, Binnengasthuisstraat 9, 1012 ZA Amsterdam, Netherlands.
    Telephone (31) 020 525 2567 **Fax** (31) 020 525 2999
    e-mail wjeeninga@bdu.uva/nl

1. **Title of scheme:** Education for marriage, parenthood, sexual education at elementary and high schools
2. **Overall purpose of scheme** Preparing tutors of psychology students, preparing subject (contents) of this education, preparing methodology for doing it at schools, preparing books and CD-ROM for students.
3. **Tutors/mentors (description and number)** 60 students of psychology.
4. **Aims for tutors/mentors** To make a longitudinal base for changing some attitudes towards family and sexual relations, resulting in reinforcement of family stability.
5. **Tutees/mentees (description and number)** More than 500.
6. **Aims for tutees/mentees** To be more prepared for real life in family. To know something about parenthood, society, drugs, AIDS, sex, nature. To have occasion to try to solve some important ethical questions, etc.
7. **Subject/substance of work** Effort to make the society better, to make family relations more stable.
8. **Year in which scheme started** 1990.
9. **Duration of each cycle** 1 year.
10. **Type and length of training of tutors/mentors** 200 hours training during 1 year, on the basis of social psychological training methods.
11. **Outcome measures** Very positive in various areas researches on attitudes (schools directors, pupils).
12. **Source and nature of finance** University grants; Ministry of Health, etc.
13. **Report(s) available** Book, methodical material, CD-ROM.
14. **Person to contact** Dr Lenka Sulovai, CSE.
15. **Address** Katedra Psychologie FFUK, Celetnai 20, Praha 1-11000, Czechoslovakia.
    Telephone 00420 2 2449 1484 **Fax** 00420 2 2449 1484

1. **Title of scheme:** Program Mentor – Pelajar UM-KP-BP (Malaysia)
2. **Overall purpose of scheme** To develop student mentoring in promoting interest in science and mathematics in secondary schools.
3. **Tutors/mentors (description and number)** 40 undergraduate student mentors doing BSc with education courses at the university.
4. **Aims for tutors/mentors** To guide school children in understanding the importance of science and technology for national development.
5. **Tutees/mentees (description and number)** 240 mentees – school pupils aged 13 to 17 from 6 schools.
6. **Aims for tutees/mentees** To encourage them to choose science and technology based as their future career.
7. **Subject/substance of work** Mentoring in secondary schools, to encourage pupils' interest in science and mathematics, discussing career opportunities and current affairs relating to science and technology.
8. **Year in which scheme started** 1997.
9. **Duration of each cycle** 6 months.
10. **Type and length of training of tutors/mentors** One day per week, plus discussions with advisers.
11. **Outcome measures** The adviser for each school monitors activity and reports back to a committee.
12. **Source and nature of finance** BP Malaysia and the University of Malaya.
13. **Report(s) available** No.
14. **Person to contact** Professor Mohd Said Mohd Kadis, Director.
15. **Address** Centre for Foundation Studies in Science, University of Malaya, 50603 Kuala Lumpur, Malaysia.
    Telephone 03 756 2239 **Fax** 603 757 6478 **e-mail** mzz@fizik.um.edu.my

1. **Title of scheme:** BP Student Tutoring and Mentoring Programme SA
2. **Overall purpose of scheme Address**ing students' problems in maths, physical science and biology. This is to improve matric students in order for them to pass/improve their matric results. So, students come on Saturdays and are tutored by senior students from the University of Fort Hare.
3. **Tutors/mentors (description and number)** 12 tutors and 3 coordinators per subject.
4. **Aims for tutors/mentors** To assist students in their matric performance in maths, biology and physical science.
5. **Tutees/mentees (description and number)** Approx 200 students.
6. **Aims for tutees/mentees** Mostly they would like to learn from tutors and be assisted in achieving better grades on their content subject. To address/supplement the poor science backgrounds they have.
7. **Subject/substance of work** Teaching content of main subjects: biology, maths, physical science.
8. **Year in which scheme started** 1996.
9. **Duration of each cycle** 1 year per group.
10. **Type and length of training of tutors/mentors** No training for tutors, but subject coordinators are trained.
11. **Outcome measures** Students who attended.
12. **Source and nature of finance** Sponsored by BP in 1995.
13. **Report(s) available** Yes.
14. **Person to contact** Jimmy Khanyile.
15. **Address** Zoology Department, University of Fort Hare, Private Bag X1314, Alice 5700, South Africa.
    Telephone +27 0404 22339 **Fax** +27 0404 22168
    e-mail khanyi@ufhcc.ufh.ac.za

1. **Title of scheme:** Lothians and Edinburgh Student Tutoring Scheme (LESTS) within Lothians Equal Access Programme for Schools (LEAPS)

2. **Overall purpose of scheme**
   1. To contribute to the delivery of quality educational experiences in the school classroom through the support provided by volunteer student tutors.
   2. To encourage high educational aspirations amongst often disadvantaged school students through contact with student tutors as role models.
   3. To provide development opportunities to students in higher/further education, especially in the fields of communication and interpersonal relationships.

3. **Tutors/mentors (description and number)** In 1996/97, 4 Edinburgh Higher Education Institutions and 1 West Lothian FE College provided 257 volunteer student tutors. Of these, 15 have proceeded to enrol for a further placement within a pilot accredited tutoring module.

4. **Aims for tutors/mentors** To improve communication skills; to develop further interpersonal skills; to gain new insights into their own knowledge through sharing it with younger learners; to gain experience of working with groups of schoolchildren, under the supervision of teachers; to function as role models for school pupils, personifying the values of a learning culture.

5. **Tutees/mentees (description and number)** Potentially all pupils of the 47 secondary schools, 239 primary schools and 24 special schools in 4 local authority areas. In 1996/97, 32 secondaries, 21 primaries and 1 special school have taken part in student tutoring.

6. **Aims for tutees/mentees** To enhance the quality of their classroom experience; to offer them role models; to encourage them to see continuing education and training as viable options; to help create for them an environment in which achievement and aspiration are the norm.

7. **Subject/substance of work** Under supervision of the class teacher, working in a variety of ways with whole class, groups or individuals. All curricular areas and all age groups are covered, including the informal curriculum and study clubs.

8. **Year in which scheme started** 1992 on a pilot basis, and developing into the present coordinated scheme.

9. **Duration of each cycle** Normally half day per week from end October/early November to Easter, with extension beyond that negotiable by school and student tutor. Semester arrangement practised by 2 HEIs requires redeployment of some tutors in February. Students of the FE college tend to be placed in schools for the summer term.

10. **Type and length of training of tutors/mentors** Half-day training by coordinators and experienced volunteer tutors, followed by induction session. Thereafter, ongoing support by school staff, HEI coordinators and scheme coordinator. Module students have more intense training in the requirements of the module as well as in tutoring itself.

11. **Outcome measures** Qualitative evaluations based on questionnaires and interviews. Possibility of more intensive evaluation is presently under review.

12. **Source and nature of finance** 4 Local Authorities and 4 HEIs, contributing in cash and in kind.

13. **Report(s) available** Interim report for 1996/97.

14. **Person to contact** Archie Pacey.

15. **Address** Carlowrie Cottage, 160 Barleyknowe Road, Gorebridge, Midlothian EH23 4PS. 16.
Telephone 01875 820 235 **Fax** 01875 820 122 **e-mail** APacey@emarkt.com

1. **Title of scheme:** CSV Learning Together
2. **Overall purpose of scheme** By means of a national network to facilitate student tutoring and mentoring in England and Northern Ireland. Supporting specific schemes as funding and other resources permit.
3. **Tutors/mentors (description and number)** Approx 7000 students throughout the UK.
4. **Aims for tutors/mentors** Development of personal and professional skills.
5. **Tutees/mentees (description and number)** Approx 70,000 school pupils through the UK.
6. **Aims for tutees/mentees** To meet their full potential and develop the habit of lifelong learning.
7. **Subject/substance of work** The National Curriculum, specific literacy projects and range of other activities.
8. **Year in which scheme started** 1992.
9. **Duration of each cycle** 1 year.
10. **Type and length of training of tutors/mentors** Minimum of 3 hours.
11. **Outcome measures** Evaluation sheets from student tutors, teachers and pupils.
12. **Source and nature of finance** Sponsorship and donations.
13. **Report(s) available** National, regional and newsletters.
14. **Person to contact** Sheila Parsons.
15. **Address** c/o National Power plc, Windmill Hill Business Park, Swindon SN2 3PS.
    Telephone 01793 892 440 **Fax** 01793 892 541
    e-mail SheilaParsons@natpower.co

1. **Title of scheme:** LSE Student Tutoring Scheme – part of the North London Connection
2. **Overall purpose of scheme** To provide additional help to school pupils with their academic work in a deprived part of inner London. To make lessons more interesting. To raise pupils' aspirations and motivation by providing positive role models. To give LSE students the opportunity to develop skills. To enable LSE students to carry out rewarding community work
3. **Tutors/mentors (description and number)** Undergraduate and postgraduate students. Approx 140 per year.
4. **Aims for tutors/mentors** To develop transferable skills and in particular communications skills. To increase confidence. To reinforce own subject knowledge. To develop understanding of difficulties faced by those less fortunate in society.
5. **Tutees/mentees (description and number)** Primary, secondary and pupils in special schools. Probably in excess of 5000.
6. **Aims for tutees/mentees** Improve academic attainment. Increase aspirations. Reinforce importance of academic effort at school for future life-chances.
7. **Subject/substance of work** A full range of subjects, but because of the nature of the LSE (and the original aims of the scheme) more students tutor in maths than any other subject.
8. **Year in which scheme started** Early 1990s.
9. **Duration of each cycle** October until April.
10. **Type and length of training of tutors/mentors** Briefing, role play, communications skills, input by past tutors.
11. **Outcome measures** Analysis of questionnaires completed by student tutors at the end of tutoring period plus feedback from schools.
12. **Source and nature of finance** Sponsorship by BP.
13. **Report(s) available** Annual reports, student tutor handbook.
14. **Person to contact** Hazel Pennell.
15. **Address** LSE Student Tutoring Coordinator, Room A236, LSE, Houghton Street, London WC2A 2AE.
    Telephone 0171 955 7379 **Fax** 0171 955 7733 **e-mail** h.pennell@lse.ac.uk

1. **Title of scheme:** The Five Year Study Programme in Engineering
2. **Overall purpose of scheme** To create a learning environment, whereby students are empowered to graduate as engineers to the benefit of themselves and their community. The scheme is aimed at students from educationally disadvantaged communities.
3. **Tutors/mentors (description and number)** 26 tutors who are senior students in the faculty.
4. **Aims for tutors/mentors** To assist/guide students through the learning process, to facilitate a learning culture, to act as role models.
5. **Tutees/mentees (description and number)** 25 first-year students; 50 second-year students.
6. **Aims for tutees/mentees** To graduate (as engineers). To be successful academically.
7. **Subject/substance of work** Mainly academic, but this cannot be done without the necessary learning, personal and social skills. Maths, physics, chemistry, statistics, drawing subjects, engineering concepts, communication, learning skills, social skills, engineering skills.
8. **Year in which scheme started** 1995.
9. **Duration of each cycle** 1 year.
10. **Type and length of training of tutors/mentors** Workshops for 1 day; weekly meetings with tutors/supervisors; individual follow-ups.
11. **Outcome measures** Questionnaires and oral feedback from students, tutors and supervisors. Academic records of students.
12. **Source and nature of finance** University funding; private sector.
13. **Report(s) available** Reports are available on scheme as a whole. Academic records are kept to date.
14. **Person to contact** Dr Ina du Plessis, Manager.
15. **Address** Academic Development Programmes, Faculty of Engineering, University of Pretoria, South Africa.
    Telephone (27) 012 420 2482 **Fax** (27) 12 432 816
    e-mail DPLE-G@Fanella.ee.up.ac.za

1. **Title of scheme:** Mentorproject 'Näktergalen'
2. **Overall purpose of scheme** A pilot project. Students will serve as role models for children with special needs and to some of the children of newly arrived immigrants as an 'entrance' to Swedish country. To give teacher students additional practice. To try out a new way of financing university studies.
3. **Tutors/mentors (description and number)** 90 each year.
4. **Aims for tutors/mentors** Students will serve as role models for children with special needs and to some of the children of newly arrived immigrants as an 'entrance' to Swedish country. To give teacher students additional practice. To try out a new way of financing university studies.
5. **Tutees/mentees (description and number)** 90 each year: 30 from one school, 30 from another and 30 children through the Immigration Office.
6. **Aims for tutees/mentees** Students will serve as role models for children with special needs and to some of the children of newly arrived immigrants as an 'entrance' to Swedish country. To give teacher students additional practice. To try out a new way of financing university studies.
7. **Subject/substance of work** Mainly outside school activities using the PERACH model in Israel.
8. **Year in which scheme started** Spring Term 1997: planning will start in August 1997.
9. **Duration of each cycle** 8 months.
10. **Type and length of training of tutors/mentors** Not yet decided; planning stage.
11. **Outcome measures** None given.
12. **Source and nature of finance** Pilot project funded by a large Swedish foundation called Wallenberg and we have money for 3 and a half years.
13. **Report(s) available** NA.
14. **Person to contact** Lena Rubinsteinreich.
15. **Address** Malmö School of Education, Lund University, Box 23501, 20045 Malmö, Sweden.
    Telephone +46 40 325 282 **Fax** +46 40 325 225
    e-mail mentorsprojekt@lhm.lu.se

1. **Title of scheme:** Scientific and Technological Literacy: Student Tutoring Project
2. **Overall purpose of scheme** To help the pupils to develop scientific knowledge, science process skills, scientific attitude, spirit of enquiry, creativity, critical thinking, expression potential and open-mindedness by tutoring approach. To help student tutors and classroom teacher learn about constructivism approach through tutoring approach.
3. **Tutors/mentors (description and number)** 2 tutors – one sophomore from chemistry department, another one from computer department, Chulalongkoon University.
4. **Aims for tutors/mentors** To help the pupils to develop scientific knowledge, science process skills, scientific attitude, spirit of enquiry, creativity, critical thinking, expression potential and open-mindedness by tutoring approach. To help student tutors and classroom teacher learn about constructivism approach through tutoring approach.
5. **Tutees/mentees (description and number)** 19 tutees from Samson nok Metropolitan Primary School.
6. **Aims for tutees/mentees** To help the pupils to develop scientific knowledge, science process skills, scientific attitude, spirit of enquiry, creativity, critical thinking, expression potential and open-mindedness by tutoring approach. To help student tutors and classroom teachers learn about constructivism approach through tutoring approach.
7. **Subject/substance of work** Scientific and technological literacy (science process skills creativity and scientific attitude).
8. **Year in which scheme started** 1996.
9. **Duration of each cycle** 6 months.
10. **Type and length of training of tutors/mentors** 2 months evaluation – life class situations (3 weeks).
11. **Outcome measures** Gain in all expected STL.
12. **Source and nature of finance** BP London/BP Thailand and the British Council.
13. **Report(s) available** Yes.
14. **Person to contact** Asst Dr Jariya Sucharukul,

15. **Address** Department of General Science, Faculty of Science, Chulalongkoon University, Bangkok or: Miss Laddaaran Sangsumlee, Chatkaur Chongkolnee Metropolitan Primary School, Bangkok Thailand.
Telephone 218 5788 **Fax** 218 5180 **e-mail** sjariya@chula.ac.th

1. **Title of scheme:** Lothians Equal Access Programme for Schools (LEAPS)
2. **Overall purpose of scheme** To encourage and facilitate entry into higher education of young people whose education has been adversely affected by economic, social or cultural factors and/or who came from families or communities where few if any people have gone on to higher education.
3. **Tutors/mentors (description and number)** Approx 450 students per annum involved in tutoring, shadowing and workshop programmes from 4 higher education institutions.
4. **Aims for tutors/mentors** Role models, study support, sources of information and encouragement, bridge between schools and universities.
5. **Tutees/mentees (description and number)** Potentially all students in 47 local authority schools – focus group approx 25 per cent of students and summer school students.
6. **Aims for tutees/mentees** To raise awareness of opportunities in, and routes into, universities. To acquire information re universities required to make an informed decision whether or not to go. Raise aspirations and achievements.
7. **Subject/substance of work** Small group/whole class/1:1 – tutors (schools and summer school). 1:1 or 2 for 2–3 days – shadows; whole year, small group – workshop facilitators.
8. **Year in which scheme started** 1995 (Pilot scheme 1991–5).
9. **Duration of each cycle** 1 year.
10. **Type and length of training of tutors/mentors** (Varies for tutors/shadows/workshop facilitators). Tutors and workshop facilitators – half-day training and induction session. Shadows – written/group discussion/personal briefing and ongoing support.
11. **Outcome measures** Percentage applying for HND or degree courses from schools was below average. Increased participation of students from families/communities with little experience of HE (any school).
12. **Source and nature of finance** 4 local authority and 4 higher education institutions. 3 year commitment.

13. **Report(s) available** Annual.
14. **Person to contact** Elspeth Turner.
15. **Address** University of Edinburgh, 58 George Square, Edinburgh EH8 9JU.
    Telephone 0131 650 4676 **Fax** 0131 650 6862 **e-mail** LEAPS@ed.ac.uk

1. **Title of scheme:** Student Tutoring Programme.
2. **Overall purpose of scheme** The placement of university student for a morning or afternoon a week over an 8–10 week period in local primary, secondary or special needs schools.
3. **Tutors/mentors (description and number)** Approx 50–60 undergraduates from the University of Wales, Bangor, and local unemployed graduates.
4. **Aims for tutors/mentors** Skills development. Role models for HE. Experience.
5. **Tutees/mentees (description and number)** School pupils from 12 primary and secondary schools with pupils from all ages.
6. **Aims for tutees/mentees** Study support. Curriculum support. Understanding of HE.
7. **Subject/substance of work** 1:1 tutoring; group work; classroom assistance.
8. **Year in which scheme started** 1991.
9. **Duration of each cycle** 8–10 week placements.
10. **Type and length of training of tutors/mentors** One evening session before placement begins.
11. **Outcome measures** Completed log sheets, evaluation of tutor and schools, certificate presentation.
12. **Source and nature of finance** BP and local TEC (Training and Enterprise Council).
13. **Report(s) available** Annual report.
14. **Person to contact** Joanne Wake or Bryn Jones.
15. **Address** Student Development, University of Wales, Bangor, Gwynedd LL57 2DG.
    Telephone 01248 382 072 **Fax** 01248 383 644

REFERENCES

Adler, G *et al.* (1997) *An Academic Development Vision for the Arts Faculty, Wits University* (South Africa: University of the Witwatersrand) in-house report.

Aiello, H and Gatewood, T (1989) 'The Glasgow Mentor Model: A Programme for At-Risk Middle Grades Students', *Mentoring International*, 3, 3, 5–8.

Albert, R S (ed.) (1992) *Genius and Eminence: the Social Psychology of Creativity and Exceptional Achievement* (2nd edn) (Oxford: Pergamon Press).

Allen, V L (ed.) (1976) *Children as Teachers* (London: Academic Press).

American River College (1993) *ARC Beacon Project: Student Catalyst Program – Peer Assisted Learning; First Semester Summary Report* (Sacramento CA: American River College) (ED 355995).

Amundsen, C L and Bernard, R M (1989) 'Institutional Support for Peer Contact in Distance Education: an Empirical Investigation', *Distance Education*, 10, 1, 7–23.

Annis, L F (1983) 'The process and effects of peer tutoring', *Human Learning*, 2, 39–47.

Arneman, K and Prosser, M (1993) 'The Development of Two Peer Tutoring Programmes in the Faculty of Dentistry, University of Sydney', in *Proceedings of Conference on Peer Tutoring at the University of Auckland 19–21 August 1993* (Auckland: Higher Education Research Office, University of Auckland).

Arnold, K D and Subotnik, R F (1994) 'Lessons from contemporary longitudinal studies', in Subotnik, R F and Arnold, K D (eds) *Beyond Terman: Contemporary Longitudinal Studies of Giftedness and Talent* (New Jersey: Ablex Publishing).

Ashman, A F and Elkins, J (1990) 'Co-operative Learning Among Special Students', in Foot, H C, Morgan, M J and Shute, R H (eds) *Children Helping Children* (Chichester: Wiley).

Astin, A W (1977) *Four critical years: Effects of college on beliefs, attitudes, and knowledge* (San Francisco: Jossey-Bass).

Astin, A W (1984) 'Student involvement: a developmental theory for higher education', *Journal of College Student Personnel*, 25, 287–300.

Atkins, M J, Beattie, J and Dockrell, W B (1993) *Assessment issues in higher education* (Sheffield, Department of Employment).

Attar, R (1976) *PERACH one-to-one tutorial project* (Rehovot, Israel: The Weizmann Institute of Science).

Babagura, A K *et al.* (1993) *The child-to-child programme of Botswana* (Gaborone: UNICEF).

Bargh, J A and Schul, Y (1980) 'On the Cognitive Benefits of Teaching', *Journal of Educational Psychology*, 72, 5, 593–604.

Barnett, R (1992) *Improving Higher Education* (Buckingham: Society for Research into Higher Education and Open University Press).

Barnett, R (1994) *The Limits of Competence* (Buckingham: Society for Research into Higher Education and Open University Press).

Beach, L R (1960) 'Sociability and Academic Achievement in Various Types of Learning Situations', *Journal of Educational Psychology*, 51, 4, 208–12.

Beardon, L A (1990) 'Cambridge STIMULUS', in Goodlad, S and Hirst, B (eds) *Explorations in Peer Tutoring* (Oxford: Basil Blackwell).

Beardon, L A (1996) 'How teachers, peer teachers and learners can together improve the quality of learning', *Proceedings of the Conference on Student Contributions to Learning, Rhodes University, South Africa*, June 1996.

Beaumont, G (1995) *Review of 100 NVQs and SVQs*, A report submitted to the Department for Education and Employment.

Beck, L (1989) 'Mentorships: benefits and effects on career development', *Gifted Child Quarterly*, 33, 22–8.

Becker, F (1993) 'The function of universities. Observations from Namibia', in CIM/DAAD/GTZ *Quality, Relevance, and Efficiency in Higher Education in Africa*. Report on the international seminar in Harare, Zimbabwe, 13–18 September 1992 (169–176) (Bonn: Education, Science and Documentation Centre).

Bell, E (1983) 'The Peer Tutor: The Writing Center's Most Valuable Resource', *Teaching English in the Two Year College*, 9, 2, 141–4.

Benard, B (1991) *Fostering Resiliency in Kids: Protective Factors in the Family, School, and Community* (Portland: Northwest Regional Educational Laboratory).

Bennet, N, Desforges, C, Cockburn, A and Wilkinson, B (1984) *The Quality of Pupils' Learning Experiences* (Hove: Lawrence Erlbaum).

Benware, C A and Deci, E L (1984) 'Quality of learning with an active versus passive motivational set', *American Educational Research Journal*, Winter, 21, 4, 755–65.

Bidgood, P (1994) 'The Success of Supplemental Instruction: The Statistical Evidence', in Rust, C and Wallace, J (eds), *Helping Students to Learn from Each Other: Supplemental Instruction* (Birmingham: Staff and Educational Development Association).

Black, J (1993) 'Peer Tutor Support in Nursing and Midwifery at Otago Polytechnic', in *Proceedings of Conference on Peer Tutoring at the University of Auckland 19–21 August 1993* (Auckland: Higher Education Research Office, University of Auckland).

Bobko, E (1984) 'The Effective Use of Undergraduates as Tutors for College Science Students', *Journal of College Science Teaching*, 14, 60–62.

Boltt, G (1996) Interview, August, Department of Science Education, Rhodes University.

Boud, D *et al.* (1985) *Reflection: Turning Experience into Learning* (London: Kogan Page).

References

Bridgham, R G and Scarborough, S (1992) 'Effects of Supplemental Instruction in Selected Medical School Science Courses', *Academic Medicine*, 67, 10, 569–71.

Bronfenbrenner, U (1974) *The Ecology of Human Development* (Cambridge: Harvard University Press).

Brookfield, S (1983) *Adult Learners, Adult Education and the Community* (Buckingham: Open University Press).

Brown, S and Saunders, D (1995) 'The Challenges of Modularisation Innovations', *Education and Training International*, 32, 2, 96–106.

Buber, M (1958) *I and Thou* (New York: Scribners).

Button, B L, White, L and Metcalfe, R (1987) 'Proctoring' *Engineering Design Education*, Autumn, 4–8.

Button, B L, Sims, R and White, L (1990) 'Experience of Proctoring Over Three Years at Nottingham Polytechnic', in Goodlad, S and Hirst, B (eds), *Explorations in Peer Tutoring* (Oxford: Basil Blackwell).

Byrd, D E (1990) 'Peer Tutoring with the learning disabled: a critical review', *Journal of Educational Research*, 84, 2, 115 –18.

Cahalan, M and Farris, E (1990) *College Sponsored Tutoring and Mentoring Programs for Disadvantaged Elementary and Secondary Students Higher Education Surveys – Report Number 12* (Washington DC: US Department of Education Office of Planning, Budget and Evaluation) (ED 323884).

Campbell, I (1995) 'Student tutoring and pupil aspirations', in Goodlad, S (ed.) *Students as Tutors and Mentors* (London: Kogan Page).

Carlitz, R D (1995) 'Kidsphere', *Internet Research-Electronic Networking Applications and Policy*, 5, 1, 16.

Carnegie Inquiry into the Third Age (1993) *Life, Work, and Livelihood in the Third Age*, (Dumferline: Carnegie Trust).

Carroll, M (1996) 'Peer Tutoring: Can medical students teach biochemistry', *Biochemical Education*, 24, 1, 13–15.

Chisholm, L and Vally, S (1996) 'Finance and Governance in Recent Conflicts over Policy', *Wits Education Policy Unit Quarterly Review of Education and Training in South Africa*, 3, 4, 15 June.

Chyriwsky, M and Kennard, R (1997) 'Attitudes to able children; a survey of mathematics teachers in English secondary schools', *High Ability Studies*, 8, June.

Clawson, J G (1979) 'Superior-Subordinate Relationships for Managerial Development', unpublished doctoral dissertation, School of Business, Harvard University.

Cloward, R (1967) 'Studies in tutoring', *Journal of Experimental Education*, 36, 1, 14–25.

Clulow, V G (1993) 'Student Perceptions of Mentoring as a Student Support System in the Bachelor of Business' (Retail Management), unpublished thesis, University of South Australia.

Clulow, V G and Brennan, L (1996) 'Student relationship constellations and their impact on study success and persistence' Southern Marketing Vol II, *Conference proceedings of the 10th Australian Marketing Educators Conference, Adelaide South Australia*, February 1996.

Cohen, P A, Kulik, J A and Kulik, C C(1982) 'Educational outcomes of tutoring: a meta-analysis of findings', *American Educational Research Journal*, 19, 237–48.

Cone, A L (1988) 'Low Tech/High Touch Criterion-Based Learning', *Psychological Reports* 63, 1, 203–7.

Conrad, E E (1975) 'The effects of tutor achievement level, reinforcement training, and expectancy on peer tutoring' (PhD Thesis, University of Arizona University Microfilms No. 76, 1407).

Corbett, A (1997) 'Unleashing the power of the Internet as a classroom learning tool', *Computer Education*, 85, 14–17.

Cornell, D G, Callahan, C M, Bassin, L E and Ramsay, S G (1991) 'Affective development in accelerated students', in W T Southern and E D Jones *The Academic Acceleration of Gifted Children* (New York: Teachers' College).

Cornwall, M G (1979) *Students as Teachers: Peer Teaching in Higher Education* (Amsterdam: COWO, University of Amsterdam).

Cowie, H and Ruddock, J (1988) *Cooperative Groupwork* (Sheffield, Sheffield University).

Craig, D and Martin, A (1986) *Gaming and simulation for capability* (Loughborough: Sagset).

Cropley, A J (1995) 'Creative intelligence: a concept of "true" giftedness', in Freeman, J, Span, P and Wagner, H (eds) *Actualising Talent: a Life-span Approach* (London: Cassell).

CSV (1995a) *Learning Together: The added value of student tutors volunteering in schools* (London: Community Service Volunteers).

CSV (1995b) *Learning Together: Student Tutoring – Research and evaluation papers on pupil aspirations and student tutor skills* (London: Community Service Volunteers).

CSV (1996) *National Student Tutoring Network: A directory of student tutoring programmes in the UK* (London: Community Service Volunteers) plus amendments 3 March 1997.

Dahme, G (1996) 'Teachers' conceptions of gifted students in Indonesia (Java), Germany and USA' Paper given at the 5th conference of the European Council for High Ability, Vienna.

Daloz, L (1986) *Effective Teaching and Mentoring* (San Francisco: Jossey-Bass).

Davidoff, S and Van den Berg, O (1990) *Changing Your Teaching: The Challenge of the Classroom* (Pietermaritzburg: Centaur).

De Groot, M (1991) *An Evaluation of the Department of Psychology's Mentoring Programme* (Johannesburg: University of the Witwatersrand, Department of Psychology) (mimeo).

Davis, C S (1978) 'Peer Tutors: Their Utility and Training in the Personalised System of Instruction', *Educational Technology*, 18, 23–6.

Davis, D, Snapiri, T and Golan, P (1984) *A survey of tutoring activities in Israel and associated evaluation studies* Publication No. 96 (Jerusalem: Research Institute for Innovation in Education, The Hebrew University of Jerusalem, School of Education).

Dennison, B and Kirk, R (1990) *Do, Review, Learn, Apply: A Simple Guide to Experiential Learning* (Oxford: Blackwell Education).

Department of Education, Pretoria (1996) *Green Paper on Higher Education Transformation*, December 1996.

Department of Employment (1994) *Enterprize in Higher Education: the first eleven* (Sheffield: Department of Employment).

Deslisle, J R (1992) *Guiding the Social and Emotional Development of Gifted Youth* (Harlow: Longman).

Devin-Sheehan, L, Feldman, R S and Allen, V L (1976) 'Research on children tutoring children: a critical review', *Review of Educational Research* 46, 355–85.

Dison, L and Pinto, D (1995) 'Collaboratively Developed Discipline-Based Materials for Academic Development Practice', *South African Journal of Higher Education*, 9, 2.

Doise, W and Mugny, G (1984) *The Social Development of the Intellect* (Oxford: Pergamon Press).

Donaldson, A J M and Topping, K (1997) *Promoting Peer Assisted Learning Among Students in Higher and Further Education* (SEDA Paper 96) (Birmingham: Staff and Educational Development Association).

Durden, W G and Tangherlini, A E (1993) *Smart Kids: How Academic Talents are Developed and Nurtured in America* (Toronto: Hogrefe and Huber).

Durling, R and Schick, C (1976) Concept Attainment By Pairs and Individuals as a Function of Vocalization, *Journal of Educational Psychology*, 68, 1, 83–91.

Ebbutt, D (1985) 'Educational Action Research: Some General Concerns and Specific Quibbles' in Burgess, R (ed), *Issues in Educational Research: Qualitative Methods* (London: Falmer Press).

Eisenberg, T, Fresko, B and Carmeli, M (1980a) *A Tutorial Project For Disadvantaged Children: An evaluation of the PERACH project* (Rehovot, Israel: PERACH, Weizmann Institute of Science).

Eisenberg, T, Fresko, B and Carmeli, M (1980b) *PERACH: A tutorial project for disadvantaged children* (Rehovot: The Weizmann Institute of Science).

Eisenberg, T, Fresko, B and Carmeli, M (1981) 'An assessment of cognitive change in socially disadvantaged children as a result of a one-to-one tutoring program', *Journal of Educational Research*, 74, 5, 311–14.

Eisenberg, T, Fresko, B and Carmeli, M (1982) 'Affective changes in socially disadvantaged children as a result of one-to-one tutoring', *Studies in Educational Evaluation* 8, 2, 141–51.

Eisenberg, T, Fresko, B and Carmeli, M (1983a) 'A follow-up study of disadvantaged children two years after being tutored', *Journal of Educational Research*, 76, 5, 302–6.

Eisenberg, T, Fresko, B and Carmeli, M (1983b) *The effect at different grade levels of one and two years of tutoring* (Rehovot, Israel: PERACH, Weizmann Institute).

Elliot, J (1978a) *Action Research in Schools – Some Guidelines* (Cambridge: Institute of Education).

Elliot, J (1978b) 'What is Action Research in Schools?', *Journal of Curriculum Studies*, 10, 4.

Ellis, R (1993) *Quality Assurance for University Teaching* (Buckingham: Open University Press).

Ellsbury, J, Wood, J and Fitz-Gibbon, C (1995) 'The impact of student tutoring on pupils' educational aspirations: evidence from Tyneside', in *Learning Together: Student Tutoring,* Research and evaluation papers on pupil aspirations and student tutor skills (London: Community Service Volunteers).

Ellson, D G (1986) 'Improving productivity in teaching', *Phi Delta Kappan*, October, 111–24.

Ellson, D G, Barber, L W and Harris, P L (1969) *A Nation-wide Evaluation of Programmed Tutoring* (Illinois: Department of Psychology, University of Indiana).

Ellson, D G, Barber, L, Engle, T L and Kampwerth, L (1965) 'Programmed tutoring: a teaching aid and a research tool', *Reading Research Quarterly*, 1, Fall, 77–127.

Ellson, D G and Harris, P L (1970) *Project Evaluation Report: Programmed Tutoring on Beginning Reading New Albany Public School System 1969–70* (Mimeo). (Illinois: Department of Psychology, University of Indiana).

Ellson, D G, Harris, P L and Barber, L (1968) 'A field test of programmed and directed tutoring', *Reading Research Quarterly*, 3, 3, Spring, 307–67.

Entwistle, N (1992) *The Impact of Teaching and Learning Outcomes in Higher Education: A Literature Review* (Sheffield: Universities and Colleges Staff Development Unit, CVCP).

Entwistle, N and Ramsden, P (1983) *Understanding Student Learning* (Beckenham: Croom Helm).

ERIC Office of Educational Research and improvement (1988) *ERIC Database: College students who tutor elementary and secondary students* (Washington DC: US Department of Education).

Erikson, E H (1950) *Childhood and Society* (New York: W W Norton and Sons).

Evans, J (1993) *Participatory evaluations of child-to-child projects in India funded by the Aga Khan Foundation* (Geneva: Aga Khan Foundation).

Evans, N (1993) *Work-based learning for academic credit* (Sheffield: Department of Employment).

Evans, T W (1992) *Mentors: Making a Difference in Our Public Schools* (Princeton: Peterson's Guides).

Eysenck, H J (1995) *Genius: the Natural History of Creativity* (Cambridge: Cambridge University Press).

Falchikov, N (1990) 'An Experiment in Same-age Peer Tutoring in Higher Education: Some Observations Concerning the Repeated Experience of Tutoring or Being Tutored', in Goodlad, S and Hirst, B (eds), *Explorations in Peer Tutoring* (Oxford: Basil Blackwell).

Fantuzzo, J W, Dimeff, L A and Fox, S L (1989) 'Reciprocal Peer Tutoring: A multimodal assessment of effectiveness with college students', *Teaching of Psychology*, 16, 3, 133–5.

Fantuzzo, J W, Riggio, R W, Connelly, S and Dimeff, L (1989) 'Effects of Reciprocal Peer Tutoring on Academic Achievement and Psychological Adjustment: A Component Analysis', *Journal of Educational Psychology*, 81, 2, 173–7.

Fineman, S (1981) 'Reflections on Peer Teaching and Peer Assessment: An Undergraduate Experience', *Assessment and Evaluation in Higher Education*, 6, 1, 82–93.

Feldman, R S, Devin-Sheehan, L and Allen, V L (1976) 'Children tutoring children: a critical review of research', in Allen, V L (ed) *Children as Teachers* (London: Academic Press).

Foot, H C, Morag, M J and Shute, R H (eds) (1990) *Children Helping Children* (Chichester: Wiley).

Foot, H C, Shute, R H, Morgan, M J and Barron, A (1990) 'Theoretical Issues in Peer Tutoring', in Foot, H C, Morgan, M J and Shute, R H (eds), *Children Helping Children* (Chichester: Wiley).

Foot, H C, Howe, C J, Anderson, A, Tolmie, A K and Warden, D A (1994) *Group and Interactive Learning* (Southampton: Computational Mechanics Publications).

Forman, E (1994) 'Peer Collaboration As Situated Activity: Examples from Research on Scientific Problem Solving', in Foot, H C, Howe, C J, Anderson, A, Tolmie, A K and Warden, D A (eds), *Group and Interactive Learning* (Southampton: Computational Mechanics).

Freedman, M (1988) *Partners in Growth: Elder Mentors and At-risk Youth* (Philadelphia, PA: Public/Private Ventures).

Freeman, J (1991) *Gifted Children Growing Up* (London: Cassell).

Freeman, J (1995) 'Conflicts In Creativity', *European Journal for High Ability*, 6, 188–200.

Freeman, J (1996) *Highly Able Girls and Boys* (London: Department of Education and Employment).

Freeman, J (in process) (1997a) *The Education of the Very Able: Current International Research* (London: OFSTED).

Freeman, J (in press) (1997b) 'Emotional development of the highly able child', *European Journal of Psychology in Education.*

Fremouw, W J and Feindler, E L (1978) 'Peer Versus Professional Models for Study Skills Training', *Journal of Counseling Psychology*, 25, 6, 576–80.

Fresko, B (1988) 'Reward salience, assessment of success and critical attitudes among tutors', *Journal of Educational Research*, 81, 341–6.

Fresko, B (1993) 'Attitudinal change among PERACH tutors: some consequences of tutoring for university student tutors', Doctoral dissertation. School of Education, Tel-Aviv University.

Fresko, B (1996) 'Effects of tutor-tutee intimacy, tutoring conditions and tutor background on college student tutor satisfaction', *Educational Studies*, 22, 2, 147–64.

Fresko, B and Carmeli, M (1990) 'PERACH: A nation-wide student tutorial project', in Goodlad, S and Hirst, B (eds) *Explorations in Peer Tutoring* (Oxford: Basil Blackwell).

Fresko, B and Chen, M (1989) 'Ethnic similarity, tutor expertise and tutor satisfaction', *American Educational Research Journal*, 26, 1, 122–40.

Fresko, B and Eisenberg, T (1985) 'The effects of two years of tutoring on mathematics and reading achievement', *Journal of Experimental Education*, 53, 4, 193–201.

Fresko, B and Kowalski, R (1995) *The relationship between the child's grade and mentoring activities, impact, and mentor satisfaction: Results from a survey of PERACH mentors in 1994* (Rehovot, Israel: The Weizmann Institute of Science) (in Hebrew).

Fresko, B and Kowalski, R (1996) *The effect of grade level and concentration of mentors on classroom learning environment and self evaluations* (Rehovot, Israel: The Weizmann Institute of Science) (in Hebrew).

Fuchs, L S, Fuchs, D, Bentz, J, Phillips, N B and Hamlett, C L (1994) 'The nature of student interactions during peer tutoring with and without prior training and experience', *American Educational Research Journal*, 31, 1, 75–103, Spring.

Fullan, M and Watson, N (1990) *The Learning Consortium. Strengthening the Links in a School/University Partnership*, Case study report, prepared for IMTEC International Conference, Oxford.

Garcia-Vazquez, E and Ehly, S W (1992) 'Peer tutoring effects on students who are perceived as not socially accepted', *Psychology in the Schools*, 29 July, 256–66.

Gardner, H (1993) *Creating Minds: An Anatomy of Creativity Seen through the lives of Freud, Einstein, Picasso, Stravinsky, Elliot, Graham, and Gandhi* (New York: Basic Books).

Garmezy, N and Rutter, M (1983) *Stress, Coping and Development in Children* (New York: McGraw-Hill).

Garson, P (1996) 'Radical proposals for higher learning', *The Mail and Guardian* 19 April (Johannesburg).

Gartner, S, Kohler, M and Riessman, F (1971) *Children Teach Children: Learning by Teaching* (New York: Harper & Row).

Gerber, M and Kauffman, J M (1981) 'Peer tutoring in academic settings', in Strain, P S (ed) *The utilization of classroom peers as behavior change agents*, 151–87 (New York: Plenum Press).

Gere, A R (1987) *Writing Groups: History, Theory and Implications* (Carbondale IL: Southern Illinois University Press).

Gibb, J (1978) *Trust. A New View of Personal and Organizational Development* (Los Angeles: Tutors Press).

Gibbs, G (1981) *Teaching Students to Learn* (Buckingham: Open University Press).

Goertzel, M G, Goertzel, V and Goertzel, T G (1978) *300 Eminent Personalities* (San Francisco: Jossey Bass).

Goldschmid, B and Goldschmid, M L (1976) 'Peer Teaching in Higher Education: A Review', *Higher Education*, 5, 9–33.

Goodlad, S (1979) *Learning by Teaching* (London: Community Service Volunteers).

Goodlad, S (ed) (1982) *Study Service: An Examination of community service as a method of study in higher education* (Windsor: NFER-Nelson).

Goodlad, S (ed) (1984) *Education for the Professions: Quis Custodiet?* (Windsor: SRHE and NFER-Nelson).

Goodlad, S (1985) 'Putting Science into Context', *Educational Research*, 27, 1, 61–7.

Goodlad, S (ed) (1995a) *Students as Tutors and Mentors* (London: Kogan Page).

Goodlad, S (1995b) *The Quest for Quality: Sixteen forms of heresy in higher education* (Buckingham: Society for Research into Higher Education and Open University Press).

Goodlad, S (1997a) 'Students as tutors and mentors', keynote address IC/BP International Conference, London, April.
Goodlad, S (1997b) 'Responding to the perceived training needs of graduate teaching assistants', *Studies in Higher Education*, 22, 1, 83–92.
Goodlad, S (1997c) 'Simulating laboratory teaching for graduate teaching assistants', in Saunders, P and Cox, B (eds) *Research into Simulations in Education: The International Simulation and Gaming Yearbook Volume 5* (London: Kogan Page).
Goodlad, S and Hirst, B (1989) *Peer Tutoring: A Guide to Learning by Teaching* (London: Kogan Page).
Goodlad, S and Hirst, B (eds) (1990) *Explorations in Peer Tutoring* (Oxford: Basil Blackwell).
Gottfried, A W, Gottfried, A E, Bathurst, K and Guerin, D W (1994) *Gifted IQ; Early Developmental Aspects* (New York: Plenum).
Graves, N B and Graves, T D (1985) 'Creating a Cooperative Learning Environment: An Ecological Approach', in Slavin, R, Shlomo, S, Kagan, S, Lazarowitz, R H, Webb C and Schmuck, R (eds) *Learning to Cooperate, Cooperating to Learn* (New York: Plenum Press).
Gray, W and Gray, M (eds) (1986) *Mentoring: Aid to Excellence in Education, the Family, and the Community* Volumes I, II (Vancouver: International Centre for Mentoring).
Green, L and Hughes, J C (1992) *Report of the 2nd BP National Workshop on Student Tutoring* (London: Imperial College).
Greenstein, R (1995) 'New Policies, Old Challenges: Reshaping the Education System', *Wits Education Policy Unit Quarterly Review of Education and Training in South Africa*, 3, 1, 15 September.
Greenwood, C R, Carta, J J and Kamps, D (1990) 'Teacher-mediated versus Peer-mediated Instruction: A Review of Educational Advantages and Disadvantages', in Foot, H C, Morgan, M J and Shute, R H (eds), *Children Helping Children* (Chichester: Wiley).
Haensly, P (1989) 'Mentoring in the Educational Setting: A Pedagogical Quintessence', *Mentoring International*, 3, 2, 25–33.
Hamburg, D (1992) *Today's Children. Creating a Future for a Generation in Crisis* (New York: Times Books).
Hamilton, S and Hamilton, M (1992) 'Mentoring Programmes: Promise and Paradox', *Phi Delta Kappan*, 73, 7, 546–50.
Hany, E A (1993) 'How teachers identify gifted students: feature processing or concept based classification', *European Journal for High Ability*, 4, 196–211.
Hany, E A (1996) 'How leisure activities correspond to the development of creative achievement: insights from a study of highly intelligent individuals', *High Ability Studies*, 7, 65–82.
Hanley, P (1996) 'Mentor involvement in a university orientation program – the James Cook experience', *Proceedings of the 2nd Pacific Rim Conference on the First Year in Higher Education, Transition to Active Learning*, Ormond College University of Melbourne, 3–5 July, 243–7.

Harrison, G V (1969) *The effects of trained and untrained tutors on criterion performance of disadvantaged first graders* (Los Angeles: University of California) (ERIC No ED 031 449)

Harrison, G V (1971a) *Structured Tutoring* (Provo, Utah: Department of Instructional Research and Development, Brigham Young University) (ERIC No 053 080).

Harrison, G V (1971b) *How to organise an inter-grade tutoring program in an elementary school* (Provo, Utah: Brigham Young University Printing Service).

Harrison, G V (1972a) *Supervisors' Guide for the Structured Tutorial Reading Program* (Provo, Utah: Brigham Young University Press).

Harrison, G V (1972b) 'Tutoring: a remedy reconsidered', *Improving Human Performance* 1, 4, 1–7.

Harrison, S R (1993) *Statistics for Business, Economics and Management* (Englewood Cliffs, NJ: Prentice Hall).

Hart, G (1990) 'Peer Learning and Support via Audio-teleconferencing in Continuing Education for Nurses', *Distance Education,* 11, 2, 308–19.

Hartman, H J (1990) 'Factors Affecting the Tutoring Process', *Journal of Educational Development* 14, 2, 2–6.

Hawes, H (1993) *Child-to-Child – Doing it better* (London: Child-to-Child Trust).

Hawksworth, A and Caplan, B (1996) *The Pimlico Connection 21st Annual Report 1995/96* (London: Imperial College of Science, Technology and Medicine and BP).

Hay, I (1993) 'Writing Groups in Geography', in *Proceedings of Conference on Peer Tutoring at the University of Auckland 19–21 August 1993* (Auckland: Higher Education Research Office, University of Auckland).

Healy, C E (1994) 'Supplemental Instruction: A Model for Supporting Student Learning', in Foot, H C, Howe, C J, Anderson, A, Tolmie, A K and Warden, D A (eds) *Group and Interactive Learning* (Southampton: Computational Mechanics).

Hector Taylor, M (1992) *Report of the Sheffield Tutoring Scheme* (Sheffield: University of Sheffield Enterprise Unit).

Hendelman, W J and Boss, M (1986) 'Reciprocal Peer Teaching by Medical Students in the Gross Anatomy Laboratory', *Journal of Medical Education,* 61, 8, 674–80.

Hill, S and Topping, K (1995) 'Cognitive and transferable skill gains for student tutors', in Goodlad, S (ed) *Students as Tutors and Mentors* (London: Kogan Page).

Hofmeister, J, Veugelers, W and Welie, L (1993) 'Improving the tie-up between pre-university and higher education', paper presented at the ATEE Conference Lisbon.

Hofmeister, J and Veugelers, W (1994) 'Recent Developments in Career Education in the Netherlands: Learning by Experience and Value Stimulation', paper presented at the AERA Conference New Orleans, USA. In: *Resources in Education,* February 1995.

Holahan, C K and Sears, R R (1995) *The Gifted Group in Later Maturity* (Stanford, CA: Stanford University Press).

Holladay, J (1989) *Monroe County Community College Writing Across the Curriculum: Annual Report 1988–89* (Michigan: Monroe County Community College) (ED 310820).

Holladay, J (1990) *Writing Across the Curriculum: Annual Report 1989–90* (Michigan: Monroe County Community College) (ED 326260).

House, J D and Wohlt, V (1990) 'The Effect of Tutoring Program Participation on the Performance of Academically Underprepared College Freshmen', *Journal of College Student Development*, 31, 365–70.

Hughes, D R (1993) 'Appropriate and distributed networks – a model for K–12 educational telecommunications', *Internet Research-Electronic Networking Applications and Policy*, 3, 4, 22–9.

Hughes, J C (ed) (1991) *Tutoring Resource Pack* (Alton: BP Educational Service).

Hughes, J (1992) *Tutoring: students as tutors in schools* (London: BP).

Hughes, J and Metcalfe, R (1994) 'Student Tutoring', in Saunders, D (ed) *The Complete Student Handbook* (Oxford: Basil Blackwell).

Hustler, D, Cassidy, T and Cuff, T (eds) (1986) *Action Research in Classrooms and Schools* (London: Allen and Unwin).

Jacobi, M (1991) 'Mentoring and Undergraduate Success: A Literature Review', *Review of Educational Research*, Winter, 61, 4, 505–32.

Johansen, M L, Martenson, D F and Bircher, J (1992) 'Students as Tutors in Problem-based Learning: Does It Work?', *Medical Education*, 26, 2, 163–5.

Johnston, C (1993) 'The Integration of Trainee Teachers in an Undergraduate Peer Tutoring Project at the University of Melbourne' in *Proceedings of Conference on Peer Tutoring at the University of Auckland 19–21 August 1993* (Auckland: Higher Education Research Office, University of Auckland).

Jones, J (1989) *Effect of Student Tutors on School Students' Attitudes and Aspirations: report to the Department of Education* (Auckland: Higher Education Research Office).

Jones, J (1990) 'Tutoring as Field-based Learning: Some New Zealand developments', in Goodlad, S and Hirst, B (eds) *Explorations in Peer Tutoring* (Oxford: Basil Blackwell).

Jones, J (1993a) 'University Students as Tutors In Secondary Schools', in *Proceedings of a conference on peer tutoring at the University of Auckland New Zealand 19–21 August 1993*, (Higher Education Research Office, University of Auckland).

Jones, J (ed) (1993b) *Peer Tutoring: Learning by Teaching*, Proceedings of Auckland Conference on Peer Tutoring, August.

Juler, P (1992) *Distance Teaching and Learning 2*, UDE604, University of South Australia.

Kampen, F, Jeeninga, W, Hofmeister, J and Woolthuis, F (1996) *Newsletter 1* (English edition) Mentor/Monitor Project VWO-UvA Crossover Programme (Amsterdam: University of Amsterdam).

Katgitcibasi, C (1992) 'Human development and societal development: linking theory and application', *Cross-cultural Psychology Bulletin*, 26, 3, 3.

Katjavivi, P H (1997) 'Commencement day address', *UNAM Forum*, 21, January/ February, 2–4.

Kaufman, F A (1992) 'What educators can learn from gifted adults', in Monks, F J and Peters, W (eds) *Talent for the Future*, (Maastricht: Van Gorcum).

Kaufman, F A, Harrel, G, Milam, C P, Woolverton, N and Miller, L B (1986) 'The nature role and influence of mentors in the lives of gifted adults', *Journal of Counselling and Development*, 64, 576–8.

Keller, F S (1968) 'Goodbye, Teacher...', *Journal of Applied Behavior Analysis*, 1, 1, 79–89.

Kennedy, M (1990) 'Cross-age tutoring – a controlled evaluation using poor readers in a comprehensive school', in Goodlad, S and Hirst, B (eds) *Explorations in Peer Tutoring* (Oxford: Basil Blackwell).

Kenney, P A and Kallison, J M (1994) 'Research Studies on the Effectiveness of Supplemental Instruction in Mathematics', *New Directions for Teaching and Learning*, 60, 4, 75–82 (Special issue on Supplemental Instruction).

Kulik, J A, Kulik, C C and Cohen, P A (1979) 'A Meta-Analysis of Outcome Studies of Keller's Personalized System of Instruction', *American Psychologist*, 34, 4, 307–18.

Klopf, G and Harrison, J (1982) *Mentoring* (New York: The Center for Leadership Development).

Kolb, D A (1984) *Experiential Learning: experience as the source of learning and development* (Englewood Cliffs, NJ: Prentice Hall).

Kozol, J (1995) *Amazing Grace: The Lives of Children and the Conscience of a Nation* (New York: HarperCollins).

Kram, K E (1980) *Mentoring Process at Work* (New Haven: Yale University Press).

Kram, K E (1985) *Mentoring at Work: Developmental Relationships in Organizational Life* (Glenview Illinois: Scott Foresman).

Kram, K E and Isabella, L A (1985) 'Mentoring alternatives: The role of peer relationships in career development', *Academy of Management Journal*, 28, 110–32.

Kram, K E (1986) 'Mentoring in the Workplace', in Hall, D T *et al. Career Development in Organisations* (San Francisco: Jossey-Bass).

Kurth-Schai, R (1988) 'The Roles of Youth in Society: A Reconceptualization', *The Educational Forum*, 52, 2, 113–32.

Lansdown, R (1995) *Child-to-child: a review of literature* (London: Child-to-Child Trust).

Laurillard, D (1993) *Rethinking University Teaching* (Buckingham: Open University Press).

Lawson, D (1989) 'Peer Helping Programs in the Colleges and Universities of Quebec and Ontario', *Canadian Journal of Counselling*, 23, 1, 41–56.

Lee, R E (1988) 'Assessing Retention Program Holding Power Effectiveness Across Smaller Community Colleges', *Journal of College Student Development*, 29, 3, 255–62.

Levin, H M, Glass, G V and Meister, G R (1987) 'A Cost-effectiveness Analysis of Computer-assisted Instruction', *Evaluation Review*, 11, 1, 50–72.

Levine, J R (1990) 'Using a Peer Tutor to Improve Writing in a Psychology Class: One Instructor's Experience', *Teaching of Psychology*, 17, 1, 57–8.

Levinson, D J, Darrow, C N, Klein, E B, Levinson, M H and McKee, B (1978) *The Seasons of a Man's Life* (New York: A Knopf).

Lidren, D M, Meier, S E and Brigham, T A (1991) 'The Effects of Minimal and Maximal Peer Tutoring Systems on the Academic Performance of College Students', *Psychological Record*, 41, 1, 69–77.

Loh, H (1993) 'Peer Assisted Study Sessions in Anatomy for Nursing Students', in *Proceedings of Conference on Peer Tutoring at the University of Auckland 19–21 August 1983* (Auckland: Higher Education Research Office, University of Auckland).

Longuevan, C and Shoemaker, J (1991) 'Using Multiple Regression to Evaluate a Peer Tutoring Program for Undergraduates', paper Presented at the Annual Meeting of the California Educational Research Association, San Diego CA, November 14–15 (ED 341717).

Louth, R, McAllister, C and McAllister, H A (1993) 'The Effects of Collaborative Writing Techniques on Freshman Writing and Attitudes', *Journal of Experimental Education*, 61, 3, 215–24.

Lorentz, E and Pascarelli, J T (1988) 'Mentoring: A Journey not a Destination', concept chapter presented for The New York State Task Force on Mentoring.

Lovell, R B (1980) *Adult Learning* (London: Routledge).

Lundeberg, M A (1990) 'Supplemental Instruction in Chemistry', *Journal of Research in Science Teaching*, 27, 2, 145–55.

McDonnell, J T (1994) 'Peer Tutoring: A Pilot Scheme Among Computer Science Undergraduates', *Mentoring and Tutoring*, 2, 2, 3–10.

McInnis, C and James, R with McNaught, C (1995) *First year on campus. Diversity in the initial experiences of Australian undergraduates* (Canberra: Australian Government Publishing Service).

McInnis, N (1972) *You Are an Environment* (Evanston, Il: The Center for Curriculum Design).

McKellar, N A (1986) 'Behaviors Used in Peer Tutoring', *Journal of Experimental Education*, 54, 3, 163–7.

McKavanagh, M, Connor, J and West, J (1996) 'It's moments like these you need mentors', *Proceedings of the 2nd Pacific Rim Conference on the First Year in Higher Education, Transition to Active Learning*, Ormond College University of Melbourne, 3–5 July, 303–14.

McPartland, J E and Slavin, R (1990) *Policy Perspectives: Increasing Achievement of At-Risk Students at Each Grade Level* (Washington, DC: Office of Educational Research and Improvement, US Department of Education, US Government Printing Office).

Magin, D and Churches, A (1993) 'Student Proctoring: Who Learns What?', *Proceedings of Conference on Peer Tutoring at the University of Auckland 19–21 August 1993* (Auckland: Higher Education Research Office, University of Auckland).

Malhotra, N K (1993) *Marketing Research: an Applied Orientation* (Englewood Cliffs, NJ: Prentice Hall).

Mallatrat, J (1994) 'Learning About The Learners – The Impact of a Peer Tutoring Scheme', in Foot, H C, Howe, C J, Anderson, A, Tolmie, A K and Warden, D A (eds), *Group and Interactive Learning* (Southampton: Computational Mechanics).

Martin, D C and Arendale, D R (1990) 'Supplemental Instruction: Improving Student Performance', *Increasing Student Persistence*, (Kansas City, MO: University of Missouri).

Martin, D C and Arendale, D R (1992) 'Supplemental Instruction: Improving First-year Student Success in High-risk Courses', *The Freshman Year Experience*: Monograph Series No.7 (Columbia SC: South Carolina University) (ED 354839).

Martin, D, Blanc, R and Debuhr, L (1983) 'Breaking the Attrition Cycle; The Effects of Supplemental Instruction on Undergraduate Performance and Attrition', *Journal of Higher Education*, 54, 80–90.

Markova, K (1987) 'On the Interaction of Opposites in Psychological Processes', paper presented at the Fourth Annual Northeast Community Psychology Conference, New Haven, CT, 24 October.

Martin, D C, Blanc, R A and DeBuhr, L (1983) 'Breaking The Attrition Cycle: The Effects of Supplemental Instruction on Undergraduate Performance and Attrition', *Journal of Higher Education*, 54, 1, 80–89.

Marton, F, Hounsell, D and Entwistle, N (1984) *The Experience of Learning* (Edinburgh: Scottish Academic Press).

Marton, F and Saljo, R (1976a) 'On qualitative differences in learning: outcome and process', *British Journal of Educational Psychology*, 46, 4–11.

Marton, F and Saljo, R (1976b) 'On qualitative differences in learning: II Outcomes as a function of the learner's conception of the task', *British Journal of Educational Psychology*, 46, 115–27.

Maslow, A (1954) *Motivation and personality* (New York: Harper & Row).

Maxwell, M (1990) 'Does Tutoring Help? A Look at the Literature', *Review of Research in Developmental Education*, 7, 4, 3–7.

Maxwell, M (1979) *Improving Student Learning Skills: A Comprehensive Guide to Successful Practices and Programs for Increasing the Performance of Underprepared Students* (San Francisco: Jossey-Bass).

Maxwell, M (1991) 'Cost Effective Alternatives to Tutoring', *Journal of Learning Improvement*, 1, 1, 1–4.

Meredith, G M and Schmitz, E D (1986) 'Student-Taught and Faculty-Taught Seminars in Undergraduate Education: Another Look', *Perceptual and Motor Skills*, 62, 2, 593–4.

Merriam, R and Caffarella, R S (1991) *Learning in Adulthood* (San Francisco: Jossey-Bass).

Meyer, M (1991) 'Evaluation of some Innovations introduced in Chemistry I'; in-house report, University of the Witwatersrand, Johannesburg.

Ministry of Basic Education and Culture (1993) *Toward Education for All. A development brief for education, culture, and training* (Windhoek: Gamsberg Macmillan).

Ministry of Basic Education and Culture Directorate of Planning and Development (1996) *Education Management Information Systems* (EMIS) A profile of education in Namibia (Windhoek: Prime Press).

Mokgalane, E and Vally, S (1996) 'Between Vision and Practice: Policy Processes and Implementation', *Wits Education Policy Unit Quarterly Review of Education and Training in South Africa*, 3, 4, 15 March.

Moody, S and McCrae, J (1994) 'Cross Year Peer Tutoring With Law Undergraduates', in Foot, H C, Howe, C J, Anderson, A, Tolmie, A K and Warden, D A (eds), *Group and Interactive Learning* (Southampton: Computational Mechanics).

Moon, J and Reynolds, S (1996) *The Welsh Higher Education Credit Framework Handbook* (Cardiff and Sheffield, Wales Access Unit and Department for Education and Employment).

Moore, M G (1989) 'Three types of interaction' (editorial), *American Journal of Distance Education* 3, 2.

Moore-West, M, Hennessy, A, Meilman, P W and O'Donnell, J F (1990) 'The Presence of Student-based Peer Advising, Peer Tutoring and Performance Evaluation Programs Among U S Medical Schools', *Academic Medicine,* 65, 10, 660–61.

Mostert, M L and Zimba, R F (1990) *Child-to-child in Namibia* (Windhoek: University of Namibia Printery)

Motala, S (1996) 'Contested Visions: Between Policy and Practice', *Wits Education Policy Unit Quarterly Review of Education and Training in South Africa*, 4, 1, 15 September.

Moust, J C, De Volder, M L and Nuy, H J P (1989) 'Peer teaching and higher level cognitive learning outcomes in problem-based learning', *Higher Education,* 18, 737–42.

Moust, J C and Schmidt, H G (1992) 'Undergraduate Students as Tutors: Are They As Effective As Faculty in Conducting Small-group Tutorials?', paper presented at the American Educational Research Association Symposium on Rewarding Teaching at Research Universities, San Francisco CA, April 23 (ED 346774).

Moust, J C and Schmidt, H G (1994a) 'Facilitating Small-Group Learning: A Comparison of Student and Staff Tutors' Behavior', *Instructional Science,* 22, 287–301.

Moust, J C and Schmidt, H G (1994b) 'Effects of Staff and Student Tutors on Student Achievement', *Higher Education,* 28, 471–82.

Mumford, A (1980) *Making Experience Pay* (Maidenhead: McGraw-Hill).

National Center for Supplemental Instruction (1994) *Review of Research Concerning the Effectiveness of SI* (Kansas City MO: NCSI, University of Missouri at Kansas City).

National Commission on Higher Education (1996) *A Framework for Expansion* (Pretoria).

National Commission on Higher Education (1996) *A Framework for Transformation* (Pretoria).

Neugarten, B L (1975) 'Adult Personality: toward the psychology of the life cycle', in Sae, W C (ed) *Human Life Cycle,* (New York: Jason-Aronson).

Niedermeyer, F C (1970) 'Effects of training on the instructional behaviors of student tutors', *Journal of Educational Research,* 64, 3, 119–23.

Njabili, A F (1996) 'Predictive validity of the 1995 IGCSE mock results as a criterion for provisional admission to the University of Namibia, 1996 academic year' (report to Senate; unpublished).

O'Donnell, A M, Dansereau, D F, Rocklin, T, Lambiotte, J G, Hythecker, V I and Larson, C O (1985) 'Co-operative Writing: Direct Effects and Transfer', *Written Communication*, 2, 3, 307–15.

OERI (1993) *National Excellence: A Case for Developing America's Talent* (Office of Educational Research and Improvement, Washington: US Department of Education)

Ogg, A (1992) *Tutor Outreach programme: a student tutoring pilot* (Glasgow: BP)

Ojanen, S and Freeman, J (1994) *The Attitudes and Experiences of Headteachers, Class-teachers, and Highly Able Pupils towards the Education of the Highly Able in Finland and Britain* (Savonlinna: University of Joensuu).

Oley, N (1992) 'Extra Credit and Peer Tutoring: Impact on the Quality of Writing in Introductory Psychology in an OA College', *Teaching of Psychology*, 19, 2, 78–81.

Olson, G A (ed) (1984) *Writing Centers: Theory and Administration* (Illinois: National Council of Teachers of English).

Otaala, B (1994a) *Child-to-Child in northern Namibia: new initiatives* (Windhoek: Frewer's Printers).

Otaala, B (1994b) *Child-to-Child in southern Namibia* (Windhoek: Frewer's Printers).

Otaala, B (1995) *Health through the school A proposed pilot project* (Windhoek).

Otaala, B (1996) *Report on participation in the distinguished Fulbright Fellowship Programme* (Windhoek: UNAM Printery).

PC (1995) *Student Tutoring in Schools, 20th Annual Report 1994-5 The Pimlico Connection* (London: Imperial College of Science, Technology and Medicine).

Pascarella, E T and Terenzini, P T (1977) 'Patterns of student-faculty information interaction beyond the classroom and voluntary freshman attrition', *Journal of Higher Education*, 48, 540–52.

Pascarelli, J (1991) 'Creating and connecting new modes of learning', paper presented at the School of Education Forum, University of Portland, Portland, Oregon.

Paul, R H (1990) *Open Learning and Open Management – Leadership and Integrity in distance education* (London: Kogan Page).

PERACH Central Office (1984) *PERACH 1974–1984: Ten years of tutoring* (Rehovot, Israel: The Weizmann Institute of Science).

Perry, W G (1970) *Forms of intellectual and ethical development in the college years – a scheme* (New York: Holt, Rinehart and Winston).

Philips-Jones, L (1982) *Mentors and Protégés* (New York: Arbor House).

Pizzini, E L (1985) 'Improving science instruction for gifted high school students', *Roeper Review*, 7, 231–4.

Potter, C S (1993) *Design for a Process of Cooperative Research in the Department of Fine Arts* (University of the Witwatersrand: Academic Support Programme) (mimeo).

Potter, C S *et al.* (1994) 'Cooperative Research with Senior Students: Towards a Methodology', unpublished paper, Wits Academic Development, University of the Witwatersrand.

Potter, C S (1995) 'The Role of Senior Students in Supporting Curriculum Development and Change', paper presented at the University of Maryland

and City University of Hong Kong: 20th IUT Conference on Improving University Teaching.

Potter, C S (1996) 'Senior Students in University Teaching: Roles in Tutoring, Undergraduate Student Support and Curriculum Development', paper presented at the Conference on Student Contributions to Learning, Grahamstown, Rhodes University.

Potter, C S, Alfred, L, Chamberlain, C, Mason, G, Rule, P, Selikow, T and Taylor, C (1993) Cooperative Research with Senior Students: Towards a Methodology (Bellville: University of the Western Cape, SAAAD Conference Proceedings).

Potter, C S, De Groot, M, Pirs, C, Pitman, M, Puterman, M and Virtue, M (1996) 'Curriculum Design and Development of the Psychology Tutorial Programme at Wits University: The Role of Senior Students in Supporting Large Group Teaching', paper presented at the Conference on Student Contributions to Learning, Grahamstown, Rhodes University.

Potter, J (1994) *CSV Learning Together Annual Review 1993–1994* (London: Community Service Volunteers).

Potter, J (1995) 'New directions in student tutoring: the UK experience', in Goodlad, S (ed) *Students as Tutors and Mentors* (London: Kogan Page).

Potter, J (1995) 'Student Tutoring in the UK: an overview', in *Learning Together: the added value of student tutors volunteering in schools* (London: Community Service Volunteers).

Pridmore, P (1996) 'Child-to-child: empowering children for health', *Journal of Practice in Education for Development*, 1, 3, 5–10.

Renzulli, J S (1995) 'New directions for the school-wide enrichment model', in Katzko, M W and Monks, F J (eds) *Nurturing Talent; Individual Needs and Social Ability* (Assen, NL: Van Gorcum).

Quintrell, N and Westwood, M (1994) 'The Influence of a Peer-Pairing Program on International Students' First Year Experience and Use of Student Services', *Higher Education Research and Development*, 13, 1, 49–57.

Ramsden, P (ed) (1986) *Improving Learning* (London: Kogan Page).

Reddy, J (1996) 'The university in contemporary society – the South African challenge', D C S Oosthuizen memorial lecture, 25 September, Grahamstown, Rhodes University.

Reisner, E R, Petry, C A and Armitage, M (1990) *Review of programs involving college students as tutors or mentors in grades K–12* (Volumes I and II) (Washington DC: Policy Studies Institute, Department of Education).

Riggio, R E, Fantuzzo, J W, Connelly, S and Dimeff, L A (1991) 'Reciprocal Peer Tutoring: A classroom strategy for promoting academic and social integration in undergraduate students', *Journal of Social Behaviour and Personality*, 6, 2, 387–96.

Richardson, J T, Eysenck, M W and Piper, D W (eds) (1987) *Student Learning: Research in Education and Cognitive Psychology* (Buckingham: Open University Press).

Riggio, R E, Fantuzzo, J W, Connelly, S and Dimeff, L A (1991) 'Reciprocal Peer Tutoring: A Classroom Strategy for Promoting Academic and Social Integration in Undergraduate Students', *Journal of Social Behavior and Personality*, 6, 2, 387–96.

Rizzolo, P (1982) 'Peer Tutors Make Good Teachers: A Successful Writing Program', *Improving College and University Teaching*, 30, 3, 115–19.

Roberts, D (1984) 'Ways and Means of Reducing Early Student Drop-out', *Distance Education*, 5, 1.

Robertson, D (1994) *Choosing to change – extending access, choice, and mobility in higher education* (London: Higher Education Quality Council).

Robin, A L and Heselton, P (1977) 'Proctor Training: The Effects of a Manual Versus Direct Training', *Journal of Personalised Instruction*, 2, 19–24,

Rogers, C (1961) *On becoming a person* (London: Constable).

Rogers, C (1983) *Freedom to learn for the 80s* (Columbus: Charles E Merrill).

Rogers, J (1977) *Adults Learning* (2nd edn) (Buckingham: Open University Press).

Rogoff, B (1990) *Apprenticeship in Thinking: Cognitive Development in Social Context* (Oxford: Oxford University Press).

Rollnick, M *et al.* (1996) 'A Team-work Approach to Workshop Delivery for Tutor Development', paper presented at the Conference of the Australian Science Education Research Association, Canberra, July.

Rosen, S, Powell, E R and Schubot, D B (1977) 'Peer-Tutoring Outcomes as Influenced by the Equity and Type of Role Assignment', *Journal of Educational Psychology*, 69, 3, 244–52.

Rust, C (1993) 'Supplemental Instruction at Oxford Brookes University', paper given at Peer Tutoring Consortium Conference, University of Glamorgan, 23 June.

Rust, C and Wallace, J (eds) (1994) *Helping Students to Learn from Each Other: Supplemental Instruction* (Birmingham: Staff and Educational Development Association).

Rutherford, M and Hofmeyr, R (1995) 'Student tutoring in developing countries: practice and possibilities' in Goodlad, S (ed) *Students as Tutors and Mentors* (London: Kogan Page).

Rye, P D, Wallace, J and Bidgood, P (1993) 'Instruction in Learning Skills: An Integrated Approach', *Medical Education*, 27, 470–73.

Saito, R and Blyth, D (1992) *Understanding Mentoring Relationships* (Minneapolis: Search Institute).

Salmon, D (ed) (1932) *The Principal Parts of Lancaster's 'Improvements' and Bell's 'Experiment'* (Cambridge: Cambridge University Press).

Saunders, D (1992a) 'Peer tutoring in higher education', *Studies in Higher Education*, 17, 2, 211–18.

Saunders, D (1992b) 'Profiling in higher education', *Journal of the National Association for Staff Development*, 26, January, 51–7.

Saunders, D and Kingdon, R (1994) *Dysgu: Student Tutoring Wales* (University of Glamorgan and BP Chemicals).

Schaffer, J L, Wile, M Z and Griggs, R C (1990) 'Students Teaching Students: A Medical School Peer Tutorial Programme', *Medical Education*, 24, 4, 336–43.

Schaie, K W (1996) *Intellectual Development in Adulthood; The Seattle Longitudinal Study* (Cambridge: Cambridge University Press).

Schmidt, H, Arend, A V D, Kokx, I and Boon, L (1995) 'Peer Versus Staff Tutoring in Problem-based Learning', *Instructional Science*, 22, 279–85.

Shochet, I M (1986) 'Manifest and Potential Performance in Advantaged and Disadvantaged Students', unpublished PhD thesis, Johannesburg: University of the Witwatersrand.

Schön, D (1987) *Educating the Reflective Practitioner* (San Francisco: Jossey-Bass).

Scruggs, T E and Osguthorpe, R T (1986) 'Tutoring Interventions Within Special Education Settings: A Comparison of Cross-age and Peer Tutoring', *Psychology in the Schools*, 23, 2, 187–93.

Sewart, D (1978) *Continuity of Concern for Students in a System of Learning at a Distance* (Hagen: Fernuniversitat ZIFF).

Sharpley, A M and Sharpley, C F (1981) 'Peer Tutoring: A Review of the Literature', *Collected Original Resources in Education*, 5, 3, 7–11 (fiche 7 and 8).

Sherman, J G (1992) 'Reflections on PSI: Good News and Bad', *Journal of Applied Behavior Analysis*, 25, 1, 59–64.

Shore, M (1995) 'Students as tutors in early childhood settings: the acquisition and transmission of problem-solving skills', in Goodlad, S (ed) *Students as Tutors and Mentors* (London: Kogan Page).

Schunk, D H (1987) 'Self-efficacy and Motivated Learning'. in Hastings, N and Schwieso, J (eds), *New Directions in Educational Psychology: Behaviour and Motivation in the Classroom* (London: Falmer Press).

Schunk, D H and Zimmermann, B J (eds) (1994) *Self-Regulation of Learning and Performance* (New York: Lawrence Erlbaum).

Slavin, R E (1985) 'An Introduction to Cooperative Learning Research', in Slavin, R, Shlomo, S, Kagan, R H, Lazarowitz, C, Webb, C and Schmuck, R (eds) *Learning to Cooperate, Cooperating to Learn* (New York: Plenum Press).

Smith, P K (1983) *Tutoring: A National Perspective* (Washington, DC: Department of Education).

Stanley, J C, Lupkowski, A E and Assouline, S G (1990) 'Eight considerations for mathematically talented youth', *The Gifted Child Today*, 2–4.

Stenhouse, L (1975) *An Introduction to Curriculum Research and Development* (Oxford: Heinemann).

Stenhouse, L (1980) 'Curriculum Research and the Art of the Teacher', *Curriculum*, 1, 1, Spring.

Stenhouse, L (1981) 'What Counts as Research?', *British Journal of Educational Studies*, 29, 2, June.

Stenhouse, L (1983) 'The Curriculum as Hypothetical', in Rudduck, J and Hopkins, D (eds), *Research as a Basis for Teaching: Readings from the Work of Lawrence Stenhouse* (Oxford: Heinemann).

Stephenson, J and Laycock, M (1993) *Using Learning Contracts in Higher Education* (London: Kogan Page).

Stephenson, J, and Weil, S (1992) *Quality in Learning* (London: Kogan Page).

Sternberg, R J (1985) *Beyond I Q* (Cambridge: Cambridge University Press).

Sternberg, R J and Lubart, T I (1995) *Defying the Crowd; Cultivating Creativity in a Culture of Conformity* (New York: Free Press).

Street, L (1986) 'Mathematics, Teachers, and an Action Research Course', in Hustler, D, Cassidy, T and Cuff, T (eds), *Action Research in Classrooms and Schools,* (London: Allen and Unwin).

Strijdom, J L (1992) 'A drug policy and strategy for Namibia', unpublished PhD thesis, University of Bophuthatswana, Mmabatho.

Subotnik, R, Kassan, L, Summers, E and Wasser, A (1993) *Genius Revisited: High IQ Children Grow Up* (New Jersey: Ablex).

Subotnik, R F (1988) 'The motivation to experiment: a study of gifted adolescents' attitudes towards scientific research', *Journal for the Education of the Gifted,* 11, 19–35.

Sutherland, J A and Topping, K J (1997) 'Collaborative Creative Writing in Eight Year Olds: Comparing Cross Ability Fixed Role and Same Ability Reciprocal Role Pairing', paper submitted for publication.

Sutherland, P (ed) (1997) *Adult Learning: A Reader* (London: Kogan Page).

Taylor, C (1995) 'Senior Student Tutors: Partnerships in Teaching and Learning – A Case Study in Social Anthropology from South Africa', in Goodlad, S (ed) *Students as Tutors and Mentors* (London: Kogan Page).

Tempest, N R (1974) *Teaching Clever Children 7-11* (London: Routledge and Kegan Paul).

Terassier, J C (1985) 'Dysynchrony: uneven development', in Freeman, J (ed) *The Psychology of Gifted Children* (Chichester: Wiley).

Terenzini, P T and Wright, T M (1987) 'Influences on students' academic growth during four years of college', *Research in Higher Education,* 26, 161–79.

Thorley, L (1994) in Saunders, D (ed) *The Complete Student Handbook* (Oxford: Basil Blackwell).

Tight, M (ed) (1983) *Adult Learning and Education* (London: Routledge).

Tinto, V (1975) 'Dropout from higher education: A theoretical synthesis of recent research', *Review of Educational Research,* 45, 89–125.

Topping, K (1988) *The Peer Tutoring Handbook* (Beckenham: Croom Helm).

Topping, K (1990) 'Peer tutored paired reading: outcome data from 10 projects', in Goodlad, S and Hirst, B (eds) *Explorations in Peer Tutoring* (Oxford: Basil Blackwell).

Topping, K (1992) 'Co-operative learning and peer tutoring: an overview', *The Psychologist,* 5, 151–61.

Topping, K (1996) *Effective Peer Tutoring in Further and Higher Education* (Birmingham: Staff and Educational Development Association) SEDA Paper 95.

Topping, K J (1997) 'Peer Assessment Between Students in Higher Education: An Examination of the Literature', paper submitted for publication.

Topping, K J and Ehly, S (eds) (1997) *Peer Assisted Learning* (Hove: Lawrence Erlbaum).

Topping, K and Hill, S (1995) 'University and college students as tutors for schoolchildren: a typology and review of evaluation research', in Goodlad, S (ed) *Students as Tutors and Mentors* (London: Kogan Page).

Topping, K J, Hill, S, McKaig, A, Rogers, C, Rushi, N and Young, D (1997) 'Paired Reciprocal Peer Tutoring in Undergraduate Economics Innovations', *Education and Training International,* 34, 2.

Topping, K J, Simpson, G, Thompson, L and Hill, S (1997) 'Evaluation of Faculty-Wide Student Supported Learning at the University of Central Lancashire', *Higher Education Review* (in press).

Topping, K J, Watson, G A, Jarvis, R J and Hill, S (1996) 'Same-Year Paired Peer Tutoring in Undergraduate Mathematics', *Teaching in Higher Education,* 1, 3, 341–56.

Torrance, E P (1984) *Mentor Relationships* (Buffalo, NY: Bearly).

Tracey, T J and Sedlacek, W E (1985) 'The relationship of non-cognitive variables to academic success: a longitudinal comparison by race', *Journal of College Student Personnel,* 26, 405–10.

Trost, G (1993) 'Prediction of excellence in school, university and work', in Heller, K A, Monks, F J and Passow, A H (eds) *International Handbook of Research and Development of Giftedness and Talent* (Oxford: Pergamon Press).

Turner, J D (1991) *Higher Education in Namibia.* Report of a presidential commission, under the chairmanship of Professor J D Turner (Windhoek: Commission on Higher Education).

Uden, T (1994) *The will to learn: individual commitment and adult learning* (Leicester: NIACE).

United Nations Institute for Namibia (UNIN) (1986) 'Education and culture', in *Namibia: perspectives for national reconstruction and development,* 505–49, (Lusaka: United Nations Institute for Namibia).

University of Namibia (UNAM) (1995) *First five year development plan 1995–1999,* compiled by Mshigeni, K E, du Pisani, A and Kiangi, G E (Windhoek: UNAM).

Van Zyl, P and Hart, F (1991) *The Mentoring Scheme* (Johannesburg: University of the Witwatersrand, SAAAD Conference Proceedings.

Veugelers, W and Hofmeister, J (eds) (1993) *Handboek Aansluitingsproject VWO-Universiteit van Amsterdam* (Amsterdam: Universiteit van Amsterdam).

Veugelers, W and Zijlstra, H (1995) 'Learning together: In-Service Education in Networks of Schools', *British Journal of In-Service Education,* 21, 1, 37–48.

Veugelers, W and Zijlstra, H (1996) 'Networks for Modernizing Secondary Schools', *Educational Leadership International* 54, 3, 76–9.

Virtue, M and Terre Blanche, M (1995) 'An Evaluation of a Tutorial Programme in Psychology', *Bulletin of Assessment and Evaluation,* 1, 25–8.

Vygotsky, L S (1978) *Mind in Society: The Development of Higher Psychological Processes* (edited by Cole, M, John-Steiner, V, Scribner, S and Souberman, E) (Cambridge, MA: MIT Press).

Wagner, L (1990) 'Social and historical perspectives on peer teaching in education', in Foot, H C, Morgan, M J and Shute, R H (eds) *Children Helping Children* (Chichester: Wiley).

Walberg, H J (1995) 'Nurturing children for adult success', in Katzko, M W and Monks, F J (eds) *Nurturing Talent: Individual Needs and Social Ability* (Assen, NL: Van Gorcum).

Wallace, J (1993) 'Supplemental Instruction at Kingston University', paper given at Peer Tutoring Consortium Conference, University of Glamorgan, 23 June.

Webb, N M (1982) 'Peer Interaction and Learning in Co-operative Small Groups', *Journal of Educational Psychology*, 5, 74, 642–55.

Werner, E E (1989) 'Children of the garden island', *Scientific American*, 260, 106–11.

West, T (1991) *In the Mind's Eye* (Buffalo: Prometheus).

Whitley, P (1980) *An Enquiry into Study Service in Institutions of Higher Education* (London: Department of Education and Science and Community Service Volunteers).

Whitley, P (1982) 'Study Service in the United Kingdom: a survey', in Goodlad, S (ed) *Study Service: An Examination of community service as a method of study in higher education* (Windsor: NFER-Nelson).

Whitman, N A (1988) *Peer Teaching: To Teach is to Learn Twice* (ASHE-ERIC Higher Education Report) (Washington DC: ERIC Clearinghouse on Higher Education).

Wilbur, F and Lambert, L (1991) *Linking America's Schools and Colleges* (Washington: American Association for Higher Education).

Wilkes, R (1975) *Peer and Cross-Age Tutoring and Related Topics: An annotated bibliography* Theoretical Paper No 53 (Madison, Wisconsin: Wisconsin Research and Development Center for Cognitive Learning, University of Wisconsin).

Wilson, M F (1995) 'Student tutors' skills gains Cardiff Institute of Higher Education', in *Learning Together: Student Tutoring*. Research and evaluation papers on pupil aspirations and student tutor skills (London: Community Service Volunteers).

Wilson, M F and Saunders, D (1994) 'Initial experiences of student tutoring at the Cardiff Institute of Higher Education', in Foot, H C *et al.* (eds) *Group and interactive learning* (Southampton: Computational Mechanics Publications).

Winner, E (1996) *Gifted Children: Myths and Realities* (New York: Basic Books).

Wits AISU (1997) Wits Academic Information and Systems Unit (Johannesburg: University of the Witwatersrand)

Zorman, R (1995) 'Mentoring and role modelling programs for the gifted', in Heller, K A, Monks, F J and Passow, A H *International Handbook of Research and Development of Giftedness and Talent* (Oxford: Pergamon Press).

Zuckerman, H (1983) 'The scientific elite: Nobel laureates' mutual influences', in Albert, R S (ed), *Genius and Eminence: the Social Psychology of Creativity and Exceptional Achievement* (Oxford: Oxford University Press).

INDEX